AMERICAN MONSTERS

Also by Jack Newfield

A Prophetic Minority

A Populist Manifesto (with Jeff Greenfield)

Bread and Roses, Too

Cruel and Unusual Justice

The Permanent Government (with Paul DuBrul)

City for Sale (with Wayne Barrett)

Only in America: The Life and Crimes of Don King

*Somebody's Gotta Tell It: The Upbeat Memoirs of
A Working-Class Journalist*

The Full Rudy: The Man, the Myth, the Mania

RFK: A Memoir

American Rebels (editor)

Also by Mark Jacobson

Gojiro

Everyone and No One

12,000 Miles in the Nick of Time

AMERICAN
✶ ✶ MONSTERS

44 Rats, Blackhats, and Plutocrats

EDITED BY **JACK NEWFIELD AND MARK JACOBSON**

THUNDER'S MOUTH PRESS
NEW YORK

American Monsters
44 Rats, Blackhats, and Plutocrats

© 2004 by Jack Newfield, Mark Jacobson, & Avalon Publishing
Group

Published by
Thunder's Mouth Press
An Imprint of Avalon Publishing Group Incorporated
245 West 17th St., 11th Floor
New York, NY 10011

AVALON
publishing group incorporated

Library of Congress Cataloging-in-Publication Data is available.

ISBN: 1-56025-554-4

9 8 7 6 5 4 3 2 1

Designed by Simon M. Sullivan
Printed in the United States of America
Distributed by Publishers Group West

Contents

COLLEGE OF LETTERS AND SCIENCE: CULTURE CRIMINALS—DISMAYING IDEAS, DISMAYING MINDS

BUMP IN THE NIGHT—CROOKS AND CRIMINALS

The Ninth Circle—Worst of the Worst

Purgatory—Either Side of the Flipped Coin

Pet Peeves

Notes on the petit *mendacities of chickenhawk warmongers* · *Alfonse D'Amato, Don King, the Reverend Al Sharpton, Jack Ruby, Jane Fonda,*

INTRODUCTION

✦

AMERICA IS THE greatest country on earth. We invented jazz and rock and roll, built the Brooklyn Bridge, wrote the Bill of Rights, were the first to extend universal suffrage. The Grand Canyon lies within our borders. We are, as so many politicians, both high minded and low, never tire of saying, the light of the world.

But we are not perfect. America has also been party to bad things, some very bad things. These include: genocide of the native populations, enslavement of people on the basis of race, invasions of numerous smaller, weaker nations, stealing of elections, blacklisting of innocent people, whole rafts of high crimes. This is to say nothing of the misdemeanors, the venal everyday business of America—payola, point shaving, and Enron-style accounting.

This is a book about these bad things, and the bad Americans who have done, and continue to do them. In *American Monsters*, we point a finger at the country's rats, blackhats, and plutocrats. We tell the stories and hand down the indictments, charges that will stick in a courtroom where there is no statute of limitations. This is the dark side between the shining seas, the blight beneath the City on the Hill, the muck of the historical record.

Here we round up (and freshly indict) some familiar names—national felons, war criminals, and mega-goniffs like Richard Nixon, Joseph McCarthy, J. Edgar Hoover, Jefferson Davis, Henry Kissinger, Roy Cohn, and the current Darth Vader/Crusader-in-charge, George W. Bush. You know: the usual suspects. But while many of the creeps lambasted in these pages have not achieved the universal opprobrium of those above, that doesn't mean they are any less repugnant. These slightly off-the-radar evildoers include Ty Cobb, the world's nastiest ballplayer, Justice Roger Taney, of the *Dred Scott* decision fame, the worst Supreme Court justice ever (until Antonin Scalia, who is also included here), and Ike Christmas, the "soldier of fortune" whose drunken, savage exploits paved the way for the United Fruit Company to take over half of Central America. Also served up for your lurid enlightenment are the sagas of some old-fashioned murderers, gangsters, and nutcases like Charles Manson, Frankie Carbo, and John Wilkes Booth.

American Monsters does not claim to present an encyclopedic, all-encompassing dossier of national rottenness. After all, evil is often in the eye of the beholder. Arranging our anointed bums into categories such as "The Ninth Circle" (for the worst of the worst), "With God on Their Side" (for the seemingly never ending stream of Elmer Gantrys who have infested the American political and spiritual landscape), and "Low Creatures in High Offices" (for the grim menagerie of officials, both elected and not) what we have attempted to present is an idiosyncratic collage of individuals who, in the opinions of the many contributors here, the nation might have been better off without. Each one of them has committed some crime, represented an idea, or fostered an attitude one of our forty-one essayists found to be reprehensible.

However, we are not black-or-white absolutists in the manner of our binary-minded "with-us-or-against-us" president. We see the gray areas. Many people in this book have their "good" sides. They might even have done exemplary things in their public career, like Lyndon Johnson, who passed the Voting Rights Act of 1965 and did more to press the cause of civil rights than any other president before falling into the maw of "escalation" and death in Vietnam. In recognition of the complexity of such figures we have provided the moral limbo of "Purgatory." In this realm one finds such "in between" figures as Huey Long, Walt Disney, Thomas Alva Edison, and Pete Rose.

Books like this are inevitably accused of blind spots. No doubt we have neglected to mention the mendacity of some hideously deserving hustler or race-hater. We understand such objections and sustain them a priori. However, there is one issue we must address in this introduction, a problem that has caused the editors a good deal of duress: there are no female American Monsters included in this volume. This does not mean the history of the Republic has been free of objectionable women. Certainly vice-presidential wife Lynn Cheney, the smug and scheming Jean Kirkpatrick, gay-hating Anita Bryant, and child killers like Susan Smith might rate an entry in one of the categories found in this book. Ayn Rand is certainly a candidate for "purgatory" (since she gives smart teenagers a template with which to confront polemical and philosophical issues, a philosophy which can later be wholly jettisoned by most thinking, feeling humans due to its self-serving mean-spiritedness).

None of these women made it, however. This is due, in part, to the fact that we couldn't find anyone who wanted to write about them. But primarily, it is our considered opinion that American sexism (a sin embraced by several of our "monsters") has prevented women from achieving the level of wealth and power that would have enabled them to compete with the male felons and fools in this book. The fact is, women have never been leaders in the extermination of native peoples, nor have they lorded over great slave populations on plantations, enforced segregation, broken unions, or led rapacious corporations in stealing taxpayers' money. Perhaps, in a more equitable society, women will soon be given a chance to rival their male counterparts in such mendacity and avarice. At that point we will be glad to include, and deride, them.

A final note on some missing favorites whose absence we truly lament. Vagaries of deadline and limitations of our Rolodexes have precluded people like Kool-Aid king Jim Jones, Louis B. Farrakhan, plus the two generations of multi-million-dollar mass murderers, John D. "Ludlow Massacre" Rockefeller and his son, Nelson "Attica Massacre" Rockefeller. Also missing are General George Custer, Robert McNamara, Benedict Arnold, and friendly old Ronald Reagan. We mention them here so readers will not imagine these villains have escaped the laser of our abhorrence. Beyond this there are many lesser figures whose craven existences were considered too puny to rate a full essay. These no-accounts have not been forgotten and are included in a final section called "Pet Peeves," a peanut gallery inhabited by the George Steinbrenners of the world.

—Jack Newfield and Mark Jacobson

LOW CREATURES IN
HIGH OFFICE—
DEAD PRESIDENTS,
IDEOLOGUES, AUTOCRATS

Andrew Jackson, William McKinley,
John Ashcroft, William J. Bennett

Democracy is not infallible. We cannot forget that Richard Nixon and Spiro Agnew carried forty-nine of fifty states and within two years both were exposed as common criminals. Sifting through many candidates we have settled on the four following reprobates as emblems of how politicians sometimes carry out the people's darker urges. Some operate on a grand, near-genocidal scale such as Andrew Jackson in his campaign to rid the American frontier of the unwanted natives. Others, such as William Bennett, deal with small-minded preoccupations of scolds and prudes, Obviously this category is underpopulated. We could have easily included John Mitchell, the Dulles boys, the Rostow boys, the whole Rumsfeld/Wolfowitz/Perle cabal, and many modern mayors, localized purveyors of sleaze and malfeasance in such municipalities as Atlantic City, Camden, Waterbury, and, more than likely, a town near you.

Andrew Jackson

✴

BY STEVE EARLE

OKAY, WORK WITH me here:

You're a Jew, living in Germany and you want to take your family to a movie. But, you're low on cash and *der kinder*, kids being kids, have visions of Gummi bears dancing in their heads, so on your way to the *kino* you stop off at a conveniently located ATM to top off your wallet. You whip out your trusty cash card, pop it into the slot, key in your access code, and the machine whirs and clicks and promptly spits out a neat stack of twenty Euro notes emblazoned with the likeness of Adolf Hitler.

Far-fetched? Maybe in Germany, but not in America. Not if you're a descendent of one of the once proud Native American nations of what is now the southeastern United States: the Creek, Chickasaw, Choctaw, Seminole, and Cherokee. And not when you consider that the face on the United States twenty dollar bill is that of none other than Andrew Jackson of Tennessee, the seventh president of the United States.

Like most Americans of his time, Jackson considered the various Native nations that lived in what is now eastern United States to be, at best, an impediment to expansion and progress, and at worst, a threat to the security of the young nation's constantly expanding borders. Many great men (among them, Thomas Jefferson) had hinted at removal of the eastern tribes to the "vacant lands" west of the Mississippi River. What set Jackson apart was his unflinching willingness to walk his talk. He was the messiah that two generations of removal advocates had been waiting for—a true believer in the concept of the manifest destiny of the white race in America and a man of action, a genuinely bad motherfucker, possessed of the gumption to prosecute that vision at any cost to life, limb, and his personal and political fortune.

Andrew Jackson arrived in Nashville in 1788 to assume the office of public prosecutor for what was then the western district of North Carolina and, through a very public string of very public altercations with the local gentry, quickly established a reputation for being quick to anger, slow to forgive, and loath to forget. In his youth he fought no less than four duels, killing one man and, on the same occasion, sustaining grave injury to his own person but never to his honor. Petulant and ambitious he made many enemies but his friends proved to be, perhaps not coincidentally, more influential. Within a few years he rose to attorney general for his district and after Tennessee was admitted to the Union in 1796 he served unremarkable terms in both houses of Congress. He resigned his Senate seat in 1798 without explanation (he was probably simply bored and homesick) and returned home where he was elected judge of the Tennessee Superior Court and, in 1802, major general of the Tennessee State Militia. It was in that capacity that he finally distinguished himself.

Jackson proved himself to be a born Indian fighter and a shrewd negotiator, wresting large tracts of land from the various nations by treaty and forming alliances that pitted one tribe against the other whenever it suited his purpose.

In retaliation for a deadly attack on settlers at Fort Mims by the Red Stick faction of Chief William Weatherford, Jackson led a successful punitive expedition into Creek Territory culminating in the nearly complete annihilation of the hostiles at the battle of Horseshoe Bend. In the aftermath the conquering hero punished the entire Creek nation (including the "friendlies" who had fought at his side) for the transgressions of a few. The ensuing treaty opened Creek lands comprising over half of what is now Alabama and a third of Georgia to white settlement and effectively ensured the demise of the Creek Nation.

Just as Jackson's victory at Horseshoe Bend resonated with his fellow frontiersmen, his stunning defeat of a British invasion force at the battle of New Orleans elevated him to a level of national fame and reverence previously reserved for the founding fathers themselves. Ironically, one of the provisions of the Treaty of Ghent, which officially ended the War of 1812, called for the return of all Native territories ceded to the United States after 1811. This included the nearly twenty-three million acres seized at the conclusion of the Creek war. Upon returning to Tennessee and assuming the mantle of Hero of the Battle of New Orleans and All-Around Six-Hundred-Pound Gorilla, Jackson simply ignored the treaty and continued his policy of removal of all Natives from all captured lands. When the Cherokee protested that the part of the Creek secession that lay in Georgia was in fact Cherokee Territory, Secretary of War William Crawford promptly returned the land to its rightful owners. The Gorilla of New Orleans howled in protest and the secretary quickly backed down, appointing a new commission to treat with the Cherokee and naming Jackson as its chairman. The results were predictable; Jackson threatened, cajoled, and in some instances bribed the chiefs, and the Cherokee surrendered an additional two million acres in return for an equal amount in what is now Oklahoma.

Jackson's newfound infallibility came to the test in 1818 when he was ordered by the administration of President James Monroe to pursue Seminole war parties into Spanish Florida. Jackson went one better. In fact he didn't stop until he had created an international incident, executing two British subjects for arming the Seminoles and capturing the Spanish capital in Pensacola. Meanwhile, back in Washington, his enemies (the list grew exponentially with his fame and his prospects for the presidency) demanded that Jackson be censured and Florida returned to Spain. In the end it was his own fearsome reputation that saved him. Other more canny politicians, Monroe and Secretary of State John Quincy Adams among them, feared the wrath of voters who would not stand for the public pilloring of their hero. The Spanish, having witnessed Jackson's humiliation of the British in New Orleans, were terrified of a similar bitch-slapping at the hands of "the Napoleon of the Woods" so they cut their losses and sold Florida to the United States for five million dollars in claims against Spain.

Back home in Tennessee, Jackson returned to the business of Indian removal, successfully negotiating the acquisition of all remaining Chickasaw lands in Tennessee and Kentucky. The Choctaw in the Mississippi Delta were next, holding out for a while, but ultimately acquiescing to Jackson's assurances that resistance would only result in a fate similar to that of their neighbors the Creeks: complete and utter annihilation.

Jackson was elected to the presidency in 1835 running on a reform platform, but his first official act was to propose Indian Removal as national policy. There was some resistance in Congress but there was no public outcry and the Indian Removal Act became law in 1828. By the time Jackson left office six years later over forty-five thousand Native Americans had been removed, some by treaty. Several thousand more followed in the early years of the Van Buren administration. In Georgia seventeen thousand die-hard Cherokee under Chief John Ross were rounded up and interred in concentration camps and subsequently shipped west by riverboat and boxcar. Somewhere between four thousand and eight thousand of them died in transit along the infamous Trail of Tears. The last holdouts were a small band of Seminole under Osceola in Florida but in the end, they were subdued and transported, and Jackson's legacy was secure. He had opened over 100 million acres of land to speculation and settlement and there was no longer any autonomous Native American Nation east of the Mississippi river. No Creek, Cherokee, Choctaw, Chickasaw, Seminole, Sac, Fox, Kickapoo, Wea, Peoria, Piankashaw, Iowa, Kakaskia, Delaware, Shawnee, Osage, Ottawa, Chippewa, Powatami, Winnebago, Saginaw, Menomini, Wyandot, Miami, Caddo, Pawnee, Seneca, Quapaw, Apalachicola, Oto, Missouri. . . . These are the names of nations, of entire distinct peoples ripped from their native soil, transported, and stranded in a strange land far from their home. Some are forgotten. Some we have appropriated in our own names for the places they once hunted and fished and raised their families; our rivers and lakes, our forests, our cities and towns. By all rights they should haunt us whenever we speak their names, but they don't, and we have Andrew Jackson to thank for that.

You see, Andrew Jackson was the template for a peculiarly American brand of national hero. He was the badass, the cowboy, the enforcer, and the lightning rod, willing and able to take the heat and go to hell for all of our sins. To break the strike, drop the bomb, and pull the switch so that we don't have to.

So the next time you go to the ATM, take a good look at that long, white face on the twenty dollar bill and then check it against your own reflection in the glass. Any resemblance? Look again. Sure, it was Andrew Jackson who burned the villages, imprisoned and executed the chiefs, made and broke the treaties—but we're still living on the land.

William McKinley

BY DANNY SCHECHTER

The Past Is Never Past: William McKinley's Imperialitis

This is a story of a man who thought he was everything until he was struck down by an assassin who called himself a nothing. It pits America's greatest writer, Mark Twain, against a president he labeled "lousy" (and was then censored for saying so).

At the center of this conflict was and is the living legacy of William McKinley, U.S. president number twenty-five, the first to ride in an automobile and use a telephone. He was known for his personal "courtesy" and as the first to run a "front porch campaign." Later, he became the third president to be assassinated. For those who require cyber verisimiltude, there is a film of him being presidential and even a Real Audio clip of a speech he gave in 1896 available online today, which is also some kind of first.

McKinley was a war hero, noticed and honored first in war for getting coffee to the men in blue on the civil war battlefield of Antietam. Before he died, he would be branded a war criminal for launching America's Vietnam before Vietnam, the largely forgotten massacre in the Philippines during the Spanish-American war. That was a long bloody Asian war like the one that emulated it years later. Both would fade too quickly into history.

The president was killed in his second term while standing at a reception line in the "Temple of Music" at the Pan-Am Expo in Buffalo in 1901. The Expo was designed to stir confidence in the new American century. He was struck down by a modest, some say deranged, anarchist, Leon Czolgosz, a Polish immigrant from Canton, Ohio.

McKinley was, in contrast, a man with an overblown sense of personal destiny. Telling a story present-day Americans are hearing yet again, McKinley said his ascent to the White House was based not on luck but providence. He kept this faith to the end. Upon dying, he said, "Good-bye, good-bye, all. It is God's way. His will, not ours, be done. Nearer my God to Thee, nearer to Thee."

Leon Czolgosz, his forgotten assassin, who often went by the alias "Fred Nobody," also spoke without remorse before his own death. "I killed the president because he was the enemy of the good people, the good working people," the sometime Fred Nobody said. "I am not sorry for my crime." He also said: "I didn't believe one man should have so much service, and another man have none."

TV aficionados of those popular crime scene investigation shows will be intrigued to learn that he was caught because he left a candy wrapper near the body he pumped two shots into. He was an admirer of the anarchist Emma Goldman, who never condemned his act. As a result she was considered guilty by association even though she never associated with the unfortunate Czolgosz.

As noted, there are a number of similarities between the Republican McKinley and the current Republican leader of the Free World. Like President George W. Bush, McKinley was a Methodist and the first Republican president at the start of a new millennium. His century, the twentieth, went on to become the bloodiest in history. (There is still time for this one to catch up.) Both politicians were denounced as imperial presidents. Like Bush, McKinley was put in office by a coalition of big business interests, and an "unprecedented advertising campaign," as one historian described it. In McKinley's case there was also the back-room maneuvering of covert operatives masterminded by a wealthy Ohio political boss named Mark Hanna. Hanna was later rewarded by McKinley, who opened up a Senate seat for his benefactor. This was Dick Cheney–style politics in the "Gilded Age." The Gilded Age was yesterday; the Enron Age is today.

Like Bush, McKinley was a tariff man, a believer in the "open door" and winning new markets, all now at the heart of the modern neo-liberal agenda. He was a one-man WTO before the WTO. His opponent, William Jennings Bryant, condemned him for his allegiance to the gold standard, for crucifying mankind on a "cross of gold." McKinley's gold trumped Bryant's silver.

Both Bush and McKinley had evangelistic inclinations. McKinley defended making war in the Philippines in order to "Christianize" the natives. Gore Vidal notes that, "When reminded that Philippines were already Roman Catholic, the president responded 'Exactly.'" Similarly, Bush's preventive war of aggression in Iraq was described as a crusade and defended in speeches laden with coded biblical language and references to "evildoers" designed to please the Christian right and outrage Islamic militants.

McKinley's story connects in a roundabout way to the present, as witnessed by Mark Twain's "To the Person Sitting in Darkness," written in February of 1901, a title that refers to Isaiah 9:2 and 49:9. Twain's broadside was understood at the time as a reference to the "hypocrites" who made brutal war on the Philippines. Twain's primary target was McKinley, whom the author said was to be condemned for massacres committed by U.S. soldiers, a practice which was condoned by American military of the time, many of whom referred to Filipinos, as Theodore Roosevelt later would, as "our little brown brothers." In many ways the Filipino War, the first true overseas instance of American imperialism, would come to serve as template for subsequent like-minded adventures. Atrocities abounded. In the heat of battle, captured Filipinos were forced to dig their own graves; then many were lined up and shot. Whole villages were set on fire, exterminating innocent men, women, and children. One American general wrote, "It may be necessary to kill half the Filipinos in order that the remaining half be advanced to a higher plane of life." (Perhaps it was fitting that the anti–Vietnam war movie *Apocalypse Now* was shot in the Philippines.)

Is it a coincidence or something more that during his now infamous "Mission Accomplished" stunt aboard the

USS *Lincoln*, George W. Bush would, clearly unknowingly, echo Twain's assault on America's first imperial president by quoting the prophet Isaiah: "To the captives, 'Come out,' and to those in darkness, 'Be free.'"

Is this history repeated? No. History continued. War on Iraq started with B-52s coming from Guam, that island which McKinley put on his world map immediately as TERRITORY, and not as a protectorate, during the "Philippine mess," as Twain used to call it. Guam, so far away from everything, nobody cared. No B-52s in those days.

Reason for war then? The Spaniards, cruising in Philippine waters with their impressive fleet of ten rusty death traps (trying to avoid contact with German, French, and whatever imperialist battleships of that time), these "Dons" were threatening the Californian and Oregon coastal lines! What a prevention! (At least this is what McKinley confessed to a Methodist congregation. I think he would not have dared to tell his brethren lies.)

Flash back to those days, to the sinking of the battleship *Maine* in Havana Harbor on McKinley's watch. It was the 9/11 of its time. Two hundred sixty Americans dead. The Spanish *must* have done it, or so the pundits of the day all agreed. We must fight back, they counseled. And we did.

Americans were indignant, fueled to war fever by the Rupert Murdoch of the pre–Fox News era of yellow journalism, William Randolph Hearst, the preeminent media mogul of the day. "I will give you the pictures. You will give me the war," Hearst said memorably, lines that were further etched into the American consciousness by Orson Welles's Citizen Kane, who said, "You provide the prose poems, I'll provide the war." It would take fifty years before definitive proof turned up that the war, which garnered America its first real whiff of world dominance, had been based on a lie not unlike another unilateral action sold on the basis of a threat of WMDs. It was later discovered those weapons too did not exist. In Cuba, it was later learned that the mighty *Maine* sank because of an accident in the engine room, not an enemy attack. But no matter, that war was fought anyway, swiftly and decisively, with the speed of Desert Storm. Superior naval power and Teddy Roosevelt's slash-and-burn Rough Riders won the day. McKinley boasted that his mission was accomplished because, "A prestige of invincibility attached to our arms." This and what McKinley assumed was "the Hand of God." The deity is always a willing partner to American adventurism, as with the current president's endless references to the help of "the Almighty" in the crusade against Saddam attest.

When the defeated Spaniards asked McKinley for his surrender terms, he humiliated them, demanding Cuba, Puerto Rico, and Guam. And then, for good measure, he asked that they throw in the Philippines, which was conquered by Admiral Dewey's fleet to keep it from falling into the hands of another power.

Here's how McKinley explained it: "When next I realized that the Philippines had dropped into our laps, I didn't know what to do with them. That there was nothing left for us to do but to take them all and educate the Filipinos and uplift and civilize and Christianize them." That's the full quote.

The war there that followed lasted more than a decade. The counter-insurgency tactics later used in Vietnam would be deployed first in the Philippines, prompting Mark Twain, who became the head of the Anti-Imperialist League, to write:

> We have pacified some thousands of the Philippine islanders and buried them, destroyed their fields, burned their villages, turned their widows and orphans out of doors, furnished heartbreak by exile to dozens of disagreeable patriots, subjugated the remaining lo million by benevolent assimilation; we are a world power.

McKinley had another word for it. "It is Manifest Destiny," he said. Some of his rhetoric then sounds eerily familiar now:

"Our flag in the Philippines [is] not the banner of imperialism, or the symbol of oppression," he wrote. "It is the flag of freedom, of hope, of civilization."

A stunning new film, *Two Bells/Two Worlds*, directed by Bernard Stone, revisits this story in the centennial anniversary year of Philippine independence. The story focuses on a rebellion on the island of Balangiga against American troops who were that very day mourning the death of President McKinley. When islanders revolted, the U.S. sent in an expeditionary force with orders to kill every male over the age of ten. Fifty thousand were slain.

In all seven hundred fifty thousand lost their lives in the war later waged by Theodore Roosevelt, whose statue graces the Museum of Natural History in New York. T. R. congratulated the general who carried out the genocidal campaign.

Emmy award-winner Stone's film documents a debate in America over the Spanish-American War that still festers with veterans' groups oblivious to the human costs of United States intervention. It has been praised by Philippine-Americans but was rejected by PBS and cable outlets for lacking "objectivity," and has still not been shown on American TV.

A century later, the crimes of William McKinley, spiritual forerunner of President Bush, are not well known even in the age of Google, except perhaps by the robust rightists of the Free Republic website who speculate longingly about what the world might have been like had McKinley lived:

> If an anarchist had not killed William McKinley, would Woodrow Wilson ever have been president? Would he have been in a position to reject the early peace offerings from the Austrian monarchy, thereby prolonging World War I? Would the die still have been cast after World War I for the rise of the Third Reich, had McKinley not been shot? Would there have been a great depression? Would there have been the New Deal? How much damage was done by the actions of an anarchist? How much to promote the growth of the state did this fanatic cause? Just some food for thought.

And so, here we have ideologues, today described as President Bush's shock troops, still waxing nostalgic about the loss of McKinley. And there's more: Theodore Roosevelt, whose own centennial was accorded museum exhibits and TV celebrations in 2002, called the man he served as veep, "the most widely loved man in all the United States."

And finally, to provide balance of the kind that our TV networks say they prize, but rarely practice, the last word belongs to this "most loved" or "lousy" man, depending on your stance towards American imperialism:

"All a man can hope for during his lifetime [is] to set an example, and, when he's dead, to be an inspiration for history."

✷ ✷ ✷

John Ashcroft

✶

BY NAT HENTOFF

NO OTHER UNITED States attorney general in American history has more thoroughly subverted the Bill of Rights and other liberty elements of the Constitution than John Ashcroft. He has the full support of George W. Bush who has publicly and repeatedly told him, "You're doing a fabulous job!"

Ashcroft, with that support, has the further advantage of advanced surveillance technology that George Orwell could not have envisioned in *1984.* As George Washington University law professor Jonathan Turley has emphasized: "For more than two hundred years, our liberties have been protected primarily by practical barriers . . . to government abuse. Because of the sheer size of the nation and its population the government could not practically abuse a great number of citizens at any given time. In the last decade, however, these practical barriers have fallen to technology."

Accordingly, Ashcroft's USA Patriot Act, and subsequent executive orders by him, have enabled the FBI and other law enforcement agencies to find out—through converged government and commercial electronic databases—a vast range of information about any American's business, medical, travel, organizational information, and his or her other life patterns.

Moreover, under the "sneak-and-peek" section of the Patriot Act, the FBI can enter your home or office when you're not there and insert the "magic lantern" (also known as the key-stroke logger) in your computer, which records every stroke you make, every letter you type, including material you never send out. The FBI then returns in your absence and downloads everything you've written. This and other government forms of electronic surveillance are being done with minimal (nearly automatic) judicial permission. And, as Lincoln Kaplan, editor of *Legal Affairs* magazine (Yale University), points out: "What is more startling about the scope of these new powers is that the government can use them on people who aren't suspected of committing a crime. Innocent people can be deprived of any clue that they are being watched and that they may need to defend themselves."

Or, as Dan Kennedy of the *Boston Phoenix* describes the increasing realization among more and more Americans that their privacy is being shredded: "It's not that you're being watched. It's that you might be, and that you have no way of knowing whether you are or not."

Ashcroft, the former senator from Missouri, who lost a re-election bid to a dead man (Governor Mel Carnahan, killed in a plane crash before Election Day), is a fundamentalist Christian who believes that this is not a secular nation because "we have no King but Jesus." He begins each day at the Justice Department with a prayer meeting, utterly convinced that he is on a God-directed mission to protect the nation from terrorists. As for his critics, he accuses them of giving aid and comfort to the enemy by creating "phantoms of lost liberties."

In 2003, Ashcroft, angered and disturbed by gathering resistance among people around the country, and some in Congress, went on a "victory tour" to defend the Patriot Act—during which he spoke only before law enforcement organizations. As a result, the resistance to the Act has grown, and there are now more than two hundred-thirty towns, cities, and counties—as well as three state legislatures (Alaska, Hawaii, and Vermont)—that have passed Bill of Rights resolutions instructing their members of Congress to pass legislation cutting out the more egregiously repressive sections of the Patriot Act. These resolutions also order state and local police to inform local officials when they have become enveloped in federal applications of the Patriot Act and other administration curbs on individual liberties.

While Congress is finally showing more irritation at the secrecy with which Ashcroft's war on the Bill of Rights is being conducted, and is contemplating various corrective measures, it deserves the harsh criticism directed at it by a lead editorial in the January 5, 2004, *Washington Post:* "Congress is supposed to be an equal branch of government, and it ought to be both aggressively overseeing the administration's work and actively exploring what laws would enhance American freedom and security. It ought not to be giving its powers away."

As for the courts, including the Supreme Court of the United States, they, too, have not been sufficiently aggressive in protecting the Bill of Rights against the serial invasions by Ashcroft, the president, and others involved in administering the much cited, but too often muted, rule of law.

"The guarantees of the Constitution and its first ten amendments, the Bill of Rights, are," Supreme Justice William O. Douglas warned, "not self-executing. As nightfall does not come all at once, neither does oppression. In both instances, there is a twilight where everything remains seemingly unchanged. And it is in such twilight that we must all be aware of change in the air . . . lest we become unwitting victims of the darkness."

The changes in the air are palpable, but the civilian courts are still open, and more Americans are coming to understand the prescience and wisdom of Thomas Jefferson: "The people are the only sure reliance for the preservation of our liberty."

But meanwhile, Ashcroft has not only eroded personal liberties. He has also attacked the independence of the federal judiciary, thereby undermining the separation of powers at the core of our system of justice. At the instigation of the Justice Department, Congress passed an amendment to a bill that orders the United States Sentencing Commission to keep records of each federal judge whose sentences are downward departures from the commission's guidelines. These reports on judges who are "soft" on sentencing must be given to Ashcroft, who is then required to inform the judiciary committees of the House and Senate about the "wayward" judges.

In addition, Ashcroft, taking command, sent an internal memorandum to all federal prosecutors around the country to report directly to the Justice Department—to "the General"—any reductions of sentences by any federal judge. There will now be a "blacklist" of judges who do not conform. Supreme Court Chief Justice William Rehnquist—hardly known to be permissive on law-and-order issues—has charged that this essentially Ashcroft attack on the separation of powers is "an unwarranted and ill-considered effort to intimidate judges in the performance of their judicial duties."

Will Ashcroft add Justice Rehnquist to his judicial blacklist?

And New York Federal District Judge John S. Martin—retiring in protest after thirteen years on the federal bench—wrote in a *New York Times* Op-Ed article: "For a judge to be deprived of the ability to consider all the factors that go into formulating a just sentence is completely at odds with the sentencing philosophy that has been a hallmark of the American system of justice."

And Southern District Judge Robert P. Patterson pointed to this "implicit threat to trial judges that, if they are considered for appellate positions, they will be subjected to the type of demeaning and unseemly treatments which nominees to the courts of appeals have undergone at the hands of Congress in recent years." These demeaning assaults have come from Republican and Democratic senators alike.

The ceaselessly energetic Attorney General, continuing to dismantle the rule of law, has convinced Congress—again with the support of the president—to place a provision in the Intelligence Authorization Act that covertly expands the USA Patriot Act to allow the FBI to demand an unprecedented range of financial and other records *without any judicial supervision.*

Since 9/11, Ashcroft has continuously pledged that any action he takes to further homeland security will certainly be under judicial supervision. But with this amendment—signed into law by George W. Bush on December 13, a Saturday—so that it would get little media attention—the definition of "financial institutions" has been expanded to include the FBI's authority to get records, as civil libertarian John Whitehead of the Rutherford Institute reveals, from: "stock brokers, car dealerships, credit card companies, insurance agencies, jewelers, airlines, the United States Post Office and . . . any other business 'whose cash transactions have a high degree of usefulness in criminal, tax, or regulatory matters.' "

As a result, Whitehead—who, in print and through his extensive network of radio commentaries, has kept unceasing vigilance on the administration's revisions of the Bill of Rights—says, "the FBI now has even more power to snoop through your business records in so-called national security investigations without any court oversight and in almost total secrecy." These subpoenas are called "national security letters," and each recipient is forbidden by law to disclose ever having received one.

With Ashcroft persistently increasing his power to revise the Constitution, and the prospect—though not yet the certainty—that Bush will win a second term and Republicans will control both the House and Senate, the essential question for the future of this nation was raised by Supreme Court Justice Ruth Bader Ginsburg last September when she spoke to more than five hndred women attorneys in Oklahoma: "The issue is whether we will be able to hang on to the liberties and freedoms that have made our country a beacon to the rest of the world."

Ominously, on the other hand, Justice Antonin Scalia—during an address at John Carroll University on March 18, 2003—insisted that "most of the rights you enjoy go way beyond what the Constitution requires," because "the Constitution just sets minimums." Scalia emphasized that in wartime, "the protections will be ratcheted down to the Constitutional minimum."

Especially if there is a horrendous equivalent of 9/11, Scalia is very likely to prevail; and so far as our constitutional rights and liberties are concerned, the "twilight" of American freedoms that William O. Douglas foretold would then descend into night. Even without another 9/11, it is all too evident—as Lawrence Goldman, former president of the National Association of Criminal Defense Lawyers, says—that "the clear lesson is that the government, in its understandable and laudable resolve to protect our security, cannot be relied on to protect our basic rights and liberties."

Furthermore, since, with few exceptions, neither the Democratic leadership in Congress, nor any prospective Democratic successor to George W. Bush, has shown much interest or alarm at the diminution of our rights and liberties, the hope for a restoration of constitutional democracy is—as Thomas Jefferson insisted—with "the people."

But, as Jefferson also said, "if we think [the people] not enlightened enough to exercise their control with a wholesome discretion, the remedy is not to take it from them, but to inform their discretion by education."

And that means, of course, that the media—in all its forms—are the sources, as James Madison knew, writing the First Amendment, of that redeeming education. However, much of the media is caught on the treadmill of the twenty-four-hour news cycle, and it reports on Ashcroft and Bush's invasions of the Bill of Rights fragmentarily and, therefore, without enough sustained context and depth to inform the people of what is being taken away from them.

But there are a few vigilant newspapers—mainstream and alternative—as well as independent magazines, publications, Web sites, and other equivalents of the pre-revolutionary pamphleteers, to keep spreading the news. This could move enough of the people to make Congress and the courts (judges and justices consume the media) hold the executive branch accountable to the Constitution—thereby ending Ashcroft and Bush's war on the Bill of Rights.

"The greatest menace to freedom," wrote Supreme Court Justice Louis Brandeis, "is an inert people." And an inert press. In the current twilight of freedom, there are growing signs that both the citizenry and the media, in part, are awakening—not to what Ashcroft calls "the phantom of lost liberties," but to the actual disappearing liberties themselves.

William J. Bennett

BY JOHN TURCHIANO

LAS VEGAS WAGS like to tell the story about a tourist couple arguing in their hotel room. The husband tells his wife that she is wasting her time playing nickel slot machines.

"You should talk," the wife responds. "You just lost five thousand dollars playing blackjack."

"There's a difference," the husband scowls. "I know how to gamble!"

This might be called the William J. Bennett line of reasoning. He expounded this kind of sanctimonious attitude as Ronald Reagan's secretary of education and as the first President Bush's drug czar. He enjoyed an additional career representing conservative views as a finger-wagging sermonizer on numerous news programs, averring right-wing mantras with an authoritative air that too many construed as a halo of credibility.

He was all over TV and op-ed pages, and he had a strong impact on Republican policy-making. He was Father Coughlin without the clerical collar. He said affirmative action had a negative effect on society. He condemned with equal ardor gay unions and labor unions. To him, a woman's right to choose was limited to deciding between raising children and putting them up for adoption. He led the relentless conservative campaign against President Clinton, even writing a book, *The Death of Outrage*, which admonished the public for not jumping on the impeachment bandwagon. He helped shape opposition to the use of stem cells for research projects. He was instrumental in pushing the second President's Bush's program of faith-based initiatives. He adored tax cuts, the bigger the better. He called Bill Clinton a "habitual liar" and Al Gore a "pathological liar." But when it was revealed in 2000 that then-presidential candidate George W. Bush had lied about an arrest for drunk driving, Bennett explained that there was a difference. Unlike Clinton, Bush wasn't under oath when he lied. Oh.

There was also a difference when it came to serving in the military. Although Bennett consistently urged others to fight, he never did. The difference was an inopportune bad back that kept him out of the military during the Vietnam War. He wrote *Why We Fight: Moral Clarity and the War on Terrorism*, and he used the tragic events of 9/11 to establish an organization with the aims of hiking military spending and stifling war dissent. To raise money for this group, he cleverly called it AVOT—Americans for Victory Over Terrorism. He became a co-director of Empower America, an organization that, among other goals, fought against the construction of new casinos.

Bennett was a principal tactician in the culture wars. He was a prominent proponent of so-called family values. He was a leading contributor to the decline of polite political discourse. He said the word "liberal" with a smug sneer and dismissed honest arguments against his positions as a reflection of society's loss of morality. Bennett didn't respond respectfully to opponents on news shows very often, he usually interrupted and scolded them.

His books and speeches preached virtues and morals but typically did so with a Rush Limbaugh–like meanness that some devout people would call un-Christian. The religious right applauded him, although other observers suspected he was more like the subject of Harry Truman's sage observation, "If the man who plays hardest Saturday night sings loudest in church Sunday morning, lock your smokehouse door."

During his tenure as Reagan's education secretary, Bennett railed against bilingual education. He insisted that schools and students themselves should be held accountable for their failures, while he did nothing to repair inner-city learning institutions or to generate the funding needed to improve education.

His term in the cabinet was marked by a precipitous decline in test scores. It didn't matter. His policies ended up having a huge influence on the second President Bush's education legislation, the Leave No Child Behind Act, a program introduced with ample flourish but then denied the funding needed to achieve its stated goals. Plenty of children are still being left behind.

As the nation's drug czar, Bennett was Ivan the Terrible. He viewed drug addiction not as a disease but as a sin. His war on drugs was a war on drug users. His entire policy on drug abuse could be reduced to two words: harsh sentences. To curtail dealers he called for laws that invaded the financial privacy rights of everyone. Addicts had a moral responsibility to admit their problem and get straight, said Bennett, who smoked three packs of cigarettes a day.

While he was head of the United States drug control program, Bennett took the same "Just Say No" approach to drug abuse as another self-anointed behavioral expert, Nancy Reagan, and had the same lack of success with it. His tenure accomplished zero in the effort to reduce the drug problem in the U.S. Crack use swelled and AIDS continued its rampage. In spite of this record, his fingerprints are all over the present Bush administration's drug program. Bennett's deputy director for supply reduction, John Walters, is the current director of the Office of National Drug Control Policy.

After lackluster performances in these two public offices, Bennett graduated to various political initiatives fueled by the funding of right-wing organizations like the Heritage, Scaife, and John M. Olin foundations. He delivered speeches before religious, conservative, and corporate groups at $50,000 a pop. He wrote and edited speeches for George W. Bush.

In the spring of 2003, *Newsweek* and the *Washington Post* reported that the former drug czar had an addiction of his own: high-stakes slot machines. Conservatives immediately defended him, arguing that his habit was perfectly legal and that the reports of his gambling were simply more examples of the "liberal media bias" that Bennett repeatedly excoriated. But even some right-wingers had to quietly fear that future news programs featuring Bennett and his haughty homilies might lead some viewers to lock their smokehouse doors.

The reports on Bennett's gambling were certainly incongruent with the reputation of a man who preached self-control. A hidden-camera photo of him sitting in front of a video slot machine revealed the same meaningful pose television viewers saw when he sat opposite Tim Russert or Ted Koppel. There was evidence that Bennett was a VIP guest at casinos in Atlantic City and Las Vegas. He had a line of credit of at least $200,000 at some of them. He had once wired $1.4 million to cover his losses at just one casino. There were reports that in two days in April 2002, Bennett dropped more than $500,000 at Bellagio in Las Vegas. On July 12, 2002, Bennett reportedly lost $340,000 at Caesars in Atlantic City. There were estimates that throughout the same decade in which he had told others how they should live their lives, he had lost as much as $8 million as a result of his undisciplined behavior in gambling halls.

There is a story, probably apocryphal, about an attempt by the National Football League to help Philadelphia Eagles owner Leonard Tose overcome the compulsive gambling problem that eventually led to his loss of the team. The NFL sent a top addiction therapist to speak with Tose. The therapist found him sitting in a casino with a cigarette in one hand and a scotch on the rocks in the other. He explained to Tose the purpose of the visit. "Why would I need your help quitting gambling?" Tose asked. "I didn't need anyone's help giving up smoking and drinking."

William Bennett would never understand the irony in the Tose story. There was a difference, he explained, between his gambling and that of others. Bennett said he gambled to relax, he didn't spend the "milk money," and his family never suffered as a result of his habit.

He later stated another reason why he didn't see his gaming hobby as a problem. Bennett, who had said Clinton and Gore were immoral because of their lies, revealed that in all the years of his lust for playing high-stakes slots and video poker machines he had "pretty much broken even."

Addiction specialists were aghast. The author of *The Book of Virtues* had displayed a classic and very public state of denial. It was clear evidence that he had never understood the throes of addiction that he had told drug users to simply shrug off.

Internet chat rooms were abuzz the night Bennett's gambling habit was exposed. There were acerbic barbs, half-hearted defenses, and partisan exchanges. Among them were:

"William Bennett's most poignant quote on family values: 'Daddy needs a new pair of shoes.' "

"Does Bill Bennett think it's virtuous to split eights?"

"Big deal. It's a report in the ultra-liberal *Washington Post*. Give me one reason why anyone should believe it."

"I'll give you three. Woodward, Bernstein, and Watergate."

"People in glass houses shouldn't throw dice."

"Unlike Clinton, Bennett is no hypocrite. Where did he lie?"

"Where did he lie? Read one of his books."

"Maybe Mr. Bennett will now see the virtues in tolerance, forgiveness, and humility from a different perspective."

"Every time I saw him on CNN I said he had a great poker face."

"Asked one time if he read his books on virtues to his kids, Bill Bennett replied that he didn't, but that his wife did. With all that time in the casinos, no wonder he didn't."

"I am a conservative Republican and I do not condone

gambling of any kind whatsoever. I am extremely disappointed by William Bennett. He obviously has been influenced by his left-wing Democrat brother, that lawyer that defended Clinton."

"$200,000 on slots? This guy was education secretary? People actually listen to him?"

Five will get you ten some people still listen to him.

The most scandalizing element of Bennett's defrocking wasn't that he had been gambling away millions of dollars while he was condemning the morals of anyone that didn't agree with him, but that he saw nothing wrong with it.

Equally revealing was that his financial backers like the Heritage Foundation, Empower America, and the John Olin Foundation apparently found nothing wrong with the fact that their generous funding may have been bankrolling Bennett's betting binges. They continued to support him, showing that denial is a condition that can be suffered by organizations as well as individuals.

Several weeks after the scandal broke, Bennett stated that he was giving up gambling. He added, however, that it was not because it was a problem, but because he was worried about people getting the wrong impression. The denial continued.

Since Bennett's "method of relaxation" was bared, his TV appearances as a political pundit have been reduced. It's understandable, of course, since news program directors would be hard pressed to have the crawl on the TV screen say, "former cabinet member and slot enthusiast William Bennett."

Though he makes far fewer television appearances Bennett is still around and still commanding large fees for his self-righteous speeches. Early in January 2004, he delivered a talk to college students in Manchester, New Hampshire. Lloyd Grove of the *New York Daily News* reported that Students for a Sensible Drug Policy passed out plastic cups for those in the audience who might want to provide Bennett with urine samples. One student got Bennett to autograph the cover of a book. It was entitled, *Winning Casino Blackjack for the Non-Counter.*

Others might have wilted under the razzing that stemmed from this fall from grace. But there's a difference with William Bennett. The nation's chief moralizer bravely persisted. Grove reported that the former education secretary used the appearance to criticize baseball legend Pete Rose for gambling on baseball.

CONFEDERATES—DOWN IN THE LAND OF COTTON, WHERE THINGS ARE ROTTEN

Jefferson Davis, John Wilkes Booth, Strom Thurmond, Ty Cobb

Slavery and white supremacy rate as America's original sin. The Founding Fathers wrote a Constitution in which a black person was considered 3/5 of a man. The Confederate States of America was the first nation in the history of the world to be founded on the declared concept that "white man is inherently superior to the black," as stated by Alexander Stephens, the vice president of the CSA, in his famous "cornerstone speech." Many say the Civil War has never quite ended, and this cannot be disproved by the long, lamentable saga of race relations in this country. The four creatures here are representative of a stream of intolerance that flows through our troubled history. We could have just as easily included George Wallace, Theodore Bilbo, Orville Faubus, Lester Maddox, Bull Conner, or Trent Lott. The depressing list goes on and on. As Andrew Johnson's wrong-headed, anti-black approach to Reconstruction, and the New York City draft riots prove, racial injustice is not limited to the South. Someday we might hope to be free of this scourge. Until then, we can hope, pray, and identify the haters.

Jefferson Davis

✳

BY ISHMAEL REED

Hurrah for Jeff Davis?

American history textbooks show the Civil War ending
with Lee's surrender at Appomattox. A very moving scene
in which Grant, a badly dressed general reeking from the
stench of cheap cigars, accepts the sword of an immacu-
lately dressed chivalrous General Robert E. Lee, who
achieved sainthood through the efforts of his Virginia fan
clubs. ("Early biographers and historians, North and
South, criticized him for major blunders. Lee . . . was
blamed for the loss at Gettysburg.") What they don't mention is that through terror and negotiation the Confederates got it all back. By 1887, Jefferson Davis, sounding
more like a victor than someone who'd been defeated, was
able to say, "There *is* no *New* South! No, it is the *Old* South
rehabilitated, and revived by the energy and virtues of
Southern men." One of those Southern men was Ten-
nessean Andrew Johnson.

During the Clinton impeachment scandal, Andrew
Johnson was presented as a noble tragic hero. President
James Polk and other contemporaries had a different view
of the seventeenth president. Polk said of Johnson, "He is
very vindictive and perverse in his temper and conduct."

Doris Kearns Goodwin and others hold that Johnson was
impeached because he stuck to his principles. In reality,

Johnson was a racist drunken bum who, on the campaign trail, got into vulgar exchanges with his hecklers. He helped to restore the Confederacy by extending amnesty to the Confederate killers. "Instead of hanging prominent rebels as he had promised, he handed out mass pardons, until every former Confederate was beyond the reach of the law. He ordered the return of seized lands to the pardoned rebels—halting efforts to provide homesteads to freedmen—and withdrew black troops from the South. At the same time, the Southern states began to pass 'black codes,' laws that virtually re-enslaved African Americans though a combination of contract-labor requirements, vagrancy laws, and apprenticeship arrangements." White violence against blacks proliferated with the approval of the Southern press. "If one had the power," said the *Memphis Daily Appeal*, "it would be a solemn duty for him to annihilate the race." Race riots broke out all over the South. In Memphis, for example, those in charge of law enforcement actually led mobs into black neighborhoods where the carnage, looting, and raping occurred.

And so what kind of system, personalities, and symbols are the supporters of the Confederacy vouching for when they praise a "country" whose economy was based upon breeding human beings like animals and whose defenders referred to those who attempted to liberate them as "nigger thieves," which is the label that the James brothers, Jesse James and Frank James, used as an excuse to execute the citizens of Lawrence, Kansas. "They killed. They shot every man and boy they saw. They pulled them out of cellars and attics, knocked them off horses, and executed them in front of their families. They clubbed them, knifed them, stole their money and valuables, burned their homes and businesses. Black and white, ministers, farmers, merchants, schoolboys, recruits: at least two hundred died in terror. . . ." After the vicious murderer Jesse James was assassinated, the mob celebrated the outlaw with the shout "Hurrah for Jeff Davis." When the Confederates were restored to power, thousands of blacks were murdered in the South by the KKK, those whom Shelby Foote likened to the French Resistance. (Shelby Foote used the N word during an interview with a San Francisco reporter, Noah Griffin. He didn't know that the reporter was black.)

Like the present occupant of the White House, President James Polk used a pretext to invade a sovereign country. He ordered Zachary Taylor, his general, to cook up something that would create hysteria for an invasion of Mexico. His administration offered to buy the Southwest, but the offer was turned down. After the defeat of a weaker opponent, the United States annexed 1,527,241 square kilometers of Mexican territory. This included Texas, New Mexico, and California. In on the slaughter of the ill-equipped Mexicans was Jefferson Davis and his "Mississippi Rifles." Then as now war fever was especially high in the South, where, to this day, the homicide rate among white males is higher than that of white males in the North. Walt Whitman blessed the war. He justified the conquest on the basis of ". . . peopling the New World with a noble race," but Sam Houston called it for what it was, land theft; he, however, also used white supremacy as the justification for stealing the Southwest. (They wanted to seize all of Mexico, but their ambitions were limited because Polk promised a short war). Henry David Thoreau was jailed for protesting the war. Tells you something about a country that has built more monuments to Jefferson

Davis, a ruthless and arrogant dictator under whose regime atrocities and massacres occurred, than to Henry David Thoreau, who represented the best of the American spirit. Of this infamous episode in American history, for which James Polk was censured, Senator Jefferson Davis said "I hold that in a just war we conquered a larger portion of Mexico, and that to it we have a title which has been regarded as valued ever since man existed in a social condition." According to historian Doug Brinkley, appearing on CNN, February 6, 2004, the idea was to pretend that Mexico was the aggressor, when, in reality, the United States was.

Davis had as much regard for Mexicans as he had for Africans, despite the attempts of these apologists to paint him as a compassionate conservative, someone who is even shown palling around with his slaves. How did his slaves feel about him? When the Union troops came upon his house, a slave pointed them to where "old Jeff's" papers were stored and one slave, who worked in the household, was a Union spy.

Under this compassionate conservative's government, a measure was passed ordering that blacks found fighting on the side of the Union be put to death. In 1863, the "chivalrous" and "gallant" Confederate army moved into Pennsylvania. "In the course of their raiding and foraging, these units searched for blacks, seized them, and sent them south into slavery. A newspaper, the *Franklin Repository*, reported, "Quite a number of negroes, free and slave, men, women, and children were captured by Jenkins and started south to be sold into bondage. . . . Some of the men were bound with ropes, and the children were mounted in front or behind the rebels on their horses." According to the book *When War Passed This Way*, "no one can estimate the number of Negroes who suffered this fate, for the practice continued throughout the time Lee's army was in Pennsylvania." Does this information make Peter Applebome and Tony Horowitz, fans of the Confederacy, want to get up in the gray—Jefferson Davis's favorite color—and join an enactment? Would the thousands of NASCAR fans who waved the Stars and Bars to greet their neo-Confederate hero George Bush put these flags away were they familiar with this history?

This wouldn't be the first time that Jefferson Davis and his colleagues enslaved people who had no way of defending themselves, whether they were slave or free, or whether they were Mexican or Native American. Those Pennsylvania blacks got off easy. On other occasions, soldiers under the order of Davis, or campaigns of which Davis was a member, murdered people even after they had surrendered! This policy of Davis's Confederacy led to what some have called the atrocity of the war. On April 12, 1864, at Fort Pillow, located fifty miles from Memphis, Tennessee, Confederate troops under the command of General Nathan Forrest, slaughtered black and white troops, even though they had begged for mercy.

"The slaughter was awful—words cannot describe the scene. The poor deluded Negroes would run up to our men, fall upon their knees, and with uplifted hands scream for mercy, but they were ordered to their feet and then shot down. The white men fared little better. Their fort turned out to be a great slaughter pen—blood, human blood, stood about in pools and brains could have been gathered up in any quantity. I with several others tried to stop the butchery and at one time had partially succeeded, but

General Forrest ordered them shot down like dogs and the carnage continued. Finally our men became sick of blood and the firing ceased." This passage from an eyewitness, a confederate soldier, Winston Grooms, Confederate apologist and author of *Forrest Gump*, a post-modernist reading of the "Lost Cause" myth, merely describes General Forrest's actions as "controversial." As an example of the hatred and spite directed at blacks, a hatred and resentment that leads to the glorification of Davis and Lee, the white citizens of Memphis, Tennessee, as a vindictive slap at black advancement, erected a statue to this monster in the 1950s. Maybe Confederate sympathizer Ted Turner will finance a movie that will enshrine Nathan Forrest's deeds.

But instead of the opprobrium cast upon foreign dictators like Joseph Stalin and Hitler for their heading regimes that engaged in genocide, Nathan Forrest, Jefferson Davis, Robert E. Lee, and their colleagues, who, Ken Burns, in a candid moment, said were responsible for more loyal American deaths than Tojo or Hitler, have been honored, as a result of one of the greatest propaganda campaigns in history. Not only has the rebel terrorist regime headed by Jefferson Davis been whitewashed by generations of apologists and historians, but by the American textbook industry and Hollywood in such films as *Birth of a Nation*, *Gone with the Wind*, *Shane*, and numerous films that celebrate the nefarious activities of the James and Younger brothers who are shown as Robin Hoods. Though film historians refer to Leni Riefenstahl's *Triumph of the Will* as the greatest propaganda film of all time, I'd choose Victor Fleming's *Gone with the Wind*. It was such an ingenious propaganda film that critics don't even see it as such. Besides, unlike *Triumph of the Will*, it was in Technicolor.

Ken Burns's *The Civil War*, which is the nonfictional redo of *Gone with The Wind*, has also contributed to a sort of Springtime for the Confederacy, showing beleaguered and courageous Southerners defending their homeland against an invasion by Yankees. This was the reading of the series by historian Leo Litwack. The Sons of the Confederacy showed Burns some love by making him a member of their organization.

Even General Stonewall Jackson was cleaned up in that neo-Confederate play, Jonathan Reynolds's *Stonewall Jackson's House*, which argued that blacks were better off in slavery. As a sign of the times, Jack Kroll, the late *Newsweek* drama critic, recommended it for a Pulitzer Prize and Robert Hurwitt of the *San Francisco Chronicle* commended the playwright for having "the guts" to pen such a play, as though shoving ugly racist projects into the faces on blacks in the 1990s required some kind of courage. Because of the often bizarre punishments meted out to his own men, Jackson was much hated by those under his command, and though Southern apologists and even a segment on National Public Radio saluted this killer, he was probably fragged by one of his own men, though the history books call it "friendly fire." Stonewall Jackson was an early believer that faith-based institutions would civilize the blacks. He sent a contribution to a black Sunday school, a fact that his defenders point to as an example of this slaveholder's enlightened attitudes toward blacks, and if television were around in those days, he'd have probably used black children as props as President Bush does.

Davis and his fellow war criminals are even venerated by monuments erected on the basis of fraudulent claims. They are listed by James W. Loewen in his book, *Lies*

Across America. Many of them were erected by the Daughters of the Confederacy, even though Davis nearly ordered Robert E. Lee, another Confederate with an inflated reputation, to fire on hungry Richmond women who were demonstrating for bread, confirming Sam Houston's description of Davis as "cold blooded as a lizard." It shows again that some white women are the last Aunt Jemimas, the last ones to vote for those who would deny them choice and praising men like Jefferson Davis, who was five minutes away from massacring their great-grandmothers in Richmond, and California's First Groper in Chief, Arnold Schwarzenegger. Can you imagine blacks honoring someone who engaged such a hostile act against them, or Native Americans building monuments throughout the West honoring Zachary Taylor or Andrew Jackson? Moreover, at least some Southern women didn't share the enthusiasm of the Daughters of the Confederacy. During the war, Richmond women of 1864 were criticized for partying while men in gray were dying on the battle-field. Augusta Jane Evans, in 1864, published an attack on her countrywomen in the *Mobile Register:* "Can mirth and reckless revelry hold high carnival in social circles while every passing breeze chants the requiem of dying heroes. . . . Shame, Shame," she wrote, "upon your degeneracy."

But lest one consigns enthusiasm for the Confederacy to the right wing, there seems to be admiration for the Confederacy among even the most enlightened circles. I remember returning from Spain, during the Christmas season of 1988, and watching CNN's Atlanta airport service celebrate the Confederacy. Something about "Christmas on the Plantation" in which all of the romance of the Confederacy was trotted out. It figures. CNN's founder Ted Turner has produced movies about the Confederacy and greets visitors to his home with loud speakers blasting the theme from *Gone with the Wind*. Turner funded a $56 million, 216-minute blockbuster film called *Gods and Generals*, directed, written, and produced by Ronald Maxwell, who made the successful Civil War film *Gettysburg*.

"This 2003 'prequel' has neo-Confederates salivating," according to the Southern Poverty Law Center. They quote Clyde Wilson, described as a neo-Confederate intellectual and founding member of the League of the South hate group, as calling the movie "an American cultural event of major significance," and "an arresting example of how a people's history should be told."

Peter Applebome, who writes about race for the *New York Times*, glorifies the Confederacy in his book, *Dixie Rising: How the South Is Shaping American Values, Politics, and Culture*. He says, "When the Supreme Court is acting as if Jefferson Davis were chief justice; when country music has become white America's music of choice and even stock car racing has become a $2 billion juggernaut; when evangelical Christians have transformed American politics; when unions are on the run across the nation much as they always have been in the South; when whites nationwide are giving up on public education just as so many Southerners did after integration—in times such as these, to understand America, you have to understand the South." Of course this wouldn't be the first time that a Northerner like Peter Applebome swooned over Southern values. Frederick Douglass, the first great African American leader, noticed a similar Northern trend in the 1890s, at a time when white terrorists had successfully destroyed reconstruction by lynching and even massacring blacks who sought to exercise their rights. In a speech made in 1894 at Rochester's Mt. Hope Cemetery he criticized those who sought to romanticize the vanquished foe, which was being done through "battlefield reunions, in popular fiction, inscribed on war memorials . . . and novels by Southern writers Joel Chandler Harris, John Easton Cooke, Thomas Nelson Page, and Sara Pryor flooded the nation's mass-circulation fiction market with local-color stories depicting the Antebellum South's refinement and civilization."

So successful has the Second Redemption of the Confederacy been that members of the president's cabinet have joined the tribute. John Ashcroft and Gale Norton have fond feelings for the land ruled by Jefferson Davis. "Secretary Norton goes so far as to describe the South's struggle as honorable and unfortunately sullied by pundits crying *slavery as 'bad facts.'* Mr. Ashcroft, in the now infamous *Southern Partisan* article, argues that as good Americans we must defend the honor and principle of the great Southern patriots Robert E. Lee, Jefferson Davis, and so forth. These men, after all, fought for so much more than 'some perverted agenda' as critics of the Confederacy claim," wrote Robert A. Soza.

South Carolina was the first state to secede from the Union and in keeping with the Confederate theme, George W. Bush often behaves as if he is the president of South Carolina in his appeal to religious fundamentalism and the homophobia that one associates with this faith. When he ran for president he pretended to remain neutral about the controversy about flying the Confederate flag over the capitol building but "slyly" used his wife, Laura, to express his views. She said of the flag, "It's not a symbol of racism to me.

I grew up in the South. Like everyone else here in Texas. And it's just a symbol of the time in our history we can't erase, really. The Civil War and, you know, there's just, that's the symbol of the Civil War."

Bush should have a painting of Jefferson Davis above his desk, because the careers of both are similar. Both were unelected. Like Bush, Davis was a fraternity cut-up. Both participated in an unprovoked attack on an adversary who did not have the equipment to make it an even fight. Jefferson Davis participated in The Black Hawk War against Indians who were attempting to defend their land against a takeover by white settlers. Black Hawk, the Sauk leader, in his autobiography, remembers the final battle. Like the black soldiers at Fort Pillow, the Sauk were murdered even after they had given up.

Early in the morning a party of whites, being in advance of the army, came upon our people, who were attempting to cross the Mississippi. They tried to give themselves up. The whites paid no attention to their entreaties, but commenced slaughtering them! In a little while the whole army arrived. Our braves, but few in number, finding that the enemy paid no regard to age or sex, and seeing that they were murdering helpless women and little children, determined to fight until they were killed. As many women as could, commenced swimming the Mississippi, with their children on their backs. A number of them were drowned, and some shot, before they could reach the opposite shore.

Besides Jefferson, another participant in this shameful war with the blame-the-victim title "The Black Hawk War" was Captain Abraham Lincoln.

Just as some of Bush's advisors convinced him that Iraq would be "a cakewalk," Davis led his followers to believe that the Civil War would not be fought on Southern soil. Like Bush, Davis also lied about the reasons his nation entered the war. No mention is made of slavery in his inaugural address and to this day, some Southerners and even historians, weighed down by the Lost Cause delusional system, insist that the war was fought over states' rights and other ideals when both Davis and Lee would have been broke had it not been for land and slaves. As for Lee, he married rich; his father, Henry (Light-Horse Harry) Lee, served time in debtor's prison. "Save for some three thousand dollars he had received from his mother's small estate, he had no inheritance." He survived by marrying well. In 1831, he married a slave-owning woman, a distant cousin, Mary Custis, the daughter of George Washington's adopted son, George Washington Parke Custis. Jefferson Davis also married up. To Zachary Taylor's daughter. After the war, and without slaves, he was in constant struggle to make ends meet.

Indeed Robert E. Lee, depicted by his apologists as a compassionate conservative, was caught red handed, participating in the very system that his apologists pretend repulsed him. On July 8, 1858, he wrote:

I have made arrangements to send down the three men on Monday . . . The man who is to carry them, is now undetermined whether to go by the mail boat, via Fredericksburg, or by Gordonsville . . . He will have orders to deliver them to you at Richmond, or in the event of not meeting you, to lodge them in jail in that city subject to your order . . . I may wish to send at the same time three women, one about 35 years old, one 22, and the other 17. They have been accustomed to house work. The eldest a good washer & ironer. But I cannot recommend them for honesty.

Lee believed, "The painful discipline they are undergoing, is necessary for their instruction as a race, & I hope will prepare & lead them to better things." Painful discipline seems to be the attitude of the Bush administration toward the poor. Discontinuing the safety net for the poor will somehow make them stronger.

Both Bush and Davis designated duties to others, Bush to his vice president and staff, and Davis, because of illness to his wife, Varina and at other times to Judah Benjamin, his secretary of war, leading General Joseph E. Johnston to complain "If that miserable little Jew is retained in his place our country will never be able to defend itself."

One thing that is different, Davis sometimes would appear on the battlefield, which was the case at Manassas, raising the morale of his troops, while George W. Bush's military activities are murky. He confines his military involvement to posturing, imitating a fighter pilot, and using soldiers and fake turkeys as photo ops before an admiring and uncritical press. (By contrast the Southern newspapers were withering in their criticism of Davis and one described him as treating the people of the South like "white negroes.")

Like Bush, Davis was an early exponent of globalization, desiring to extend a system of cheap labor to other states and to Cuba . . . etc. just as the president is a sort of P.R. man for doing the same for multinationals on the hunt internationally for wage slaves. Also, like Bush, Jefferson Davis was known for a hot head, an attitude that Bush has kept private. Davis once challenged Zachary Taylor, his future father-in-law to a duel, while Bush, under the influence of alcohol, is rumored to have challenged his father to a fight.

Bush seems to acknowledge his connection to Davis. "Last Memorial Day," reports Andrew Sullivan, "for the second year in a row, Bush's White House sent a floral wreath to the Confederate Memorial in Arlington National Cemetery. Six days later, as the United Daughters of the Confederacy celebrated Jefferson Davis's birthday there, Washington chapter president Vicki Heilig offered a 'word of gratitude to George W. Bush' for 'honoring' the Old South's dead. And, why not? In 2004, Jeff Davis is hip. As Peter Applebome said, ". . . like Elvis, Jefferson Davis had never been better." Even Davis's arguments about race are also current, but instead of wisely hiding behind questionable graphs and statistics, and op-ed columns of pompous rhetoric, or hiding behind black faces for hire, Davis was up-front with his opinions. He simply believed that black people were inferior to white people. "We recognize the negro as God and God's Book and God's Laws, in nature, tell us to recognize him—our inferior, fitted expressly for servitude . . . the innate stamp of inferiority is beyond the reach of change. . . . You cannot transform the negro into anything one-tenth as useful or as good as what slavery enables him to be."

Charles Murray's *The Bell Curve*, which says the same thing, but in a pseudo-scientific manner, not only received praise from the *Irish American National Review*, and *Commentary*, published by Jewish Americans, but from the *New York Times* and so-called "attack-queer" journalist Andrew Sullivan. Richard Bernstein of the *Times* even asked that some thought be given to a theory that blacks excel at basketball because of genetic differences. (But now that Bryant Gumbel has done a show about Eastern Europeans dominating the NBA, do you suppose that those

players received a genetic transplant from the blacks?)
Even the popular media have gotten into the act. For
example, in an 2003 episode of the television show *Law
and Order: Special Victims Unit,* the script invited the audience to contemplate whether there existed a rape gene
passed from black males to their sons. In this episode, a
Chinese-American youth became a rapist because his
mother was raped by a black; clearly, Jefferson Davis was
ahead of his time, which might account for his popularity
in the strangest of places.

And so when contemporary Southerners and North-
erners praise characters like Davis and Lee are they also
endorsing the policies of the system that these men represented or do they separate the men from their deeds and the
consequences of their ideas? Is the Confederate "battle"
flag a symbol of this system or merely an object revered by
art-loving Southerners? One can excuse Ms. Bush. Her
biographer reveals that she has led the life of the typical
Southern belle, a sort of stateside Saudi princess, isolated
from blacks until she attended college and even then, not
knowing the significance of Martin Luther King, Jr.'s, visit
to her Austin campus. Otherwise, how would someone as
literate as she praise a flag that represented a system that
led to the destruction of millions of human beings and the
forced separation of families? These family members were
sent to death and enslavement camps called plantations,
the subject of Harriet Beecher Stowe's great novel, *Uncle
Tom's Cabin.* African women were sexually exploited so
much that according to Joel Williamson and Chester Himes
a new race emerged in the United States and while the contemporary press casts Thomas Jefferson and Strom Thurmond as the lone perpetrators of what a contemporary

writer, and ex-slave, William Wells Brown called a "decadent" practice, the practice was widespread. Mary Chesnutt, the Martha Mitchell of the Confederacy and a friend of the Davises said that every woman was aware of other women's husbands carrying on with African-American women, but not their own.

And what part of the Confederate history are its champions celebrating? The part where they fought against the Union? Or the postwar part where ex-Confederates fought against the granting of rights to the former African captives. Eric Foner, in his book, *Reconstruction: America's Unfinished Revolution, 1863–1877*, reports a massacre committed by the ex-Confederates, who are depicted in films like *Gone with the Wind*, as the cream of Knighthood. When blacks met to reconvene a constitutional convention, they were met by the city police, which was made up of Confederate veterans. "Fighting broke out in the streets, police converged on the area, and the scene quickly degenerated into what General Philip H. Sheridan later called 'an absolute massacre,' with blacks assaulted indiscriminately and the delegates and their supporters besieged in the convention hall and shot down when they fled, despite hoisting white flags of surrender.... The son of former vice president Hannibal Hamlin, a veteran of the Civil War, wrote that 'the wholesale slaughter and the little regard paid to human life I witnessed here' surpassed anything he had seen on the battlefield."

Jefferson Davis might not have been the "Lucifer" that Sam Houston said he was, but clearly the "country" over which he presided and the legacy that it formed was certainly a hell.

John Wilkes Booth

BY LEW GROSSBERGER

What Everyone Knows About John Wilkes Booth

He was a madman. He operated alone. He was an actor. His brother Edwin was a better actor. He sneaked into the presidential box at Ford's Theater and shot Lincoln in the back of the head. Then he vaulted over the balcony railing, snagging his spur in a draped flag, and broke his leg when he landed onstage. He shouted: "Sic semper tyrannis," (thus always to tyrants), hobbled off, and vanished. A couple of weeks later, he died under slightly ambiguous circumstances in a burning barn.

Much of that is true. Except that Booth probably wasn't insane and did not operate alone. Oh and his acting was quite good.

What Nobody Knows About John Wilkes Booth

Even now, 138 years later, we don't know for sure whether Booth's scheme of multiple assassinations was planned or sanctioned by the Confederate leadership, or whether it was merely a home-cooked plot for which Booth recruited old school friends, drinking buddies, malcontents, and assorted rebel riffraff. Was Booth a dedicated Confederate agent on an official mission, just a very determined freelance hater with connections, or something in between? Mainstream historians tend to accept the second option but the argument goes on.

Why Did Booth Hate Lincoln So Much, Anyway?

Booth, a dedicated white supremacist, was in love with the Antebellum South and its charming customs, such as slavery. "The country was formed for the white, not for the black," he proclaimed. Booth admired the Southern gentry and the fragrance of genteel chivalry they emitted. There was perhaps a certain wistful snobbery in him. He was ready to thrash any man who spoke a word against Robert E. Lee or those dashing boys in gray, whose ranks, however, he never saw fit to join.

How Booth got that way, though, is a mystery. True, he was born and raised in Maryland, a border state full of Southern sympathizers. But no one else in his family was pro-slavery or secessionist; indeed, he and brother Edwin argued bitterly on the issue.

There is no mystery about the focus of Booth's hatred. In his eyes, Lincoln was the emblem of abolition, the dispatcher of armies raining destruction upon the South, and a power-mad tyrant. The hate became very personal. Booth was given to furious rants about Lincoln's homely face, his country expressions, his plain dress and earthy humor. To Booth, Lincoln was a crude, clownish yet evil oaf, the opposite of the polished, courtly Southern gentlemen he so revered. The man's eloquence, his basic fairness and decency, his magnanimity were qualities Booth somehow missed. When Lincoln gave one of his greatest speeches—the second inaugural—Booth stood in the crowd outside the Capitol. There is actually in existence a photograph of the scene with both men visible. It was that day that Lincoln uttered his moving plea for reconciliation: "With malice toward none, with charity to all." Booth had malice toward one.

Everyone Loves Show Biz

The man had talent; give him that.

Booth's career got off to a bad start; his father, also a renowned actor, did not believe in teaching. But Booth improved and once he hit his stride, he started getting good notices and lead roles. At the end, he was a star, magnetic, handsome enough to make women swoon. He was athletic, too, and was known for making his entrances with spectacular leaps. He was especially popular in the South but was famous everywhere, and was able to cross army lines without difficulty. (Always a nice benefit for a spy or assassin.) In 1864, Booth's last full year of work, he earned $20,000, far more than General Lee.

For Abraham Lincoln, plays, opera, and concerts were a refuge from the grinding, brutal war. He and Mary Todd Lincoln went often to the theater. Shakespeare was a favorite. They had seen John Wilkes Booth before; Lincoln had even sent him an admiring note and asked to meet. Booth snubbed him.

How much did Booth hate Lincoln? Imagine: He killed a fan.

Hey, Gang, Let's Kidnap the President

In March 1865, Booth and five henchmen waited in the woods near a veterans' hospital, where Lincoln was scheduled to visit wounded soldiers. Booth planned to kidnap the president and exchange him for Confederate prisoners of war. But Lincoln canceled at the last moment.

Then came Lee's surrender at Appomattox. "Our cause being almost lost, something decisive and great must be done," Booth said. The great thing would be multiple murders: Lincoln, his vice president, his cabinet, General

Grant. When Booth informed his colleagues of the switch, two of them quit the plot.

Plan B

April. The war had gone on for four bloody years. The great battles had all been fought. Richmond had fallen. The remaining rebel armies were leaving the field. Jefferson Davis was on the lam, soon to be nabbed by Union cavalry. He called for guerrilla war but the wiser heads—notably Lee—rejected the notion. But for a formal document of surrender, the Confederacy was a dead letter.

Only now does the bitter ender hatch his murder plan. Loathing Lincoln as he does, Booth is blind to the fact that the man in the White House is now the white South's best friend, that Lincoln's greatest desire is to reunite the fractured country, to heal and forgive. Booth is too late to save the Confederacy. But he is in time to increase the power of the vengeful radicals in the North, foster mutual hatred, and help remove the country's best chance for moderation.

Never a Cop Around When You Need One

There was no Secret Service in 1865. Protecting the president was a ridiculously haphazard affair and Lincoln cared little for bodyguards. Just one man, Washington city policeman John Parker, had been assigned to guard Lincoln's box that night. Parker left his post. Why? No one knows. Booth talked his way past an unarmed presidential aide and walked right into the box.

The Lincolns had two guests with them that night, April 14. Army Major Henry Rathbone rose up after the shot and grappled with the assassin. But Booth whipped out a knife and slashed the major's arm to the bone, ending the struggle. "Stop that man!" screamed Rathbone's fiancée, Clara Harris, as Booth jumped for the stage. No one did.

Other Than That, Mrs. Lincoln, How Was the Play?

It was tripe. *Our American Cousin* was a tired old farce with a predictable plot and cheap gags, but still a long-running crowd pleaser. American bumpkin inherits an English title, heads for Blighty and shows up the snobby bluebloods. Before firing his single-shot derringer into the back of Lincoln's head, Booth waited for the reliable laugh line of Act II: "Don't know the manners of good society, eh? Well, I guess I know enough to turn you inside out, old gal, you sockdologizing old man-trap!" These were the last words Abraham Lincoln heard.

Some Friends of JWB

Lewis Powell, a.k.a. Paine, Confederate Army veteran, assigned by Booth to kill the secretary of state (but only wounded him). Hanged. David Herold, twenty-three-year-old drifter, helped Powell find his way to Seward's house. Hanged. George Atzerodt, German immigrant, assigned to kill Vice President Andrew Johnson. Chickened out. Hanged. Mary Surratt, owner of the Washington boarding house where Booth and his henchmen plotted. Hanged. Dr. Samuel Mudd, set Booth's leg. Served four years in prison. (Despite the fervent lobbying of his descendants, Mudd was probably in on the conspiracy.) Edman Spangler, stagehand and carpenter. Held Booth's horse behind the theater. Four years in prison.

Any Chance He Could Have Gotten Away With It?

Slim. While the murder succeeded either through amazing

luck or the machinations of a powerful super-conspiracy (you may believe whichever you like), the escape plan was flawed. Booth was famous. Everyone in the theater knew him—even, as noted—his victim. You'd think an actor would have availed himself of disguise but no. Booth needed to take a bow onstage.

The plan was to head for the Deep South, where sympathetic folk might shelter him until he could reach Mexico. Problem was the shallow South, now overrun with bluecoats. Of course the leg slowed him down. Nor had he reckoned on the wrathful alacrity of Edwin Stanton. As Lincoln lay dying and others gave in to grief and confusion, the secretary of war seized control of the government and flung into action the largest manhunt in the nation's history. Wanted posters went up. Armies of man and horse combed the capital and outlying districts. They blocked river crossings, thundered up and down country roads and town streets, banging on doors in the night, questioning everyone, arresting and interrogating all of dubious identity, shattering the silence of wood, field, and village square. It took them twelve days.

I Really Hate This Part

According to one biographer, Booth had a Jewish ancestor. Several generations back in his genealogy was this Spanish Jew who allegedly left for England in the Seventeenth century. The original family name was Botha. There is no indication that Booth ever brought this up in conversation.

How, Exactly, Did Booth Die?

Bullet in the throat.

Getting out of Washington was easy. Booth rode ahead of the news. Crossing a bridge out of Washington, he rendezvoused with co-conspirator Herold, picked up firearms from friends, and was treated by the subsequently controversial Dr. Mudd. After that, Booth's dwindling time on earth devolved into the nightmare of the hunted prey (not that I feel the slightest sympathy) as he was hounded through the swamps, woods, and back roads of Maryland and Northern Virginia by the Union dragnet.

Finally, fifty miles from the scene of his crime, around two in the morning of April 26, the assassin was cornered while hiding in a tobacco barn. (Apparently, some farmer had tipped off a Union patrol.) Herold came out, hands up. Not Booth. Armed with a carbine and a pistol, he asked, absurdly, for "a fighting chance." Instead, the troopers set the barn on fire. Seeing his quarry outlined against the flames, a soldier shot through a crack in the structure. Booth fell, paralyzed. Dragged to the farmhouse porch, he lay dying as the sun came up, his captors staring down at him.

A doctor arrived, took a look, said nothing could be done. Booth's last request was to have his no-longer functioning hands held up before him. He stared at them. "Useless. useless," he muttered.

He certainly was.

You Sure Booth Wasn't Nuts?

Not so you would notice. It was his father, Junius Brutus Booth, who was truly insane. Wish I had the space to recount his many outrageous and sometimes hilarious escapades, only some of which were alcohol fueled. Junius probably would have been locked away in an asylum except that he was recognized as one of the best actors in both America and England. One minor eccentricity that unfortunately failed to rub off: On his property, he refused to allow any killing, even of insects.

But the son, could he cop an insanity plea in a courtroom of today? Put it this way: You wouldn't want to be his lawyer. True, he had, as they say now, issues. He was given to depression. He was a binge drinker. Madness galloped in the family. He could easily be described as obsessed, perhaps even unhinged, by his hatred of Lincoln. But John Wilkes Booth was always rational, coherent, and composed. He knew exactly what he was doing. After all, he commanded a cell of wartime spies and conspirators, which tends to rule out the deranged-loner motif.

And self-defense is definitely a nonstarter.

Accomplishments of JWB

1. Made himself perhaps the most hated man in American history.
2. Cast a blight on the family name. Edwin stopped acting for years. A sister, Asia, left the country.
3. Killed any chance for the kind of moderate reconciliation Lincoln wanted. The political atmosphere turned poisonous. There would be hell to pay.
4. Became the spiritual ancestor—or perhaps founding father is the term—of the Great American Assassination Tradition. Later would come Guiteau, Czolgosz, Oswald, Ray, Hinckley, et al, the politicians of the bullet.

So that's what you did for us, Booth. There is your legacy. Thanks for your time. You may now go back to rotting in hell . . . if there is one. If not, just rot.

Strom Thurmond

✹

BY KEVIN ALEXANDER GRAY

The Legacy of Strom Thurmond

I grew up next to the tracks in a black neighborhood called Freyline in what was then rural Spartanburg, South Carolina. Some called it "Niggerline." There was (and still is) one road in, one road out. A main Southern railway line and Mr. Jack Dobson's cow pastures and cornfields locked us in. Dobson lived at the top of the hill in the traditional white big house complete with those huge white columns on the big porch that rung the house. The house sat framed by centuries-old pecan, magnolia, and weeping willow trees that kept it cool in the summer.

As a youngster I cut both black and white folks' grass to make school money. Saturday was generally white folks' day. I had my regulars and was usually hired for the whole day for a variety of chores. And although change was in the air, I was their boy back in a day when most white folk still had at least one, usually named Leroy, Charlie, or Bo (as in short for boy). And if your name wasn't Leroy, Charlie, or Bo, it was by the end of the day. Straight up rednecks called you boy right off the bat.

Labor was cheap and many moderate-income white families also had a black maid. Polite whites referred to their "colored" housekeepers as "domestics." The others called them "girls." The younger women made the daily early morning one-to-three mile walk to their employers' neighborhoods or to the bus stop, but some of the more benevolent white wives would pick up "Mama," as older workers were often called, around the time the morning school bus ran. At the end of the day, after the floors were mopped, the clothes were hung on the line and the kids fed, about a half hour or so before the sun went down, white women in their shiny cars would make the regular trip back to "Niggerline" or "Niggertown" to their workers' home. Almost always, the black housekeeper would sit in the back seat of the car. I remember wanting to hurl a rock but Mrs. Alberteen or someone else I knew was also in the car.

One of my Saturday customers was someone we all knew to be in the Ku Klux Klan. Word had it he was a Great Titan, Giant, or Exalted Cyclops. Whatever his title, he was the local leader. He was a redneck when a redneck was someone to avoid. This particular fellow stayed just off the main road at the entrance to our neighborhood. Looking back he was a pretty stereotypical Southern cracker, complete with that chewing tobacco lump in his lower lip. He wore his white shirt tucked into his blue khaki work pants, sleeves rolled up. Most memorable was that bad smelling, stomach turning Brylcreem grease in his always-wet hair, the small black clip comb in his shirt pocket, and his hands, ever wet from constant preening. I did my best to keep a safe distance between us and I was always prepared to bolt, leaving my lawn mower if necessary.

He may have been a cotton mill supervisor although I don't really know for sure. In the class of white people to work for it was always better to get a teacher, preacher, or some type of professional than a mill supervisor whom we regarded as low class but with power to misuse. Polite whites did not constantly remind you of their power; it was clearly understood.

Yet knowing the boss man was Klan didn't stop us from dealing with him. And although he probably burned the cross in the cornfield in front of our house, he still umpired the integrated little league baseball games and his son played catcher for our team. I cut his and his father-in-law's grass. After integration I went to school with his kid. My uncle's wife was his maid. My first cousin is his daughter.

That's how the South was when I was growing up in the sixties and early seventies. The white man burning crosses and ranting about race-mixing would also buy all the little black boys sodas after the game and still have enough hypocrisy left to screw the black housekeeper and dare her to tell. Whether it was a young James Strom Thurmond or the neighborhood Klansmen, rape and race-mixing have always been part of the story of the South. Thurmond's contradictions only mirrored those of South Carolina and the nation.

The Reverend Joseph Lowery, former head of the Southern Christian Leadership Conference, called Thurmond "a racist by day and a hypocrite by night" when it was revealed that, at age twenty-two, he had fathered a child, Essie Mae Butler (Washington-Williams), by Carrie Butler, his family's sixteen-year-old black maid. But many black South Carolinians saw Thurmond as a life-long hypocrite because they saw him through the race, sex, and power prism.

South Carolina activist Modjeska Simkins, who died in 1992 at the age of ninety-two, kept the "Essie" (as she called her) story alive through her years on earth. Simkins, a feisty woman not afraid to poke her finger in a raw sore, was an NAACP organizer during the years Thurmond was governor. She often told of the "biracial baby born to a teenage domestic in the Thurmond home, a girl so poor that her neighbors had to help feed and clothe the child."

Still, knowing about Thurmond's black daughter may have actually softened black feelings toward him even though blacks knew it was no coincidence or mystery that Butler and her six-month-old child left, fled, or were relocated to a northern state. As Nadine Cohodas, author of the biography *Strom Thurmond and the Politics of Southern Changes*, said after hearing confirmation of Washington-Williams's paternity, "The black teenage servant must have figured that if she spoke out, she might not be believed and might put herself in extreme danger." It is also not surprising that Butler died shortly after her baby's birth, as a young girl carrying a secret child may not have sought or had access to much medical care.

Washington was following custom when she returned to be educated at South Carolina State College, the state's public black college. Throughout the South, many of the "colored" offspring of patrician white males were educated at state-supported black colleges and received "loans" from white "patrons." As John Wrighten, who attended South Carolina State Law School with Julius Williams, who later married Essie Mae Washington, said, "There were so many half-white children at South Carolina State College when I was there; there were five or six girls you couldn't distinguish from white girls." He said Washington was in that group.

Many interracial sexual trysts, long-term relationships, or accommodations were seemingly consensual. That is unless you were the unlucky black guy caught having consensual sex with a white gal. Even if the women didn't holler "rape" (which was usually how the scene played out), she may as well, or someone did it for her. Still, on the southern social class ladder, being "high-yellow" (light skinned) often meant a ticket to the black middle and upper class, a better job, house, college, and a different kind of treatment by whites. And there were those who may have naively hoped that having sexual relations with a black woman might lead a white man to treat black people better.

Since Washington-Williams's announcement, some people have speculated that perhaps Butler intentionally became pregnant with a conscious plan to have a child who would have a better life than her own. This helps Thurmond apologists avoid the subject of rape. But rape, like racism, is about power. Carrie Butler was fifteen years old when Thurmond impregnated her. And although at the time, the age of statutory rape in South Carolina was fourteen, Butler still had no power in the relationship—only a vagina. The relationship, if one wishes to call it that, seems more akin to that of master and sex tool or toy. For even as Jim Crow was eroding, the ultimate expression of white male power was the ability to do to a black woman anything, anytime, anyway they wanted to with absolutely no guilt and no fear of consequence or responsibility. It was common for a young white boy, such as Thurmond, to "learn about sex on the colored side of town." Some "did right" by the children they sired while many others did not even acknowledge their black offsprings' existence. Yet, even if Thurmond was not a deadbeat dad, Washington-Williams's revelation of her long held "secret" and her expression of affection for her biological father were more like the delusional yearnings of a neglected child lost in the hope that one day her cruel parent would see what a wonderful offspring he had produced and embrace her. And this pretty much explains the psychosis afflicting African-Americans in their relationship with white America.

Those attempting to put a positive face on Thurmond's legacy ignore the issue of the strong possibility of rape in the Butler story because it not only clashes with their contrived heroic image of the lawmaker but it also gives Butler rights she did not possess during the Jim Crow period of American history. Their refusal to recognize Butler as more than a necessary detail in this story is their refusal to recognize black humanity. And that refusal is rooted in an unwavering belief in white supremacy that goes far beyond bare-boned race hatred. As a white Southerner once told me, "That's the mistake people make about Southerners. The masters never hated the slaves. Whites, in particular powerful white men, during Jim Crow didn't hate blacks. That would have been like hating your mule or your dog."

Miscegenation was one of the first big words I learned as a youth. From white lips it was a sinister thing. Blacks saw it as the white man's greatest fear and weakness. Obviously, the hypocrisy of it all was and is evident in the faces of all the high yellow and light brown kids running around. And while the anti-miscegenators fretted over white racial purity and advocated—and committed—murder as punishment for black men and white women having sex, most mixed-raced kids were a result of race mixing between white men and black women. Not only was the sexual contact an expression of white male power; it was also a psychological response to the stereotypical fear of the black man as hyper-sexed beast: Mandingo.

The Mandingo myth originated in the Old South where white slave owners believed that the Mandinkas were the fiercest warriors of Africa. After a Caribbean slave revolt in the 1800s, John C. Calhoun of South Carolina, the leading intellectual of the Southern gentry, invoked the specter of Mandingo slaughtering white masters as justification for their enslavement. Black male sexual prowess was also a big part of the myth. The often used colloquialism, "once you go black you never go back," is the myth of the big black, well-endowed buck, Mandingo.

In the 1970s, the myth became the movie *Mandingo* in which one-time heavyweight champ Ken Norton played a noble slave who burns down the white man's plantation and escapes to freedom with the blonde Southern belle in his arms. My mother took us kids to see the "controversial" movie when it was shown at the local drive-in theater. And at the top of her stack of romance novels was a book whose cover displayed a muscular, caramel-colored black man caressing a buxom, blonde lass, her ample white breast barely covered by the straps of her torn hoop dress, her long blonde ringlets cascading over her shoulder, with the title *Mandingo* emblazoned across the cover.

The Mandingo stereotype entraps black males to this day as evidenced by the pop culture embrace of the pimp, gangsta rappers along with a host of psycho-sexual-social illusions. The myth fuels denial over homosexuality and feeds rampant homophobia in the black community. As black gay and bisexual men practice a dangerous sexual secrecy, the AIDS crisis in the black community worsens. As a friend told me, "One of the worst things to be is a gay black man in the South. The preacher wants you to lead the choir, and maybe even give him a blowjob every now and again, while condemning, denying, or damning your very existence from the pulpit."

As for white women, during slavery, a white woman marrying or consensually having a child by a black man usually found herself in legally sanctioned bondage. "Defilement" or being "spoiled" during the Jim Crow era most often meant being banished—stripped of being "white" for one's "nigger-loving" ways. White men used "protecting white womanhood," the first plank in the Klan platform, as a pretext for controlling white women, but in some respects it trapped the men in a psychotic effort to prove their own sexual dominance.

In Thurmond's youth and political prime, lynching and the fear of it was the primary weapon to discourage black men from even looking the "wrong way" at white women let alone having sexual relations with them. And lynching was accepted at all levels of white society as a means of controlling race mixing. Even in the late seventies, my first organizing job, with the Southern Christian Leadership Conference back when Ralph Abernathy was the head, was over the death of a black man, Mickey McClendon, murdered for dating a white woman. McClendon, from Chester, South Carolina, was shot, tied behind a pick-up truck, set on fire, and dragged down a road, much the way James Byrd, Jr. was in Jasper, Texas, in 1998. Today, whether it's Kobe Bryant in Colorado or high school football star Marcus Dixon in Georgia, whenever a black man is accused of the rape of a white woman, black Americans view the alleged crime in the context of history.

Sex is the prevailing theme of Thurmond's life. While he was alive and after death, the local press gleefully retold the story of a young Strom "sneaking out his upstairs bedroom for a romantic tryst with unnamed women." Thurmond's "virility," his marrying a twenty-two-year-old, Nancy Moore, at age sixty-six, having four children even as an old man, and his "secret" black child were all a testimony to Southern white male power.

Thurmond's initiation into the "customs and traditions" of segregation, sex, and white supremacy began with his political mentor Benjamin Ryan Tillman. "Pitchfork" Ben Tillman, a virulent white supremacist, also from Edgefield, Thurmond's home county, constitutionally (and otherwise) reinstituted white rule after Reconstruction. Pitchfork Ben was proud to have driven blacks demanding rights out of the state at gunpoint. He and his Sweetwater Sabre Club members wore white shirts stained in red to represent the blood of black men. When Tillman came to power as governor in 1890, blacks were the majority in the state. Today, blacks represent a third of the population. The decrease is directly due to Tillman's political legacy. Tillman's assault on black rights was immediate. He quickly revised the state constitution to ensure legal segregation of the races, stripping blacks of all political and economic power. As a United States senator, Tillman declared, "We of the South have never recognized the right of the Negro to govern white men, and we never will."

Thurmond's father, J. William, himself a state legislator, once served as Tillman's campaign manager. Tillman later rewarded J. William by naming him U.S. attorney (a job currently held by Strom's son—Strom Jr.) in a new South Carolina district even though Thurmond had killed a man in an argument over Tillman's politics. Tillman was a frequent visitor to the Thurmond home, a "symbolic part of the family," according to Cohodas, and a godfather of sorts to the Thurmond children. But to blacks, Pitchfork Ben was the prime purveyor of Negrophobia. And wrapped around Tillmanism was the ideal of the "pure, defenseless, southern white woman." "There is only one crime that warrants lynching," he said, "and governor as I am, I would lead a mob to lynch the Negro who ravishes a white woman." During Tillman's first term there had been five lynchings, in his second term there were thirteen.

Still, black South Carolinians were initially optimistic about Thurmond, who began his career as a Democrat. As a South Carolina state senator in 1938, despite the Tillman influence, he publicly opposed lynching and declared that the Ku Klux Klan stood for "the most abominable type of lawlessness." Thurmond called himself a "progressive" and upon election as governor in 1946 he declared, "We need a progressive outlook, a progressive program, a progressive leadership." He spoke of improving black schools, revising the Tillman Constitution of 1895, and abolishing the Tillman poll tax that was used to keep blacks from voting. He supported "equal rights for women in every respect," saying, "women should serve on boards, commissions, and other positions of importance in the state government." He also called for "equal pay for equal work for women."

At his inaugural Thurmond said, "more attention should be given to Negro education. The low standing of South Carolina educationally is due primarily to the high illiteracy and lack of education among our Negroes. If we provide better educational facilities for them, not only will much be accomplished in human values, but we shall raise our per capita income as well as the educational standing of the state." But Thurmond was not calling for an end to segregation, he was hoping for a new and improved "separate but equal." It would take the federal courts to strike down "separate but equal" and to force desegregation, or "integration," as the Thurmond forces would define it. Thurmond stood squarely with Tillman on race mixing—he was against it and let stand the constitutional prohibition against it. It took 103 years before South Carolina finally voted to remove a ban on interracial marriage from its state constitution. Although it was not actively enforced, Tillman added the clause to the state's constitution in 1895 prohibiting "marriage of a white person with a Negro or mulatto or a person who shall have one-eighth or more of Negro blood." Up until 1997, state legislators refused to allow voters to decide whether to remove the ban. A constitutional amendment, passed in 1998, finally deleted the line.

Still, at the start of his career blacks gave Thurmond high marks for his handling of the Willie Earle lynching, which stamped his administration as "liberal without being radical" by whites outside the South. On February 16, 1947, a young black man from Pickens County was arrested and charged with the murder of Thomas Brown, a white Greenville taxicab driver. The next day a mob broke into the Pickens County jail, took Earle, shot him, stabbed him, and then beat him to death on the outskirts of town. The FBI and state officials investigated the crime at the behest of Thurmond, who also called for the prosecution of those accused of lynching. But after a highly public trial the jury acquitted the accused men.

However, when President Harry Truman desegregated the armed forces and announced his broad civil rights program in 1948, Thurmond could not tolerate the challenge thus posed to the "customs and traditions" that defined his deepest beliefs. Thurmond ran for president that year as the "Dixiecrat" States' Rights candidate, admonishing the faithful that holding power boiled down to one thing—race—and he would make sure that only white men held it. As Northern Democrats pushed for civil rights, Thurmond and his fellow Southern Democratic governors cried "states' rights" just as their ancestors did to justify African enslavement. As author Kari Frederickson wrote, Thurmond and other Dixiecrat governors appealed to racist, "conservative white men suffering from a self-diagnosed case of political impotency."

Thurmond as Tillman's political heir was the icon of the new "anti-miscegenation" movement. In his acceptance speech at the Birmingham meeting announcing his presidential bid he speechified, "All the bayonets in the Army cannot force the 'Negrah' into our home, our schools, our churches, and our places of recreation."

Candidate Thurmond's platform stood for segregation and against race mixing. When the votes were counted Thurmond had 1.1 million votes, won four states and garnered thirty-eight electoral votes. 1.1 million Americans voted in favor of segregation—it was not enough to defeat Truman, but the Democratic Party was never the same.

Eventually Thurmond was elected to the Senate as a write-in candidate in 1954, a post he would retain for a half century, until his retirement in January 2003. Throughout his congressional career, he opposed almost every major civil rights initiative. In 1956, he authored the infamous Southern Manifesto, a document signed by nineteen of the twenty-two Southern senators that urged the South to defy, as they put it, the Supreme Court's "clear abuse of judicial power" in outlawing segregation in public schools. In 1957, he executed the longest filibuster in history while trying to halt the first Civil Rights Act proposed in the Senate and backed by Eisenhower.

Lyndon Johnson's success in passing the Civil Rights Act of 1964 was the last straw for Thurmond. He left the Democratic Party and signed on with Republican Barry Goldwater. Upon leaving, Thurmond declared, "The party of our fathers is dead."

Thurmond's departure signaled a major shift in American politics. It was the birth of South Carolinian Lee Atwater, Jesse Helms, Newt Gingrich, and Trent Lott's Republican Party. The Thurmond defection prompted the GOP appeal to white southern conservatives and foreshadowed Richard Nixon's race-inspired "Southern strategy." This framework exists today. Race supremacy is the ideological glue that keeps white men in the South in the Republican Party. Today they are called the "Bubba vote" and NASCAR dads, but the appeal is build on Tillmanism, the Dixiecrat Movement, the Southern Manifesto. It's almost always couched in the language of "states' rights," but race and social control is the subtext.

Race politics explains Ronald Reagan beginning his 1980 campaign at the Neshoba County Fair in Philadelphia, Mississippi, the place where civil rights workers Michael Schwerner, James Earl Chaney, and Andrew Goodman were murdered. His declaration then, "I believe in states' rights," sent the same message as George W. Bush's 2000 sojourn to the fundamentalist college Bob Jones University in Greenville, South Carolina. The school's founder has often been linked to the Klan and for years provided a Biblical sanction for racism. The school refused to admit blacks until 1971 and banned interracial dating until 2000.

In the seventies, as the country's racial attitudes changed, Thurmond did as the self-serving do to stay in office—he changed, at least cosmetically. With blacks representing a third of the voters in South Carolina he hired the first black man ever employed by a Southern senator and actively re-courted the black vote. Thomas Moss, a Korean War veteran and organizer with the meat packers union (in the "right to work state") in Orangeburg, South Carolina, headed the Voter Education Project, a program that encouraged blacks to register to vote. Working with Moss, Thurmond began championing grants to black colleges, businesses, and municipalities. He voted in favor of extending the Voting Rights Act—a law that guaranteed the federal government's right to enforce a citizen's right to vote. He also voted in favor of the Fair Housing Act and the Martin Luther King federal holiday. His reward? During his 1978 re-election bid, ten of South Carolina's eleven black mayors endorsed him.

Back in 1996, I was organizing a national conference on the epidemic of church fires in the South. As it just so happened, South Carolina led the nation in the number of church fires and the National Council of Churches was sponsoring the conference being held in the state. An old friend and NAACP member, Joann Watson of Detroit, made the trip down south. And as fate would have it, Joann and I were talking in the lobby of the Downtown Holiday Inn when who should stroll in? Strom in the flesh, looking kind of dazed but still moving, his aide not a step away. Joann immediately threw her two arms up in the air and, like Moses appealing to Pharaoh, cried in a strong but not loud voice, "Senator, let my people go!" Strom, leaning just a little, stopped, stuck his hand out to Joann, and said in a clear twangy voice, "Go where? I love everybody. Everybody's my friend!"

Thurmond was the epitome of the classic pork-belly politician. Graduate from high school and you'd probably get a letter from Thurmond. If a parent had trouble reaching a kid in the military, call Thurmond's office. Need help with the V.A.? Call ole Strom. The "rural myth" is that Strom shook the hand of almost every South Carolinian. His apologists want us to remember that Thurmond.

When black State Senator Kay Patterson of Columbia agreed to eulogize Thurmond, it was front-page news all across the state. Patterson said, "Strom's experience is on the road to Damascus. I have supported him since he left his segregationist ways and became a real American citizen and tried to be the senator for all the people of the state." Patterson's attitude mirrored African-Americans' optimistic hope for Thurmond when he began his career.

But a new generation was reminded of Thurmond's legacy and iconic status at his 100th birthday party. Mississippi Senator Trent Lott praised Thurmond's 1948 campaign saying, "I want to say this about my state. When Strom ran for president, we voted for him. We're proud of him. And if the rest of the country had followed our lead, we wouldn't have had all these problems over all these years, either." Although Lott fell on his sword and apologized all over himself, his signal was unmistakable. Had it not been for blacks getting rights and race-mixing, the world of white men with total power would be intact.

In the end, regardless of whatever changes Thurmond made later in life, his legacy can be described in two words—"Segregation Forever." Or maybe, "Segregation and Hypocrisy Forever!" Even if Essie Mae Washington-Williams's name is chiseled alongside the names of his other children onto the Strom Thurmond statue that stands facing the Confederate Women's Monument on the Statehouse grounds, his contradictions and hypocrisy will still be etched in stone. But maybe, in a way, the day they chisel that name will be the day white South Carolina finally begins to confront its own contradictions.

Ty Cobb

BY RAY ROBINSON

ON JULY 17, 1961, Tyrus Raymond Cobb, seventy-five, the greatest baseball player of his generation—and certainly the meanest, cruelest, and richest—was put to rest in the red clay of his native state of Georgia. There were only three ballplayers on hand to pay their last respects to him. Why former catchers Mickey Cochrane and Ray Schalk and pitcher Nap Rucker bothered to show up is anybody's guess. Perhaps they wanted to make certain that Cobb was dead. The major leagues didn't send an official representative to the funeral, but those who were there said that the demonic Cobb looked ghastly in his coffin.

There wasn't a single facet of the game of baseball in which Cobb didn't excel—hitting, fielding, throwing, fighting. But if there was ever an opponent or teammate who had a good word to say about him, he hasn't yet been quoted. Cobb himself had his own enemies list, longer even than Richard Nixon's. He called it his "son-of-a-bitch list." Some of the mildest-mannered men in baseball, who generally had kind words to say about everybody, despised Cobb.

"He's about as welcome in ballparks as a rattlesnake," said the icon Lou Gehrig. Charlie Gehringer, the talented Detroit second baseman who suffered under Cobb's managerial aegis for two years, described Cobb as "a really hateful guy," and Charlie Schmidt, a burly catcher, called Cobb a "rotten skunk." Paul Gallico, the sportswriting troubadour of Cobb's era, thought Ty was "mentally deranged." Other "endorsements" were unprintable.

Cobb's reputation was well deserved. He was involved in a number of unseemly on-field and off-field incidents during a career that lasted from 1905, when he joined the Detroit club, until 1929, when he finished up under Philadelphia's Connie Mack. He fought with umpires, teammates, foes, spectators, waiters, taxi drivers, parking lot attendants, bellhops, wives, and several of his children. From all accounts he had few congenial relationships with anyone, except his father, but that's another story.

He was often caught mouthing bigoted remarks about black people. On one occasion he assaulted an aged black chambermaid who had complained that he called her "a nigger." Perhaps Cobb's most infamous misadventure occurred on the afternoon of May 15, 1912, at Hilltop Park in upper Manhattan, the first home of the Yankees (then called the Highlanders). During the game between Detroit and the Yankees, the fans had been making vile comments about Cobb, some suggesting that he had black blood. That, of course, was the worst thing you could say about a man, in Ty's mind. With a runner on first in the top of the fourth inning, Cobb suddenly lurched from the dugout and leaped into the stands. Within seconds he was beating up on an unfortunate citizen named Claude Lucker. In the post-fight inquiry it turned out Lucker didn't have any hands.

Lucker denied that he'd been one of Cobb's detractors. American League President Bancroft Johnson, who had little use for Cobb to begin with, happened to be in the stands that day. Immediately, he issued an indefinite suspension against the malefactor. Cobb was furious, which was generally his state of mind, anyway. But, ironically, Cobb's teammates joined him in his protest, overcoming, for the moment, their loathing of him. They insisted that a great injustice had been done, overlooking the fact that Cobb had no right to assault an innocent fan. "We want him reinstated for tomorrow's game," said the players' petition, or there will be no game. If the players have no protection, we must protect ourselves."

When Johnson refused to budge from his position, Manager Hughey Jennings of Detroit had to corral a group of sandlot players to fill out his lineup, since his regulars refused to play against the Athletics. The toothless Tigers were trampled, 24-2. Though they threatened to remain out for the rest of the season, the striking Tigers gave up within twenty-four hours and went back to work. Johnson ended up fining Cobb $50, as well as plastering him with a ten-day suspension. Each rebellious Tiger was fined $100, a considerable sum in those days.

Lucker threatened to sue Cobb, but never did. Oddly, a part of the baseball public seemed to support Cobb, and certainly, in his own southland the word went forth that Cobb was an exemplar of "real manhood." A local clergyman, however, in his Sunday sermon, expressed the feeling that for a player to pummel a spectator was "undignified and unworthy of a true sportsman."

The episode did little to mellow The Georgia Peach, as he was called, and in the ensuing years he changed not at all. He came to be known as "The Butcher" and his own manager, Jennings, said he would have traded him in a minute if he could have received decent value for him. Cobb's tactics on the bases continued to intimidate rival fielders. Third basemen Ossie Bluege of Washington once told baseball historian Donald Honig that Cobb really went out of his mind if he felt he was going to be thrown out. "It seemed to make him crazy, like a cornered animal. That's when he was most dangerous," Bluege said. Apparently, Cobb couldn't be on the losing side of any situation. When he roomed with someone, he insisted on being the first into the bathroom in the morning and he threatened to attack his roomie if he dared venture into the shower before he did.

Off the field Cobb was equally nasty and paranoid. Even when he had an opportunity to be judicious he couldn't bring himself to act in such a way. Late in his life, when he was asked to rate players on his all-time team, he was disparaging to most of the modern stars. Ted Williams, Joe DiMaggio, Bob Feller, Willie Mays, and others were dismissed as a "fragile lot," who couldn't play the game the way it was supposed to be played. He did have some kind words for Yankees' shortstop Phil Rizzuto (who probably pleased Cobb because of his bunting ability) and Stan Musial, the Cardinals' brilliant hitter. (Had Cobb suddenly gone soft when he delivered his words of praise for Rizzuto and Musial?)

Cobb went to his grave feeling that those players who came along after he left the game were little more than fakers and couldn't carry his spikes. The irony, of course, was that was close to the truth, for Cobb's record was truly astounding. His lifetime batting average of .367 was unequalled. Even in his final year he hit .323, and he stole home one last time that season, giving him thirty-six such steals in his career. In one game in 1915 he stole home twice against Washington. In 11,429 times at bat he struck out only 357 times, an accomplishment that measures out to about one whiffing for every thirty-two plate appearances. In the early 1900s Cobb put together nine consecutive batting titles. Then he picked up three more after that skein was broken. In a phase of the game that he appeared to glory in the most—stolen bases—he led the American league six times.

Cobb's fondness for numbers extended to his finances. He amassed more money than any man in baseball during his time. When most ballplayers knew little about the workings of the economic system, Cobb was sophisticated about it. He even made the first endorsement of Coca-Cola in 1908. He became fast friends, or at least a golf contact, with Robert Woodruff, who was named chief of Coca-Cola operations in 1923. Conveniently, the soft drink company was based in Atlanta. As a result of the Woodruff association, Cobb continued to buy into Coca-Cola. Eventually he owned over 20,000 shares, enough to purchase all of the guns he needed. In his declining years Cobb was never without a weapon. He also developed the habit of carrying generous amounts of cash with him. When he slept he often had large denomination bills tucked under his pillow. His other main investment was General Motors stock, which, like Coca-Cola, held up remarkably well during the Great Depression years.

His success in baseball and at accumulating money got Cobb invited into a White House poker game with President Warren G. Harding. Some of the pots in those games mounted to $10,000 and Cobb invariably walked away as a winner. Harding and his cronies were lousy poker players, just the kind of targets that Cobb liked.

There were many low points in Cobb's tempestuous sojourn through life. But the nadir arrived in 1927, when he was suddenly cashiered as manager of Detroit. He had never shown much patience with young players. With veterans he was often harsh and overly critical. One observer remarked about Cobb's tenure as manager that each day for the players was "like nine innings of hell." However, the event that caused Cobb's dismissal had nothing to do with his team's dismal record. Rather it was precipitated by an accusation that he had been involved in trying to fix the result of a ball game back in 1919 between Detroit and Cleveland. Allegedly, he had joined in a little conspiracy with his old pal, outfielder Tris Speaker (who, incidentally, was once a member of the Ku Klux Klan) in trying to make certain that the Tigers would qualify for the third-place money. The scandal was revealed by baseball's Commissioner Kenesaw Mountain Landis, whose granitic countenance had become famous for his tough role against the eight fixers of the 1919 Black Sox World Series. After a lengthy investigation of the Cobb-Speaker matter, during which Landis was burned in effigy in Georgia, the commissioner ruled that the chief witnesses were not to be believed. Therefore, he concluded, Cobb and Speaker were exonerated of charges and were reinstated.

For years baseball's amateur psychologists have tried to solve the riddle of Ty Cobb. What caused his constant rage and despicable behavior? Why had he become a man full of relentless hate for almost all human beings? It is not necessary to retreat to the man's youth in search for pertinent clues. Born in December 1886 in rural Northeast Georgia, close to the town of Royston, Cobb had many advantages as he grew up. After the fratricidal Civil War, Cobb's family still was well off, and he was raised in a comfortable antebellum house. Ty's father, William Herschel Cobb, married Amanda Chitwood when she was only twelve years old, but such a linkage was not that uncommon in those years.

Ty, it is said, worshipped his father, who boasted all manner of credentials as a prominent man of the area, which included the towns of Lavonia, Harmony Grove, and Carnesville. William Cobb had served variously as editor of the local newspaper, mayor, state senator, mathematics teacher, county school commissioner, and aphorist. In many respects William Cobb epitomized the type of romanticized Southern gentleman portrayed in Margaret Mitchell's *Gone with the Wind*. He was demanding and a disciplinarian, but the young Cobb respected his father's commands. Father Cobb didn't care much for the fact that Ty wanted to play baseball for money. He would much have preferred a doctor in the family. But William Cobb gave his approval for Ty's incipient baseball career with the Augusta ball club, as long as his boy "didn't come home a failure."

On the night of August 8, 1905, when Ty was eighteen and away from home playing for Augusta, the relationship between father and son came to an abrupt, shocking end. That end, perhaps, provides the major clue and road map to

Ty Cobb's monstrous behavior for the rest of his life. William Cobb had left the house early in the evening in his buggy, presumably to contract some business in the area. He told Amanda he would be back the next day. But he seemingly had other plans, which he kept from Amanda. She retired a bit after ten o'clock, but was awakened a few hours later by a scratching noise at her window. She jumped out of bed and reached for her revolver, which she kept handy in a drawer. Approaching the window, she spied the figure of a person trying to enter her bedroom. Without hesitation, and sparked by fear, she fired her weapon through the curtain at the shadowy figure. Two bullets struck the man, who Amanda believed was an intruder—and he fell dead. Within minutes it became clear that Amanda Cobb had killed her husband William Cobb.

What William Cobb was doing at the window at that hour of the night has never been fully explained. The rumormongers in town whispered that William Cobb returned to his house in order to spy on his wife, who he thought was having a romantic liaison with a neighbor. Whatever the truth of the matter, Amanda Cobb was cleared of the killing, and the case was dropped.

Did this traumatic incident set off the hounds of hell within the young Tyrus? Was he forever haunted in his daily life and in his dreams by the image of his murdered father? Some who knew him at the time, and others who have studied his life, believe that Ty Cobb's psyche was indelibly damaged on that night in 1905.

Paul Gallico supported that theory. Gallico also blamed the brutal hazing that Ty was subjected to from his uncouth teammates when he first arrived in the big leagues.

No excuses—but at last an explanation.

BLACK ROBES, BLACK HEARTS— JUSTICE DENIED

Roger Taney, Webster Thayer, Antonin Scalia

In many cases judges are just lawyers who knew a politician. Judges sit on thrones above the courtroom, wrapped in black robes and insist on being called "Your Honor." Some judges, like William Douglas, Thurgood Marshall, and Benjamin Cardozo, actually were honorable. Others have had murderous prejudices and could not spell impartial. The following trio by no means represents the full spectrum of American judicial iniquity. Certainly we could have James Bradley, who single-handedly swayed the election of 1876; fixer Abe Fortas; Nixon's rejected Supreme Court nominee Harold Carswell; and, of course, Clarence Thomas. The list is long and inglorious, but these three will do for now.

Roger Taney

BY ERROL LOUIS

The Unjust Justice

Experts on constitutional law disagree about nearly everything, but there are two matters on which scholars are virtually unanimous: that the single most destructive,
worst-reasoned Supreme Court ruling in American history
was the *Dred Scott* decision of 1857—and that full responsibility for the decision lies with its author, Chief Justice
Roger Brooke Taney.

It is difficult to overstate the impact of the forty-page
judicial disaster, which announced to a divided nation,
already on the brink of civil war over the question of
slavery, that millions of black bondsmen and their descendants would remain trapped in chains forever, with no possibility of becoming American citizens.

Not only slavery, but racism, was declared by Taney to
be the unalterable law of the land. Reading the decision
from the bench, from pages held in trembling hands, the
seventy-nine-year-old judge (whose name is pronounced
TAW-nee) decreed that all blacks, including free men and
women who were descended from slaves, were "beings of
an inferior order, and altogether unfit to associate with the
white race, either in social or political relations; and so far
inferior, that they had no rights which the white man was
bound to respect."

The decision helped convince anti-slavery agitators like John Brown and his followers to take up arms, since lawful opposition to the peculiar institution had been exhausted: Brown's bloody, doomed uprising at Harper's Ferry took place two years after *Dred Scott*. In the political mainstream, the ruling helped pulverize the rapidly shrinking common ground of compromise between Northern and Southern leaders: the nation would, four years later, be plunged into a savage civil war that claimed six hundred-thousand American lives, more than all other wars combined.

Dred Scott, as legal scholar Andrew Finkelman has written, "has come to stand for all that can go wrong in a Supreme Court decision, and all that did go wrong under the pro-slavery Constitution. It remains the most infamous decision in American constitutional history, and its author suffers accordingly. . . . Whenever the name of Taney comes up, there will always be the echo of hooting."

Political leaders never forgave Taney for *Dred Scott*. One justice of the Supreme Court, Benjamin Curtis, penned a lengthy dissent and resigned from the court in protest. A young ex-congressman from Illinois named Abraham Lincoln regularly launched salvos against the decision during a failed 1858 campaign for senate and a successful 1860 run for president. Indeed, on the day he took office in 1861, Lincoln—after being sworn in as president by Taney— proceeded to attack the decision in his inaugural speech.

But that's getting ahead of the story.

Taney occupied the chief justice's center seat on the Supreme Court for twenty-eight years—longer than any other justice except his predecessor, Chief Justice John Marshall—and authored about three hundred judicial opinions. Only once in all that time, with *Dred Scott*, did the Taney court strike down an act of Congress as unconstitutional—the Compromise of 1820 that limited the expansion of slavery to newly created Western territories. That was the central question the high court was asked to rule on in *Dred Scott.*

Striking down Congress's right to decide which territories would be slave or free would have been troubling enough in a country about to come apart at the seams due to lack of compromise. But Taney, unbidden, rummaged through history and concluded that Dred Scott had no standing to sue in any federal court: all black Americans lacked basic citizenship rights, such as the right to sue, because the country's founding documents never authorized any such degree of equality.

The problem with the latter argument, as pointed out in Justice Curtis' dissent in *Dred Scott,* is that it simply isn't true. In five of the thirteen founding colonies, free black men had the right to vote, and participated in votes to ratify the Constitution in roughly the same proportion their white countrymen did.

Dred Scott couldn't have come at a worse time in the nation's history. In the 1850s, the pro-slavery Southern states had reached a tense, uneasy political standoff with their Northern counterparts. Congressional leaders kept pasting together compromises to keep the union intact; the deals involved carefully defining each of the new Western territories—which would soon become states—as either allowing or prohibiting slavery. The general idea was to maintain the existing balance of power in Washington by adding slave states and free states in rough parity.

It was a dubious, volatile political bargain born of expedience rather than morality, and it required constant political and legal tweaking. In 1846, a slave named Dred Scott filed a lawsuit claiming that he, his wife, and his two daughters should be freed because, over a twelve-year period, his owner, an Army doctor named John Emerson, had brought Dred to live for extended periods in Illinois (a free state) and the Wisconsin Territory (where, pursuant to an 1820 act of Congress, slavery was banned forever).

At the time of the lawsuit, Dr. Emerson had died, and Dred and his family were owned by Emerson's wife and living in Missouri, a slave state. The question was whether the years Dred spent living in free territory rendered him free. The case wandered through the judicial system for a decade before arriving at the Supreme Court.

Waiting at the high court, much to the misfortune of Dred Scott and millions of black Americans being held in bondage, was Robert Brooke Taney. Born in 1777 to a family of Maryland planters, Taney as a young man had no chance of inheriting the family plantation—he was the second-born son, not the first—and instead studied law and began dabbling in local politics.

By 1806, Taney had passed the bar, begun building a successful legal practice in Frederick, Maryland, and married Anne Phoebe Charlton Key (who, trivia buffs should note, was the sister of Francis Scott Key, author of "The Star-Spangled Banner"). Active in the Federalist Party, Taney won election to a five-year term in the Maryland state senate.

At this point, the record shows Taney to be a moderate on racial matters. He freed his own slaves, and supported the movement to send black Americans back to Africa as colonizers. In 1819, Taney even defended a minister, Jacob Gruber, who'd been accused of inciting rebellion by delivering a sermon against slavery. Taney won acquittal for Gruber, denouncing slavery as "a blot on our national character." "Every real lover of freedom confidently hopes that it will be effectually, though it must be gradually, wiped away, and earnestly looks for the means by which this necessary object may be attained," Taney told the jury.

That attitude wouldn't last. By 1827, Taney had become a leader in the Democratic-Republican Party (the ancestor of today's Democratic Party), and was elected attorney general of Maryland. He also threw his state's party organization behind Andrew Jackson, a rising political star from Tennessee. In 1828, when Jackson won the White House, he named Taney as his attorney general.

Recently uncovered papers by Taney during his tenure as attorney general show the evolution of his thinking on race. Shortly after taking office, the Jackson White House faced an international incident triggered in the Carolinas: British ships had docked, only to have their free black sailors seized and jailed by local officials. When Secretary of State Edward Livingston asked Taney for a legal opinion on the dispute, the response was a precursor of the logic of *Dred Scott*. The individual slave states were within their rights in seizing the free black sailors, said the future judge: state's rights trumped federal power and even foreign treaties.

That wasn't the only justification for letting free foreign sailors be seized based on the color of their skin. Blacks, Taney added, were "a separate and degraded people," who were "not looked upon as citizens by the contracting parties who formed the Constitution."

But Taney wasn't publicly known for his views on race or his strange and inaccurate reading of history; not yet.

He came to public attention in the early 1830s as a loyal fixer for President Jackson, ready to take on distasteful and controversial tasks for a president whose dynamic, frontier populism was sweeping the young nation. Taney took on political battles for Jackson, and in the process began creating enemies in Congress.

In 1832, for instance, Jackson wanted to shut down the Second Bank of the United States, which Jackson and his followers viewed as a symbol of wealthy, Northern interests. Jackson's enemies in Congress set a trap for the president by holding a sudden, early vote to re-authorize the bank's charter. The idea was to force Jackson to choose between signing the bill—thereby extending the life of the hated bank—or issuing a veto that would hurt Jackson politically while leaving the bank open and untouched.

The confrontation, let us remember, took place decades before the Federal Reserve was created: At the time, the Second Bank was responsible for 15 to 20 percent of all lending in the United States, and 40 percent of the currency in circulation. Despite the economic turmoil that might result, Taney suggested to Jackson a sly, gutsy course of action: veto the bill to extend the bank's charter, and also withdraw $10 million in federal deposits, a move that would make the bank's collapse inevitable.

Jackson duly ordered his secretary of the treasury, William Duane, to transfer federal funds out of the bank; when he refused to do so, Old Hickory promptly fired the secretary and named Taney to the post while the Senate was in recess. The funds were yanked; the Second National Bank went into decline, and eventually closed its doors in 1836 (a dissolution that contributed, within months, to the Panic of 1837, the worst economic panic the republic had ever experienced).

Taney's actions enraged the Senate, and when the law-makers returned to Washington they lost no time in refusing to make Taney's recess appointment to Treasury permanent. Thus did Taney become the first cabinet nom-inee in history to be denied office by the Senate. He returned to Maryland in disgrace.

Two years later, when John Marshall retired from the Supreme Court, Jackson nominated Taney, his right hand, as a replacement. A still-angry Senate killed Taney's nomi-nation by postponing a vote indefinitely on the last day of the Senate session. When Jackson re-nominated Taney, some senators went so far as to introduce a bill to reduce the size of the Supreme Court from seven to six, which would elim-inate the seat altogether. But the House of Representatives refused to go along with the scheme. In the end, Taney won approval by a Senate vote of twenty-nine to fifteen.

As the dissenting senators knew, throwing judicial robes around Taney—a partisan battler down to his finger-nails—would not suddenly make him detached or even-handed. Their fears were realized in *Dred Scott*, where Taney argued that blacks had no role in the shaping of the Declaration of Independence or the Constitution, which was why they could claim no rights as American citizens.

Lincoln quietly demolished Taney's opinion about ninety days after it was handed down, noting in an Illinois speech that "the *Dred Scott* decision was, in part, based on assumed historical facts which were not really true." In reality, said Lincoln, quoting the dissenting opinion of Benjamin Curtis, "in five of the then thirteen states, to wit, New Hampshire, Massachusetts, New York, New Jersey and North Carolina, free negroes were voters, and, in proportion to their numbers, had the same part in making the Constitution that the white people had."

Taney dug in his heels and never backed down from his opinion, which tarnished the reputation of the court. "The Supreme Court is gradually becoming a mere party machine," wrote the *New York Tribune* pointedly, "to do the bidding of the dominant faction and to supply places to reward party hacks."

Even after Taney died in 1864, his enemies were eager to settle accounts. "He slandered the memory of the founders of the government and framers of the Declaration," wrote the *Atlantic Monthly*, referring to Taney's most famous decision as a "combination of ignorance, injustice, falsehood, and impiety."

An anonymous pamphlet, titled *The Unjust Judge*, was even more vicious, noting that the *Dred Scott* ruling "would disgrace any man or jurist in Christendom." "As a Jurist," the broadside read, "he was, next to Pontius Pilate, perhaps the worst that ever occupied the seat of judgment."

Webster Thayer

BY NICK PILEGGI

WHEN MASSACHUSETTS JUDGE Webster Thayer sentenced Nicola Sacco and Bartolomeo Vanzetti, a pair of Italian immigrant anarchists, to death for a payroll robbery and murder in 1927, he knew that the eyewitnesses could not identify them, that the defendant's gun presented as evidence did not match the murder weapon, that Vanzetti, identified as the getaway driver, could not drive a car, and that a key prosecution witness was testifying under a false name because he had just pleaded guilty in an unrelated larceny case and had been promised probation instead of prison for his testimony.

Still, with Judge Webster Thayer in charge of their case, Sacco and Vanzetti never had a chance.

Thayer knew the local police chief suspected the robbery was the work of the notorious Morelli gang and that the description of the gunmen matched the Morelli gang much more than it did either of the defendants, but it made no difference. Before the trial, Judge Thayer made sure of the outcome by allowing sheriff's deputies to round up potential jurors at Masonic lodges, veterans' halls, and volunteer firemen's clubs—the kinds of locations least likely to be sympathetic to newly arrived immigrants.

Judge Thayer so clearly demonstrated his bias in the case that Harvard law professor Felix Frankfurter, who later became a United States Supreme Court justice, wrote that Judge Thayer's opinion was "a farrago of misquotations, misrepresentations, suppressions, and mutilations.

"The opinion," Frankfurter wrote in the *Atlantic Monthly* at the time, "was literally honeycombed with demonstrable errors, and infused by a spirit alien to judicial utterance. . . . By systematic exploitation of the defendants' alien blood, their imperfect knowledge of English, their unpopular social views, and their opposition to the war [World War I] the District Attorney invoked against them a riot of political passion and patriotic sentiment; and the trial court connived at—one had almost written, *cooperated in*—the process." Frankfurter wrote that every reasonable probability pointed away from Sacco and Vanzetti and toward the Morelli gang.

Though Judge Thayer's decision was riddled with error, and he was ridiculed and condemned around the world as the poster boy for the politically biased judge in a political court—he even became the butt of a Woody Guthrie lyric imploring *"Old Judge Thayer, take your shackle off of me"*—there was no chance that his death sentence could ever be reversed.

At the time, Massachusetts law held that the trial judge ruled on all appeals and motions involving his own cases. This meant that it was Judge Thayer to whom Sacco and Vanzetti's defense attorneys had to take their appeals.

According to friends and attorneys who knew him, Judge Thayer seemed absolutely gleeful turning down eight consecutive appeals over a tortuous seven-year period before Sacco and Vanzetti's execution in 1927.

James P. Richardson, a Dartmouth professor and friend, quoted Judge Thayer saying over lunch, "Did you see what I did with those anarchistic bastards the other day? I guess that will hold them for a while."

George Crocker, another prominent Boston lawyer, said that Judge Thayer told him, "We got to protect ourselves against 'em; there are so many Reds in the country."

And Charles Curtis, an attorney who visited the judge in his chambers shortly after he gave Sacco and Vanzetti the death penalty, said: "He [Thayer] was standing between me and the window, so that when I looked out . . . behind him I saw the top of the Charlestown Jail where the death house was. I wasn't thinking much about it until I realized that Judge Thayer was no longer talking about our case, but strutting up and down boasting that he had been fortunate enough to be on the bench when those sons of bitches were convicted. I had a chill. . . ."

Judge Thayer's bias did not come out of a vacuum. During World War I, anti-immigrant sentiment was already in full fury. Foremost of these rabble-rousers was George Creel, chairman of the United States Committee on Public Information, who championed the nation's patriotism by saying that while our "boys" were fighting the "Huns" abroad, Americans at home should fight the unpatriotic slackers such as draft dodgers, conscientious objectors, German-Americans, immigrants, and Communists.

When the war ended in 1918, the nine million Americans employed in wartime industries and the four million who had served in the military, suddenly found themselves without jobs about twenty years before anyone thought about unemployment insurance. While the economic collapse caused worker unrest and violent strikes across the country, many Americans felt that the strikers were unpatriotic. Strikers were branded as "Reds," colleges were deemed to be hotbeds of Bolshevism, and many teachers were fired for current or prior membership in the most moderate of leftist organizations.

The American Legion was founded in St. Louis at this time (May 8, 1919) "to foster and perpetuate a one hundred percent Americanism," and by the end of the year the Legion had a million members. While most were engaged in distributing anti-Communist patriotic pamphlets, the more zealous Legionnaires formed vigilante groups that pursued their own variety of "justice" against radicals, both real and suspect. "Leave the Reds to the Legion," became the call of the day. The Red Scare also breathed new life into the Ku Klux Klan, now able to add "radical immigrants" to their hate-fueled campaign against blacks, Catholics, and Jews.

There was so much hysteria that very little attention was paid to distinguishing between the millions of arriving immigrants and the relatively tiny percentage of radicals among them. An editorial in the Tulsa *Daily World* urged its readers to "strangle" radicals, "kill them, just like you would kill a snake. Don't waste money on a trial. All that is necessary is the evidence and a firing squad."

The newly elected president, Woodrow Wilson, didn't help. He had already gone on record expressing his contempt for the new immigrants "who have poured the poison of disloyalty into the very arteries of our national life . . . such creatures of passion, disloyalty, and anarchy must be crushed out."

To deal with the "Red Crisis," the Justice Department started the general intelligence division of the Federal Bureau of Investigation and put young J. Edgar Hoover in charge of breaking up Bolshevik plots by jailing and deporting radicals. Arrests were often made without warrants and for all kinds of reasons. In Newark, New Jersey, for instance, one man was arrested for looking like a radical. Another man was deported because a government witness said he "ran" like a foreigner. It was not until the 1920s, after a report by highly regarded independent lawyers detailed the Justice Department's abuses, that the Red Scare hysteria began to die down. By then, however, it was too late for Sacco and Vanzetti. They were already caught up in the judicial machinery.

On April 15, 1920, a paymaster and guard were killed during a $16,000 robbery of the Slater and Morrill shoe factory in South Braintree, Massachusetts. While eyewitnesses could not identify any of the robbers, they did see a car pull up with several other men inside. The gunmen threw two cashboxes into the car before it sped off. Two days later the car was found abandoned in some woods about five miles from the crime scene.

Sacco and Vanzetti were picked up almost by accident. They had gone to meet up with a friend who was going to help them transport and temporarily hide boxes of radical pamphlets and tracts. What they did not know was that a police tipster had erroneously reported that their friend's car was the getaway vehicle used in a robbery similar to the one in South Braintree.

Sacco and Vanzetti may have been anarchists and radicals, but they were clearly not guilty of killing the paymaster and guard and making off with the payroll. Sacco, thirty-two, and Vanzetti, twenty-nine, were, like millions of newly arrived immigrants, spending their days working at menial jobs. They were, as Vanzetti later wrote, "nameless, in a crowd of nameless ones." Sacco was a shoemaker living with his wife and two children in Stoughton, Massachusetts, and the unmarried Vanzetti was a fish peddler in North Portsmouth.

When police started questioning the two men about the car, and about why they needed the car—they lied. At first, Sacco and Vanzetti had no idea they were being questioned about the Braintree murders. They thought they were being questioned about their radical beliefs, which is why they lied. They knew they could have been deported or imprisoned for twenty years for their political views. Sacco had the draft of a handbill in his pocket about an upcoming anarchist meeting featuring Vanzetti as a main speaker. They lied because a few weeks earlier, a fellow anarchist, Andrea Salsedo, jumped, fell, or was pushed to his death from the fourteenth floor of the Justice Department's New York offices.

Salsedo had been arrested by federal agents and held incommunicado for several weeks after they traced a revolutionary leaflet found at a bombing site to his Brooklyn print shop. Before Salsedo fell to his death, Attorney General Palmer announced that Salsedo had made important disclosures.

As a result, Sacco and Vanzetti panicked. They knew Salsedo personally and were worried he might have pointed a finger at them. They immediately began making plans to get rid of any incriminating evidence they might have in their apartments, such as radical pamphlets, leaflets, and brochures. That is why they had gone to the garage to meet up with their friend. They had intended to store their boxes of radical literature at a safe hiding place until the Red Scare pressure had subsided. For them, it never did.

Webster Thayer was born in 1857, graduated from Dartmouth College in 1879, and became a prominent member of the Worcester, Massachussetts, social elite. While he became a Superior Court judge in 1917, according to those who knew him, Judge Thayer was not so much a man of the twentieth century as a nineteenth-century nativist. Thayer was one of those northern European puritan patriots who loathed the flood of southern European immigrants who were invading his country and despoiling the American gene pool. He did not hide his bias. Thayer would often pontificate at the University Club about how the United States had to "protect itself against the anarchists and Reds" as well as the dangers inherent to the country as a result of southern European mass migrations.

For Sacco and Vanzetti, however, with or without Judge Thayer, 1921 was a bad time to be Italian immigrants, avowed anarchists, and on trial for murder. Chances are they were doomed no matter what they or their lawyers did. For instance, once Sacco and Vanzetti were arrested, there was no effort on the part of police to find out who really committed the robbery. The evidence against the pair was non-existent. The police had no eyewitnesses, no weapons, and no sign of Sacco and Vanzetti spending any of the loot during the three-week period between the robbery and their arrest. Not a penny of the payroll was ever traced to Sacco or Vanzetti. In fact, not a penny of the money was ever found.

Meanwhile, the head of the Morelli gang, Joe Morelli, who had been the prime suspect before the Sacco and Vanzetti arrest, bought a new car shortly after the robbery and took off for a motor trip out west. But no police questioned any members of the Morelli gang in connection with the South Braintree murders and robbery.

By the time Sacco and Vanzetti were brought before the bench, it was decided that the lies they'd told to hide their radical beliefs were proof of what Judge Thayer described as a "consciousness of guilt." Because they had lied once, Thayer reasoned, they were not only guilty of being anarchists, but also culpable in the Braintree robbery and murder. The judge felt so strongly about his theory that he emphasized it to jury at the end of the trial.

It did not help that Sacco and Vanzetti spoke very broken English, and their testimony shows how often they misunderstood the questions put to them. Nor did it help that the prosecutor, Frederick Katzmann, the Norfolk district attorney, was essentially objection-proof. Judge Thayer allowed his witnesses to exaggerate, contradict themselves, and even alter their own earlier grand jury testimony.

Fred Moore, the defendants' California-based defense lawyer, whose services had been paid for by labor activists and anarchist groups, was either ignored, overruled, or told to sit down by the judge. The trial was riddled with inconsistencies and outright falsehood. When one eyewitness, Mary Splaine, was first questioned by the police, she said she could not identify Sacco because she was standing at a second-floor window about sixty feet from where the car sped away. Yet, a year later, during the trial, Katzmann got her to identify Sacco in extraordinary detail.

"He had a gray shirt," Mary Splaine testified, ". . . and what we would call a clean-cut face. . . . The forehead was high. The hair was brushed back and it was between, I should think, two inches and two-and-one-half inches in length, and dark."

When Fred Moore attempted to question the witness's suddenly recovered memory, Thayer dismissed his objections as petty.

Another witness, Louis Pelzer, a shoe cutter, testified at the trial that he thought Sacco was a "dead ringer" for the shooter. Yet under cross examination by Fred Moore, Pelzer admitted that he had originally told police he was unable to identify anyone because he wasn't at the window. But, before Moore could discredit Pelzer's "eyewitness" testimony further, Judge Thayer interceded and told the jury that even if Pelzer had lied earlier, he was currently showing the jury that he was "big enough and manly enough now to tell you of his prior falsehoods."

The fact that Sacco and Vanzetti owned guns (not unusual at the time) was also distorted for the jury by Judge Thayer. Sacco had a gun because he was a night watchman at a shoe factory and Vanzetti had one because he carried large sums of cash (between $100 and $125) in his fish business. However, despite knowing that the guns did not match the murder weapons, Judge Thayer allowed the prosecutor to call Colonel William Proctor, a police ballistics expert, who told the jury that the gun used in the robbery was a Colt .32, the same "type" as Sacco's. Despite repeated objections by the defense, Judge Thayer never told the jury that the bullets from Sacco's .32 Colt did not match the gun used in the murder.

After the seven-week trial, Judge Thayer's charge to the jury guaranteed Sacco and Vanzetti's guilt. A judge's charge is supposed to help a jury find its way through complicated laws and the maze of conflicting testimony. Since there was no direct evidence linking the two men to the crime, Judge Thayer devoted much of his twenty-five thousand-word charge to his "consciousness of guilt" theory. He also instructed the jury that "it was Sacco's gun that fired the fatal bullet," when in fact he knew that that was not Colonel Proctor's testimony.

Judge Thayer's charge to the jury was so biased that Justice Frankfurter wrote, "I assert with deep regret, but without the slightest fear of disproof, that certainly in modern times, Judge Thayer's opinion stands unmatched for discrepancies between what the record discloses and what the opinion conveys."

Judge Thayer was apparently undaunted by criticism. His charge to the jury called for a fair verdict, and he phrased his charge in such a way that patriots and native-born Americans would understand. By thanking the jury for enduring a seven-week trial, Judge Thayer said the jurors were "rendering a most important service" like "true soldiers, responding to the spirit of

American loyalty. There is no better word in the English language than 'loyalty.' "

He took obvious relish in his use of baroque oratory in a courtroom where English was a second language to the defendants and their supporters.

"Let your eyes be blinded to every ray of sympathy and prejudice," he told the jurors, who were all non-immigrants. "Let me beseech you not to allow the fact that the defendants are Italian to influence or prejudice you in the least degree. They are entitled, under the law, to the same rights and considerations as though their ancestors came over on the Mayflower."

The jury's guilty verdict and Judge Thayer's death penalty sentence might have taken place in the Dedham, Massachussetts, courthouse, but the decision was heard round the world.

"*Sono innocento!*" Sacco said. "They kill innocent men. Don't forget. They're killing innocent men!"

Hundreds of thousands protested on streets all over the world. In Paris, the United States embassy had to be protected by tanks from angry protestors. A riot in London resulted in forty injuries. The United States Consulate in Geneva was surrounded by five thousand. Huge crowds protested in New York and Boston.

Their appeals, which went on for seven years and were all denied by Judge Thayer, aroused people like Robert Benchley, Dorothy Parker, Edna St. Vincent Millay, Felix Frankfurter, Oliver Wendell Holmes, H. L. Mencken, and Katherine Anne Porter to write and protest against the sentence. Six plays, including Maxwell Anderson's *Winterset* and James Thurber and Elliott Nugent's *The Male Animal*, dealt with the Sacco and Vanzetti case. A film, *She's*

Working Her Way Through College, starred Ronald Reagan as the heroic professor whose job is threatened when he proposes to read some of Vanzetti's letters in one of his classes. There were at least nine novels based heavily on Sacco and Vanzetti.

There was so much clamor about the case that Massachusetts Governor Alvan T. Fuller, a successful automobile dealer before getting elected, was asked to consider executive clemency for the flawed trial. Fuller appointed "the Lowell committee," so-called because the most prominent member was A. Lawrence Lowell, president of Harvard. A Boston Brahmin and descendant of wealthy New England mill owners, Lowell was known to harbor an intense hatred for Jews, especially Felix Frankfurter, a professor at his own law school.

Lowell wrote a final report excluding or deliberately misinterpreting evidence supporting Sacco and Vanzetti's innocence. He conceded that some of Judge Thayer's comments about "Reds" were "inappropriate," but that the judicial process had been correct and that clemency was not warranted.

On August 23, 1927, the day of the execution, police set up machine guns atop the prison walls. Streets around the prison were blocked off to protestors. Gunboats patrolled Boston Harbor. Two days later a funeral procession of many thousands followed the hearse from the prison to the Joseph A. Langone funeral home where the bodies of Sacco and Vanzetti were cremated. A floral arrangement with banner reading *"Aspettando l'ora di vendetta"* (await the hour of vengeance), was placed nearby.

Six months after their death, the executioner's house was bombed, though no one was injured. On September 27,

1932, Judge Thayer's house was bombed, but he was unhurt. He moved to his club in Boston, and seven months later he died.

Sacco and Vanzetti's death certificates are in the Boston Public Library, along with a canister of their ashes and their death masks. The cause of death is given as: "Electric shock. Judicial homicide."

Antonin Scalia
✴
BY JACK NEWFIELD

The Learned Primitive

Imagine the bigoted Archie Bunker of Queens, New York, sitting on the majestic Supreme Court, with a lifetime appointment, and no capacity for shame, doubt, or empathy with anyone different.

This is what we have now with Antonin Scalia, also out of Queens, New York. Instead of a stained undershirt, he wears a black robe. Instead of making us laugh, he makes us cringe. Scalia is not as uneducated, or as crude, as the sitcom character played so brilliantly by Carroll O'Connor. The cerebral Scalia enjoys opera, fine wines, texts in Latin, and obscure theologians. But the public record of his life reveals a man just as intolerant, just as insulting, and just as arrogant as the fictional pop culture primitive sitting around his kitchen table with a perpetual sneer of superiority.

In reading many of Justice Scalia's opinions, and interviewing law school professors, I could not find a single opinion he has written that found discrimination to exist against a racial minority, a woman, an immigrant, a worker, a disabled person, or a senior citizen, that he thought was unconstitutional.

The performance of Scalia in *Bush v. Gore* helped produce the most fraudulent and politicized Supreme Court decision since *Dred Scott* in 1857.

Scalia helped steal the presidency for George Bush. He suddenly abandoned his philosophy of federalism—states' rights—to justify this theft, this nullification of the votes of fifty million Americans, to reach a conclusion that satisfied Scalia's political bias, even though the facts and the law were not on George Bush's side.

The central event in this drama was the emergency order of December 9, 2000, written by Scalia, that stopped the counting of votes in Florida at the moment Al Gore had narrowed Bush's lead to 154 votes. The Florida Supreme Court—the highest jurisdiction of states' rights—had ordered sixty thousand disputed "under-votes" to be re-counted.

Scalia's stay, agreed to by Justices Thomas, Rehnquist, Kennedy, and O'Connor, reversed this order, and froze the counting before Gore could take the lead. If Gore had been ahead in the counting before the case reached the Supreme Court, this would have transformed the political, media, and psychological dynamics in which the High Court had to deliberate and decide.

In his emergency stay, Scalia wrote—incredibly—that Bush has "a substantial probability of success" with his case. No impartial jurist with an open mind could have put that thought on paper, on December 9 of 2000, given the factual chaos of that day. He was emboldened by the fact that he had Justice Thomas's vote in his pocket, as usual.

Once the vote counting was frozen by Scalia's order, the Court's five-to-four selection of Bush to be president became the inevitable final scene of this partisan script. The aborted Florida re-count might have produced a legitimate majority for Bush if all the votes had been counted in good faith, but we will never know the actual will of the people.

Scalia's intervention in the democratic process—plus his stubborn partisanship in conference—made the Supreme Court look like a bunch of bought boxing judges, or Olympic ice skating judges trading votes.

Few news organizations have even mentioned that Scalia's two sons worked for law firms representing Bush's campaign. Right after Bush's inauguration, Scalia's son, Eugene, got the job as the solicitor at the Department of Labor. His bias against labor unions was flagrant at the federal agency created to defend the rights of workers.

In June of 2003, this Supreme Court, dominated by Republican appointees, finally began to moderate its intolerant views in two landmark cases. These Ford, Reagan, and Bush appointees ruled in favor of affirmative action in the University of Michigan case, and they ruled that gay sexual relations in private are constitutionally protected by the right of privacy, in *Lawrence v. Texas.*

But Scalia dissented in both these cases. All through the 2000 campaign, George Bush kept invoking Scalia and Thomas as his "two favorite justices," in a not-so-subtle pandering message to the Christian right about who he would nominate once he has a vacancy. The sacred trust of high judicial office was being offered as a patronage job to an extremist faction.

During the oral arguments in the affirmative action case, Scalia told the university's attorney that if the law school was so determined to be more inclusive, it should simply lower its admission standards. This was dangerously close to saying, from the bench, that blacks had inferior intelligence and could not meet high intellectual standards.

Most of the written opinions in the Michigan case revealed troubled jurists struggling with complex ideas. The majority five-to-four opinion, drafted by Ronald Reagan appointee Sandra Day O'Connor, ratified the consideration of race as a factor in admissions, while barring quotas. It was a compromise ruling, close to the American consensus.

But Scalia's dissent to O'Connor's opinion was sarcastic, scornful, simplistic, and smug. It was the opposite of judicious. It had no balance or nuance. It was weirdly insulting to O'Connor, warning that her opinion opened the gates to "racial discrimination."

Scalia's nasty dissent went on to say, sarcastically, that, "The non-minority individuals who are deprived of a legal education, a civil service job, or any job at all, by reason of their skin color, will surely understand."

This was almost a copycat version of Jesse Helm's hideous TV campaign commercial of 1990, showing a pair of white hands crumpling up a rejection letter in the context of affirmative action. In that election, Helms was running against an African-American, Harvey Gantt, the mayor of Charlotte.

Three days after this dissent, Scalia issued another bitter rant in reaction to the court's six-to-three majority decision overturning the Texas sodomy statute. This time he proclaimed himself on the side of those who "do not want persons who openly engage in homosexual conduct as part of their business, as scoutmasters for their children, and teachers in their children's schools, or as boarders in their homes."

This homophobic hysteria fell a little short of those deeply reasoned prophetic dissents by Oliver Wendell Holmes and Louis Brandeis that would be vindicated by history a generation later. This was not a minority opinion ahead of its time. This was just bloviating about bogeymen, like some right-wing talk show host in a second-rate media market. Scalia's words had nothing to do with the case at hand. It was a cheap shot in a lost culture war.

Having already rigged the outcome of a presidential election, Scalia didn't think twice about engaging in a flagrant conflict-of-interest with the vice president, perhaps anticipating another five-to-four decision to bail out the GOP.

In January of 2004, Scalia went duck hunting in Louisiana with Vice President Dick Cheney. The problem was that Supreme Court had just agreed to hear Cheney's appeal of a lower court order requiring him to disclose the members of his secret energy task force that devised national policy behind closed doors, to profit polluters.

Public interest and environmental organizations had been trying for two years to discover the names of those oil, gas, energy, and nuclear industry executives, many of whom were also large donors to the Bush-Cheney campaign. They were living proof of crony capitalism. Finally a federal appeals court ruled that at least some of these corporate names had to be made public. The plaintiffs suspected that disgraced Enron cheaters and tainted Halliburton executives were among these privileged, cozy insiders, and the public had a right to know this prior to the 2004 election. But Cheney appealed this ruling, in a move that smelled like stalling.

Three weeks after notice of this appeal was filed, Scalia went on his duck hunt with the powerful defendant in a case pending before him—a case with vast implications for the limits of government secrecy. Scalia also accepted free air travel on Air Force 2.

This extended *ex-parte* time, spent in a convivial recreational setting, violated all the judicial rules of impartiality and fairness. They don't even do this in a zoning case in Bridgeport or Atlantic City! The logical remedy to such contaminating contact, and free travel, was for Scalia to recuse himself from judging the case. The law says a federal judge must recuse himself when his "impartiality might be questioned." But Scalia, acting like he was above this law, ignored all demands that he step aside—including two stiff *New York Times* editorials.

Since 2000, there have been fourteen instances where members of the Supreme Court have recused themselves to avoid the appearance of favoritism and conflicts of interest. In the celebrated 1971 case, when the Court overturned Muhammad Ali's draft resistance conviction eight-to-zero, Thurgood Marshall recused himself, because he knew Ali. Few justices in history had more deeply held convictions than Marshall, but he also had a sense of personal integrity, and a reverence for the reputation of the Supreme Court, as its first black member.

Justice Scalia sometimes pays lips service to the First Amendment, but, in practice, he violates it and seems to resent those who keep it alive, such as working reporters doing their job.

In 2003, a group in Ohio gave Scalia an award for his alleged support of free speech. He used the occasion to prevent radio and television coverage of this event celebrating free speech and open society, saying it was his nonnegotiable policy never to allow reporters to film or tape record his public speeches.

In April of 2004, Scalia was giving a speech in the gym at Presbyterian Christian High School in Hattiesburg, Mississippi, before three hundred people. Two reporters were present, taping his remarks for accuracy—Antoinette Konz of the *Hattiesburg American*, and Denise Grones of the Associated Press. Thirty-five minutes into the speech, the two reporters were approached by a deputy U.S. marshal, who demanded their tapes be erased.

After some initial resistance, the two reporters reluctantly complied with the demand, which was consistent with Scalia's long-standing policy.

This was a historic moment. Here was a Supreme Court Justice of the United States, in public, violating the First Amendment! And trashing the Fourth Amendment's prohibition against unreasonable search and seizure! And he was giving a speech lamenting the loss of respect for the Constitution! After a week of blistering mockery by editorialists, Scalia did issue an apology to the two local reporters. But he also said he would continue his ban on the recording of his speeches by the electronic media, because he has often been "misquoted." Scalia also wrote to a reporters' committee that, "people don't revere" the Constitution "like they used to."

For all his learned primitivism and moralistic cynicism, Scalia will be remembered as among the most political and least judicious Supreme Court jurists in our history—as the stark opposite of giants like Holmes, Brandeis, Black, Douglas, Brennan, Blackmun, and Stevens.

Scalia's reputation will forever give off the same odor as Chief Justice Roger Taney and Joseph Bradley, the partisan Republican justice who decided the disputed election of 1876 in favor of Rutherford Hayes, ending Reconstruction with another stolen presidency.

WITH GOD ON THEIR SIDE—
UNHOLY HOLYMEN

Jonathan Edwards, Brigham Young, Gerald L. K. Smith, Cardinal Francis Joseph Spellman, Billy Graham, Elijah Muhammad

America is the most church-going of all industrialized nations, which means it has most true believers, a situation which can make the rational-minded among us nervous, especially when the government seems to be under the control of men and women who plan foreign policy according to the Book of Revelations. This is not a screed against worship; a bit of the Spirit never hurt anybody. But even if religion isn't the opiate of the people, it sure can make the preacher rich, and powerful, if he plays his consecrated cards right. For every Mother Teresa there is an Elmer Gantry. Wanton hucksterism and abuse of people's spiritual trust is a dangerous and deplorable malfeasance not limited to priestly sexual misadventures with altar boys. Here is a sampling of Godly monsters.

Jonathan Edwards
※

BY ADA CALHOUN

JONATHAN EDWARDS (1703–58) is one of those pre-Revolutionary religious leaders whose names are written on blackboards in sixth-grade classrooms at good schools every year around Thanksgiving, along with John Calvin, Cotton Mather, and John Wesley. Even though he's sure to be forgotten over Christmas break, Edwards is still there, perched at the top of our nation's cultural family tree, glaring at us from under his wig, the prototype for generation upon generation of cold, judgmental father-figures with the one true God on their side.

It's easy to bash him on the grounds that Puritans were just plain mean. Like the dad in *Footloose*, Edwards didn't want his congregation getting carried away with what he called "party spirit." Like Anna Wintour, he despised chitchat. He liked having money (he did have nearly a dozen children to support) and could be fantastically long-winded. He could be proud, although he preached against the sin of pride. He was forever telling everyone they were going to hell unless they were, by some glorious chance, part of the Elect and therefore endowed with the potential to receive God's grace. Overall, he was probably not someone you'd want to have dinner with.

Mark Twain called him "a resplendent intellectual gone mad," and said the experience of reading Edwards left him with "the strange and haunting sense of having been on a three days' tear with a drunken lunatic." There is indeed something of the genius madman about Edwards, who spent much of his childhood hanging out in a prayer booth he constructed in a swamp near his family home, obsessively observing spiders, about whom he later wrote an essay that's often held up as an example of early natural science. He had a fascinating mind and wrote reasoned, nuanced philosophy and theology, spending page after page wondering, for example, whether or not all love arises from self-love.

(An encouraging aside for those prone to anxiety: One benefit of self-love's being the source of all evil is that if you're comfortable with yourself, you're deluded and hovering over the pit of hell, whereas if you're really nervous, you might be okay.)

There are various kinds of virtue, but its essence, Edwards said, is love of God. Since the physical world is analogous to the spiritual world, God is manifest in our surroundings, although He's embodied by some things more than others. Naturally, your love will be strongest for things that manifest God most. It's kind of murky how you quantify God-manifestation (one gets the image of that carnival game where you hit the lever with a hammer and watch the piece of metal rise to indicate manifestation level, with bell-ringing signaling ultimate deity-ness).

Anyway, the phrase Edwards used to indicate the disposition you attained when you were in fact in possession of true virtue was "disinterested benevolence," a phrase that bears an unfortunate resemblance in its connotations of detached thoughtfulness and thoughtful detachment to the term "compassionate conservatism."

Edwards helped ignite the great awakening, the flurry of revivals that brought great swaths of the country to God. He encouraged mission work and himself acted as a missionary among the Indians for several years. American evangelical Christianity got a real push from Edwards and his cohorts at a time when the whole church-state thing, and so much else about how America would or would not be religious, was still up in the air. The pre-Revolutionary country's strict English-inherited hierarchies were just starting to be challenged when the dissent-loathing Edwards reinforced the right of the Godly to isolate and condemn those outside the fold. For posterity, Edwards's most enduring idea is perhaps that fantasy of the "city set upon a hill," a place occupied solely by the Godly (specifically, in this case, he was talking about Northampton).

After dutifully sorting the unconverted from the saved, he then kept the faithful on the right path by, essentially, scaring the shit out of them. He preached what is probably the most famous (and is certainly the best titled) sermon in our country's history: "Sinners in the Hands of an Angry God" (1741). Predictably, it contains spiders. Here's a sample:

"The God that holds you over the pit of hell, much as one holds a spider, or some loathsome insect, over the fire, abhors you, and is dreadfully provoked; his wrath towards you burns like fire; he looks upon you as worthy of nothing else, but to be cast into the fire; he is of purer eyes than to bear to have you in his sight; you are ten thousand times so abominable in his eyes as the most hateful venomous serpent is in ours. . . ."

When Northampton's crops failed in 1743, Edwards told his followers that it was their fault for not taking better care of the poor. When the roof collapsed during a sermon, it was God's warning to them, and it was a sign of God's mercy that no one died beneath the rubble. He made God present in America long before Joseph Smith claimed Jesus had in his lifetime jetted over to the New World to preach to the Indians. Sure, all ministers made God a daily presence—the Catholics and Anglicans were busy doing it at the time, too—but Edwards and his spider army were particularly effective in instilling that sense that, as the Bette Midler song goes, God is watching us. (And, by the way, is he ever pissed off.)

Of course, it's hard to be watched all the time by a bloodthirsty, omnipotent being, and Edwards's followers showed their appreciation for twenty-three years of his paternal concern by kicking their leader out of his own congregation in 1750.

That firing may or may not have had something to do with the American Revolution's approach. Society was, after all, becoming more liberal and more open, whereas Edwards, a Calvinist who didn't believe in free will, had attempted to restrict church membership to what he called "visible saints."

The vote the parishioners held to kick him out is a vote we wind up having every day: Is poverty in fact a punishment for sin? Are some of us born with the potential for redemption while others are lost causes? Should we make society more exclusive or more inclusive?

Edwards willed many things to us Americans, and one, it may be argued, is a creeping sense of collective doom. Something about those sermons is embedded in our national psyche.

"Unconverted men walk over the pit of hell on a rotten

covering," Edwards preached, "and there are innumerable places in this covering so weak that they won't bear their weight, and these places are not seen. The arrows of death fly unseen at noonday; the sharpest sight can't discern them."

Unhappiness is, Edwards suggested, our natural and proper condition. From his pulpit, he put a potent guilt cocktail into our drinking water. It's a back-brain sense of self-loathing, a funk that's passed like a virus through the ages. There's a line in Doutcronomy, 32.35, that Edwards enjoyed quoting, and it's a warning to those who get too comfortable: "Their foot shall slide in due time."

Brigham Young

BY THOMAS GOLTZ

YOU SEE THEM everywhere, adjusting their thin and proper black ties on their starchy white shirts, getting ready to knock on doors everywhere from Egypt to Estonia and even the side streets of my hometown of Livingston, Montana.

They are the direct spiritual descendants of a man who certainly made his mark in this world, and, depending on your beliefs and concepts of heaven and hell, probably in the next one, too. This man started out as a lonely and largely illiterate journeyman paint mixer, and ended up pursued by such literati as Mark Twain and Sir Richard Francis Burton. He was run out of several towns in Ohio, Missouri, and Iowa for general quackitude, then marched on by the United States Army in his desert exile for fornication, yet went on to inspire his squeaky-clean heirs to more or less take over the CIA and FBI (and, no doubt, the newly created Office of Homeland Security).

Not bad for a man who took a marginal (and largely despised) group of nineteenth-century odd-ball believers, convinced sixty-five thousand of said outcasts to walk over a mountain range in mid-winter to found a socialist utopia in the wilderness, and then ended up with twenty-seven wives and fifty-six children and God knows how many great-great-grandkids, who now sport the best-looking butts and healthiest-looking complexions of anyone boogie-boarding down Park City ski slopes.

Yes, yes, I am talking about the Big Bee, as in Brigham, as in Young, as in the real American Moses and re-founder of the folks known to them as the Latter Day Saints, who most of the rest of us call Mormons.

That guy.

I mean, let's give credit where credit is due. Think about the People's Temple and Jim Jones and the Kool-Aid disaster in Jonestown. Think about Heaven's Gate and Marshall "Do" Applewhite and his San Diego–based crowd of Hale-Bopp–chasing space cadets in their Nike trainer shoes. Think of the Branch Davidians and David Koresh and the shoot-out at Waco. Think about virtually any effort to form a new religion either from scratch or from an older, accepted one over the past two hundred years of American history and you will be obliged to admit that whatever else you might say about the Man From Whitingham, Vermont—modern day messiah or manipulating mad-man—this must be said right now: *he succeeded*, where lesser would-be prophets and social engineers failed, and usually at the cost of their lives as well as those of their followers.

Not so with Brigham Young.

Born in 1801 as the ninth of eleven children in a poor family of farmers who moved to New York State when he was three, young Brigham first left home at age sixteen (and allegedly after only eleven days of school) to start life as an itinerant carpenter and handyman to help the family get by. (Members of the LDS church like to stress the idea that a number of homes in upstate New York still boast Young Original chairs, tables, and fireplace mantels, and that he devised some new way to mix paint and lacquer.) In 1823, he met and married Miriam Angeline Works and moved to the town of Mendon, where the couple joined the Reformed Methodist Church and had two children before Miriam sickened, forcing Brigham to work outside the house as well as to perform chores normally done by the ladies.

Life might well have continued on in that fashion but for one of those flukes of fate that always seem to happen in other centuries than one's own. In 1830, a stranger came through town bearing not the Good Word but the Real Word, namely the newly printed Book of Mormon, the message of God as revealed in the golden tablets by the Angel Moroni to the first prophet of the Church of Christ, Joseph Smith. The LDS first prophet was then a visionary young man of twenty-three years with a tendency to make enemies, not only of God-fearing Christian folk—thanks to the discrepancies between the Book of Mormon and the Gospels—but even with many of his followers due not only to his tendency to meddle and revise the revelations bestowed upon him by Moroni from time to time, but also his tendency to meddle with his followers' wives. *Four thousand corrections* have been made to the Book of

Mormon and other LDS scripture since first revealed in 1830; it is not known how many saintly wives were tampered with in the process, but anti-Mormon Christian fundamentalist literature provided by such groups as the Watchtower suggests that there have been quite a few.

Whatever the case, young Brigham was reticent at first, but clearly seeking something that Methodism could not give and that Joseph Smith's new text offered. After two years, he finally decided to embrace the faith, as did most of his brothers, and almost immediately sallied forth to give witness in Canada—the first of a score of missions to seek converts over the next two decades.

His return to Mendon was marred by a further deterioration in Miriam's health, and after she died in 1832, he gathered several friends together in 1833 to travel to Kirtland, Ohio, to join Smith's small colony of Church of Christ believers, as the Mormon Church was then known. There, he met Mary Ann Angell, who would become Brigham's second wife and mother of his next six children. One presumes that he also assisted Prophet Smith in the inspired speaking-in-tongues translation of the Egyptian papyrus manuscripts that served as the theoretical proof that the golden tablets shown Smith by the Angel Moroni were actually written by Abraham, and thus thousands of years older than any extant manuscript of the Bible. The school of cracking the codes and symbols embedded on the Rosetta Stone in Egypt was still in its infancy, and there were few around to disprove Smith's translation or, for that matter, the claim by the man who sold Smith the papyrus manuscripts of their antiquity.

There were other activities, too, ranging from doing theological battle with leaders of splinter groups to participation

in self-defense units sent to embattled knots of persecuted members of the renamed Church of Latter Day
Saints. There was even one reported self-imposed exodus
in 1937 when some of the splinter groups thought that
Young was exercising too much influence on Smith, possibly resulting in yet another change of name in 1838 of
the followers of the True Faith, namely, to that of the
Church of Jesus Christ of Latter Day Saints, now head-
quartered not in Kirtland, Ohio, but Nauvoo, Illinois. All
in all, it was an important time of development, culminating in Brigham's appointment by Smith in 1941 to
president of the Quorum of the Twelve Apostles after the
church had been driven out of Ohio and Missouri by
armed detractors of Smith's mission accompanied by
allegations of the LDS practice of fornication and
polygamy. Curiously, part of the testimony came from one
of Young's fellow twelve apostles, a certain Orson Pratt,
who came close to accusing Smith of trying to seduce his
wife in the name of God.

After "much reluctance and considerable thought and
prayer," Brigham first embraced Smith's new doctrine of
Plural Marriage in 1842, taking Lucy Ann Decker Seeley
as the first of his eventual twenty-five polygamous wives.
All in all he had twenty-seven, sixteen of whom would
bear him a total of fifty-six children.

Then, in 1844, and under a cloud of obscure circum-
stance and while Brigham was away preaching on the East
Coast, Prophet Smith and several other leading members
of the church were picked up in Carthage, Illinois, and
jailed on charges of treason. An irate mob of vicious anti-
Mormons attacked the jail, and after Smith killed two
assailants with a hidden pistol, he was murdered by the

mob. Upon hearing of the evil event, Brigham rushed back to the colony, but all seemed to be in shambles, with any number of former associates claiming the mantel of the martyred prophet.

Young had no other choice. To hold the church together, he began the first of a series of great western treks—first to Winter Quarters (now Florence, Nebraska) in 1846, and then, after assuming the title of prophet and the authority of Joseph Smith, onward and over the Rocky Mountains to the Great Salt Basin—and the future Salt Lake City. He arrived with the forward group on July 24, 1847, and in the role of a real-life, modern, American Moses.

A visitor to today's Salt Lake City will find a large, clean, "conservative" western American city replete with the standard hotels and convention centers, a handful of bars (actually, "clubs"), as well as small knots of Jack Mormon drunks and very non-Mormon punks hanging out down by the slightly sleazy bus station. Aside from the Temple Square and attendant buildings in the center of town (temporary visitors with a lengthy layover at Salt Lake International Airport can take a free shuttle in and back on the hour for a free, guided walking tour of the facilities, including the massive computer room devoted to the study of genealogies), there is not much to suggest that this was once a frontier town made by saints for saints, and at the explicitly revealed instruction of the biggest saint of them all—Brigham Young.

His own abode was a row of log cabins on what is today's South Temple Street built by and for Young and his growing collection of wives and children. Known as Harmony House, it served as the governorate of the self-described State of Deseret that Young declared in 1849. It was then augmented by a two-story adobe structure with a tower surmounted by a gilded beehive, which thus gave the name of the place as Beehive House, which in turn became the official residence of the governor of Utah Territory in 1851, a position Young acquired and held until stripped of it in 1857, when President James Buchanan attempted to appoint a new, non-Mormon governor from Georgia. That was also the year that Buchanan sent the army to suppress the LDS "rebellion" against federal authority—meaning the now officially accepted dogma of polygamy announced in 1852—as well as to investigate the so-called Mountain Meadow Massacre, in which 120 new emigrants were killed by Paiute Indians in cahoots with a band of Mormons led by one John D. Lee, a crime thought to be traceable back to Brigham Young himself. The American Moses, however, declined to engage the federal forces, choosing rather an Indian-style tactic of indirect harassment of supply routes until the garrisoned forces marched back East with the commencement of the Civil War, leaving the LDS more or less in peace.

The concept "more or less" stems from the fact that while outsiders were suddenly no longer capable of long-distance interference in church affairs, a new round of internal conflict had broken out over church doctrine, including theological disputes between Brigham the prophet and the same Brother Orson Pratt who had accused Joseph Smith of attempted adultery. This time, most of these disputes related to Young's interpretations of Smith's revelations concerning Blood Atonement, the impossibility of blacks becoming priests due to the Mark of Cain, as well as the practice of polygamy as being not only divinely ordained, but necessary for man's becoming sons of God as well as God himself, a complex theological dispute known in Mormon circles as the Adam-God Doctrine. Once again, Brother Pratt was on the losing end of the stick and was eventually stripped of apostleship.

Brother Pratt was not alone in his protest, however. Back in Iowa, those Mormons left behind (or unwilling to follow Young during the great exodus) were busy creating the single largest splinter group of the LDS under Joseph Smith III, the Reformed Church of Jesus Christ of Latter Day Saints.

But Brigham Young had more on his mind than obtuse theological dispute. He entertained visitors as diverse as the young Samuel Clemens and Captain Richard Francis Burton. The former loathed Young, but failed in being able to provoke the prophet to do more than pat him on the head and ask if he were a boy or a girl, while the latter asked—and was denied with a smile—for temporary membership in the church in order to make a little comparative, on-the-spot research into the relative merits of polygamy in Islam and the LDS. At the same time Brigham was busy building up his City of the Saints as the mothership of Mormonism that would spawn four hundred colonies in Utah, Nevada, and Idaho territories over the next two decades, and, thanks to a special permanent emigration fund, draw in LDS settlers from all over the United States, Britain and its dominions, as well as Scandinavia and western Europe. Young's policy of Mormon self-sufficiency (almost socialist in nature, including collective works projects for roads and canals as well as a tithing for tax) kept in-migration of non-Mormons to the Utah territories to a minimum. When by 1869, a sufficient number of non-Mormon men had settled in the territory to upset the demographic balance, the prophet took the radical step of instituting women's suffrage—thus hugely increasing the number of Mormon voters on election lists, and off-setting non-Mormon settlers' claims to change in everything from land deed distribution and registration to mining laws.

Friction between the quasi-theocratic state and the central authorities, however, continued. In 1871, for example, Young was charged with violating the anti-polygamy laws of the United States, but never convicted. More seriously, the specter of the Mountain Meadow Massacre of 1857 returned, and although twenty years after the act, John D. Lee was once more put on trial and condemned to death for his participation, and executed that same year.

Brigham Young was not far behind, leaving this vale of tears on August 29, 1877, a victim of appendicitis. His statue now stands in the rotunda of the capital in Washington, D.C., and the number of people registered as members of his church is now well over ten million, worldwide.

As for the City of Saints he built, the last time I was in town I did indeed stop in to the Temple grounds, and even visited the genealogy center for several hours, playing around on the computers until I had established to my own satisfaction that my immediate family, down to three generations, just does not exist, or have collectively been damned to hell for at least as long as the LDS has existed.

And, as I left Salt Lake, I noticed the arrival of the most recent batch of conventioneers coming to the city: a group of Southern Baptists, who regarded their three-day public meetings as a fine time to start going around and knocking on Mormon doors, spreading the Word of God in its original form.

✳ ✳ ✳

Gerald L. K. Smith

BY JAMES RIDGEWAY

"THE GREATEST RABBLE-ROUSER seen on earth since Apostolic times," was the way H. L. Mencken described Gerald L. K. Smith, the flamboyant, right-wing, preacher-politician who drew crowds by the tens of thousands during the 1930s. Smith got hot when he met Henry Ford and the two of them pored over the details of what they thought was a Jewish conspiracy to run the world. Smith thereupon embarked on a campaign to search out the Jews, get them out of the film business and the government, and to make lists of where they lived so they could be rounded up on a moment's notice. What made Smith different from the other Jew haters of the time was his ability to push his political views into mainstream American politics.

His life spanned much of the last century and ran from Huey Long's populist crusade up through Nixon and into the Carter years. Unlike most of the far-right politicians of today, he spoke to immense crowds, far larger than any of the throngs turning out for mainstream politicians who do most of their politicking through TV. Smith was a huckster, pumping out his wild rants and exposés with the gusto of one of today's tabloids. He rode the crosscurrents of nativism, populism, and nationalism, and his influence lingers in the contemporary far right. Among Smith's supporters was Wesley Swift, who provided a direct link to the Fifth Era Klan, Aryan Nations, and Posse Comitatus, and the groups that plotted the bombing of the Federal Building in Oklahoma City beginning in the 1980s and culminating in the successful attack on April 1995. And

Smith himself supported Christian Identity, an offshoot sect of Christianity that provides an underpinning for many of the contemporary far right groups. (I have set out in greater detail the evolution of nativist politics in *Blood in the Face: The Ku Klux Klan, Aryan Nations, Nazi Skinheads, and the Rise of a New White Culture*, published by Thunder's Mouth Press.)

Smith's wild version of nativism, nationalism, and populism provided the seed bed for much of the content of the Reagan-Bush years; religious fundamentalism, cultural conservatism, anti-intellectual, anti-tax, anti-UN, etc. trace their recent origins back into the political hothouse of the 1930s.

A Wisconsin-born fundamentalist minister and an early member of the Nazi-wannabe group the Silver Shirts, Smith got his start in national politics through Huey Long, the charismatic and corrupt populist United States senator and former governor of Louisiana. Long hired Smith as national organizer for his "Share Our Wealth" campaign, which sought to cap the income of the rich and redistribute wealth throughout the country. In his biography of Huey Long, Harry T. Williams recounts how, while barnstorming across Louisiana in 1934, "Smith spoke to over one million people. It was rousing stuff for a nation in the depth of the Great Depression: 'Let's pull down those huge piles of gold until there shall be a real job,' he shouted. 'Not a little old sow-belly, black-eyed pea job, but a real spending money, beefsteak and gravy, Chevrolet, Ford in the garage, new suit, Thomas Jefferson, Jesus Christ, red, white, and blue job for every man.' " Smith's spaniel-like devotion to Long extended to sleeping at the foot of his bed, and when Long died, Smith delivered the eulogy to a huge crowd of the Kingfish's supporters.

With his idol gone, Smith devoted himself to launching his own third party. He joined forces with Father Charles Coughlin of the Church of the Little Flower in Michigan, who had gained notoriety with his vitriolic radio sermons that attacked the Federal Reserve System and Franklin Roosevelt and over time grew more and more virulently anti-Semitic. Along with Francis Townsend, an elderly physician who sought to establish a system of pensions for the masses, they created the Union Party and ran Wiliam Lemke against FDR in 1936. Lemke proved to be an uninspiring figure, drawing fewer than one million votes, and the partnership among the three men broke up—in part because Coughlin's and Smith's competing egos meant they couldn't stand to be on the same platform.

Smith soon went to New York, where he set up the Committee of One Million (with nine founding members). The committee ostensibly fought the twin evils of the New Deal and Communism, warning that a violent Communist revolution would soon be launched. In fact the committee was an instrument used by businessmen to attack the labor unions. And as with all of Smith's short-lived organizations, it provided a focus for raising money. (In addition to passing the hat at public events, Smith became a pioneer of direct-mail fundraising.)

When little came of his efforts in New York, Smith moved to Detroit, where he met auto tycoon Henry Ford. Ford gave the preacher money and loaned him detectives, who put together the Ford Company Red File of supposed Communists. Smith had always been leery of Jews, but after getting to know Ford and reading Ford's *Dearborn Independent* series on the threat of "The International Jew," he found his true mantra, which he would repeat until the end of his life: "The day came when I embraced the research of Mr. Ford and his associates and became courageous enough and honest enough and informed enough to use the words: 'Communism is Jewish.' " The best single account of Smith's life is contained in Glen Jeansonne's *Gerald L. K. Smith, Minister of Hate*. I am indebted to him for much of the information in this article.

An isolationist in World War II, Smith created the America First Party—later the Christian Nationalist Party—and in 1942 founded a monthly magazine, *The Cross and the Flag* (which continued publishing until 1977). He thought Hitler was misunderstood and the idea that six million European Jews had been killed was ridiculous. In fact, he said, these same Jews were walking around in American cities, having been smuggled in to keep Roosevelt in power. Under the guidance of an all-powerful Jewish aide named "Sammy the Rose," and with the support of Stalin, the Jews had even faked FDR's death, stashing him in an insane asylum until the day when they would attempt to make him President of the World.

After an unsuccessful run for the United States Senate, Smith drifted from Detroit down to St. Louis, where he tried to stir up trouble between the white working-class and the black sections of the city, and eventually settled in Los Angeles. He was a keen supporter of Joe McCarthy and curried favor with various chairmen of the House Un-American Activities Committee, to whom he presented lists of people he claimed were Communists. Smith testified on several occasions before the committee, claiming, among other things, that he was being persecuted by a "left-wing cabal" that included Frank Sinatra, Orson

Welles, Eddie Cantor, and Walter Winchell, among others. He took personal credit for persuading the committee to investigate the film industry.

In 1948 and 1952 Smith supported General Douglas MacArthur for the Republican nomination. He circulated stories that Harry S. Truman's middle initial stood for "Solomon" and that Truman and his wife had engaged in Talmudic study, and came down hard against Eisenhower, claiming that the Episcopalian war hero was actually a Swedish Jew, and worse, had diddled his secretary while he was leading the allied forces in Europe. In 1952, Smith once again threw his hat into the ring and ran on the Christian Nationalist party ticket, pledging himself to fight interracial marriage, guarantee white supremacy, eliminate the income tax, and get the United States out of the UN. He failed to get on one ballot. Disheartened at what America had come to, he talked of throwing in the towel for good. But not before he led an effort to impeach and imprison all nine members of the Warren Supreme Court.

While he didn't claim that John F. Kennedy was a Jew, Smith did peg him as pro-Jewish and soft on Communism, and denounced his family as a bunch of drunken whore-mongers. In 1964, Smith initially backed George Wallace for president, calling him "the white man's Martin Luther King," but he soon ditched Wallace for Barry Goldwater, whom he admired for standing up for the John Birch Society, voting against the Civil Rights Act, and holding firm behind Joe McCarthy. The fact that Goldwater actually had Jewish blood could be excused because the Arizona senator was a practicing Christian. Smith's backing of Goldwater became ever more fervent when the Democrats nominated the detested Lyndon Johnson. "I saw pimps in command," Smith wrote at the time of the Democratic Convention. "I witnessed the glorification of whoremongers . . . mealy-mouthed Southerners behaving like Judas Iscariot on the night of our Lord's betrayal . . . fine, self-respecting citizens of Mississippi kicked out, and the bloc of blacks manipulated from New York and Moscow permitted to sit in their places." As Smith saw things, Johnson got his Great Society measures through Congress because he proffered the members of Congress whisky and women. "I think he's guilty of murder, homosexuality, a wide variety of perversions, thievery, treason, and corruption."

In 1968, Smith turned his attacks to Hubert Humphrey ("gabby, repulsive, aggressive, offensive, arrogant, egotistical, over ambitious, radical, opportunistic") Eugene McCarthy ("a bad man"), and Bobby Kennedy, who would turn the treasury over to Jews and "mongrelizers," and who had "deliberately groomed his hair in a goofy manner to strike the sex chord impulse stimulated by the disgraceful and scandalous Beetles [sic]."

Instead Smith embraced the "wholesome" Nixon, and in 1972, after Wallace was shot, he strongly backed Nixon as an alternative to George McGovern, whose supporters comprised "perverts, lesbians, women-lib fakers, demagogues, and downright traitors." Smith later argued that the Watergate burglars were after evidence showing McGovern took money from Fidel Castro, and declared: "My one criticism of Nixon is that he didn't personally supervise the Watergate raid so that it would have been done right." He saw Nixon's eventual resignation as the work of Zionists.

Smith spent his golden years in Eureka Springs, Arkansas, turning the town into a religious tourist attraction featuring the Christ Only Art Gallery, the Bible Museum, the Passion Play theater, and a seven-foot-high statue, Christ of the Ozarks, beside which lies the grave of Gerald L.K. Smith.

Cardinal Francis Joseph Spellman

BY DAN BISCHOFF

EARLY ON THE afternoon of Dec. 5, 1967, Marine Corps One scattered pigeons as it landed unannounced in New York's Central Park. President Lyndon Johnson got out of the helicopter and climbed into the back of a black armored limousine for the short drive to St. Patrick's Cathedral. He had a funeral to attend.

All the secrecy was necessary because Johnson was a war president, and the man he meant to honor had been one of the greatest proponents of American involvement in the Vietnam War. More than three thousand mourners had lined up outside the cathedral to pay their respects, but hundreds more had been arrested protesting against the war that morning in front of the church. Johnson did not want his presence to swamp the funeral; as it was, crowds started chanting, *"Hey, hey, LBJ/How many kids did you kill today?"* as Johnson slipped into St. Pat's and took his place in a pew near the casket holding Cardinal Francis Joseph Spellman. The chanting was loud enough to be heard above the obsequies inside.

The two men have been forever linked by their war, but they had far more in common than that. Cardinal

Spellman was a prince of the Catholic Church, educated at the American College in Rome, an old-school, Irish-Catholic prelate who loved the pomp and splendor of his Church and its elaborate, incense-scented Latin rites—a far cry from the Southern Baptist pol from the banks of the Pedernales who liked to carry on policy discussions through the bathroom door.

But just underneath they were two of a kind, natural political fixers who first rose through their respective ranks by finding out what men of power needed (money, of course, but much else besides) and providing it. And Spellman represented more than just political moxie: secular power in the hands of religious clerics. It is an old story in the United States, especially wherever the fires of prejudice have burned the brightest. But as Americans prepare to open a new chapter in that story, it might help to remember what tax-exempt clerics can do with faith in a capitalist democracy—and Frank Spellman was, well, a cardinal case.

Today, in the wake of its ongoing child abuse scandals, the precipitous decline in American priestly vocations, and the virtual disappearance of convents, it's difficult even to think of the Catholic Church in the United States as a powerful national force that could shape everything from popular entertainment to official foreign policy. But drop back just two generations and you would be amazed.

Cardinal Spellman headed the American Catholic Church during its period of greatest cohesion and power, from 1939, when he became archbishop of the Diocese of New York, until his death in 1967. The cardinal oversaw a tremendous boom in the physical assets of the Church, particularly in New York. In just four years, from 1955 through 1959, Spellman spent a staggering $168 million to build fifteen churches, ninety-four schools, twenty-two rectories, sixty convents, and thirty-four other major institutions, from hospitals to public charities.

You could pass through your entire life, from birth through college, and conceivably until your death and display in a Catholic funeral home, without ever having to deal with any social organization that was not specifically Catholic. Thousands of priests and nuns staffed these facilities, organized charities, and led lay-religious retreats for the faithful. Most Catholics knew nothing about the private lives of priests or nuns, but they saw every day their impact on the society around them.

This vast apparatus was overseen by an autocratic hierarchy that had shown itself to be independent of Rome in the past. It was Spellman who reined in this army of idealistic priests and established the modern Irish-American Catholic clergy's style of governance—secretive, image-conscious, occasionally Machiavellian, and always instinctively conservative—that has marked it to this day.

It was a style that grew as the Church itself had grown, out of the deep prejudices of the nineteenth century (the Ku Klux Klan was originally organized as much to combat Catholics as blacks; cartoonist Thomas Nast, the inventor of Santa Claus, showed Irish bishops' mitred hats rising from the East River like the gaping maws of crocodiles). The Irish in America were both more numerous and more loyal to their Church than Catholics of other nationalities, and they have always dominated the American clergy.

Joseph Francis Spellman—his friends, from lawyer Roy Cohn to Pope Pius XII, always called him Frank—grew up in an era when an ambitious young Irish-American was thought only to have a choice among the "four P's": politics, the police, prison, or the priesthood. But Frank Spellman was different. He was born in 1889, not in the teeming Irish neighborhoods of Boston, but in Whitman, Massachusetts, a thoroughly Yankee Protestant town of pleasant frame houses and giant red-brick shoe factories. His father, William Spellman, was the child of workers who labored in the shoe plants, but William had become a successful grocer. Young Frank, the first of five siblings, grew up in a large home with a carriage house and a stable, on a five-acre spread dotted with fruit trees.

It was Spellman's gruff, driven father who provided him with a model for success; his mother, formerly Nellie Conway, by all accounts as soft and sweetly loving as her husband was a whippet, was the daughter of an ox-cart driver for the shoe factories. When he was old enough, they sent their eldest son to Fordham University, a Jesuit institution in New York City, where they had relatives.

But it wasn't his scholarship that set Frank Spellman apart. It was his desire to succeed. As a young seminarian in Rome, Spellman cultivated powerful clergy and wealthy American visitors alike by snapping them with his new-fangled camera, developing the pictures, and then sending them along with a note soon thereafter. Flattery was all he had to offer, yet Spellman quickly began moving among diplomatic circles in Rome, and many of his fellow students began to resent him.

Later, when he had larger resources (millions of dollars flowed through his hands as a bishop, with virtually no oversight from either the United States or the Vatican), Spellman could be more generous. He sent gold watches, jewels, tapestries, grand pianos, even limousines; Pope Pius XII used a white-and-gold electric shaver shipped from New York. Spellman's friendship with the rabidly anti-Communist Pius would be the key to his own elevation (on naming Spellman cardinal in 1946, Pius put his own red hat on the little Irishman's head). After World War II, Spellman acted as a conduit for millions of dollars from United States intelligence sources ($350 million in relief and political slush funds in 1947 and 1948 alone) to help stave off Communist electoral victories in Italy, a source of constant worry to the pope.

The money to build St. Pat's, as the saying goes, came from the pittances of a million Irish maids in New York City. But Spellman pooled parish funds in such a way that the Church was suddenly able to be a financial player, leveraged by vast real estate holdings and working with wealthy Catholics (like Joseph P. Kennedy—who went into business with Spellman's realtor to buy the huge Chicago Mart, still the foundation of the family fortune).

Even more importantly, Spellman came to play an equally significant role in secular American politics. Founder of the annual Al Smith Dinner (nominally a benefit for Catholic charities, the banquet has always been a forum for national politicians to pay fealty to the Catholic vote), Spellman was military vicar to United States armed forces during World War II, a confidante of FDR, and later a spirited defender of Joe McCarthy and the anti-Communist crusade he led. The cardinal routinely traded information with the FBI and CIA throughout his tenure.

Spellman dominated local politics in his diocese, too, so much so that during his time as archbishop of New York, few city appointments were made without first getting the cardinal's nod. His rectory near St. Patrick's Cathedral became known as "the Powerhouse" to New York pols, and many journalists feared crossing the little man in round, gold-rimmed glasses.

Of course, the source of Spellman's power wasn't so much the capital budgets he controlled as his position as chief arbiter of morality for the city's Catholics. How this power worked its way through the bureaucracies was never clear, but it was unmistakable. When City College hired famed philosopher Bertrand Russell (who had written a libertine book called *Marriage and Morals* that mocked Church positions) in 1940, Mayor LaGuardia soon had him fired. Russell denounced the Church for using its influence against him, and Spellman frostily replied that he "challenged the wisdom of subsidizing the dissemination of falsehood under the guise of liberty."

Perhaps we can take the measure of how Spellman's power worked in the city—and engage in full disclosure—by looking at how the cardinal managed to stop subscriptions to the *Nation* by all the public school libraries in New York City.

In those days, the nine-member public school board was divided among the city's main religious groups, with three Catholics (even though they had their own sprawling school system), three Protestants, and three Jews. But there was little doubt who carried the most clout. In 1947, the *Nation* ran a series of articles by Paul Blanshard that questioned the Church's influence in the state over issues of abortion, birth control, and divorce. The cardinal insisted that all the public school libraries give up their subscriptions, and the board quietly went along.

The *New York Herald Tribune* found out about Spellman's hand in the decision, and overnight it became a real public donnybrook. Poet Archibald MacLeish led an impromptu Committee to Lift the Ban, but it was upheld in the courts. The battle over the *Nation* was one of the few times during Spellman's career when his behind-the-scenes methods were exposed in the press, and one of the first times they boomeranged (Blanshard wound up with a bestselling book, *American Freedom and Catholic Power*).

The default mode of Spellman's secular politicking was anti-Communism. Beyond his support for Joe McCarthy's crusade, Spellman shared information about Catholic labor leaders whom he suspected of being Communist with the FBI, and even accused striking gravediggers at one of New York's Catholic cemeteries of being Communists themselves (he backed down after using seminarians as scabs failed to break the union). He went so far as to have the Catechetical Guild print a four-color comic book, *Is This Tomorrow?*, which featured a panel showing a mob of depraved Commies crucifying a cherubic-looking Spellman on St. Pat's door.

Spellman could occasionally use his influence to lean on right-wing extremists, too. He was instrumental in the silencing of the anti–New Deal radio priest, Father Charles E. Coughlin, in 1940—though only after FDR suggested that the IRS might do a little audit of how Catholic bishops spent their money. But Spellman's model for Church-state relations would always be Generalissimo Francisco Franco, who declared the Spanish Civil War to be a crusade for "Holy Mother Church" and restored many ecclesiastical privileges, including complete control of the national film industry. Spellman found Franco to be "a very sincere, serious, and healthy middle-aged man."

The movies were a power center no man could ignore by

the 1930s. The cardinal was responsible in his lifetime for a striking rehabilitation of the Irish in popular American culture, thanks to the enormous influence wielded by lists of "forbidden" films put out by the Catholic Legion of Decency. In particular, Hollywood concocted a series of sentimental priest movies that were meant to flatter Spellman (*Going My Way*, which won Bing Crosby his Oscar, and *Boys Town*, with Spencer Tracy, were only the beginning; scores of Catholic melodramas were produced, from *Angels with Dirty Faces* to *The Shoes of the Fisherman*, over three decades). And they worked, both with the cardinal and at the box office.

Throughout his career, cardinal Spellman's public image was anything but that of a hard-nosed political fixer. Short and round, with clean-shaven pink cheeks and long robes, Spellman spoke in a high, squeaky voice. He generally conveyed a sweetness that was almost akin to fainting spells. Virtually all of his public moralizing involved sexual matters, which he seemed to oppose as mere subjects of discussion; even salty old Joe Kennedy bit his tongue around the cardinal, who was uncomfortable with off-color jokes. Lying, hypocrisy, or cheating were almost never castigated by the Powerhouse.

According to John Cooney's 1984 *The American Pope*, on which much of this account has been based, many of the priests who worked in the Powerhouse simply assumed Spellman was homosexual (others steadfastly dismissed the very idea). Certainly, among his many powerful friends the cardinal counted any number of closeted gays: Spellman never seemed so relaxed as he did on Roy Cohn's yacht off the coast of Key West, or when he took in a few horse races with FBI Director J. Edgar Hoover.

Nonetheless, speculation about the cardinal's sexuality is probably bootless, and there are no known accusations against him. But the dissimulation that was key to his political effectiveness during his lifetime did leave a profound mark on the Church he helped to build. Free discussion was never encouraged, in matters of faith and morals it was dismissed as dangerous, and wherever possible, ancient, impossibly conservative answers to life's questions were touted as the only response to changing realities. When the sexual revolution of the mid-1960s swept through the United States the Catholic clergy was entirely unprepared, and many simply left their vocations.

The secrecy and administrative juggling that were Spellman's style ultimately led to a clergy that was so out of touch with the faithful as to be resented by most of the laity. When the sex scandals started to come out in the 1990s, the ranks of the clergy were so depleted, and their fund of practical ideas for running the Church so scanty, that the institution seemed to implode overnight.

Of course, the cardinal died in 1967, long before all these things had been made clear to Catholics and the public at large, and before the war in Vietnam had had its Tet offensive. In that much, at least, Cardinal Spellman was lucky.

Lyndon Johnson, and the rest of us, less so.

✳   ✳   ✳

Billy Graham

BY TERRY BISSON

Caesar's Man

Like many of the great American performers of his generation, Billy Graham got his start in vaudeville. Chicago's Youth for Christ was designed to appeal to GIs back from World War II and kids just off the farm. They put on quite a show, featuring flashing electric bowties and neon "glo-sox," a praying horse that knelt at the cross, trombones, and even a "consecrated saxophone."

The handsome young Southerner was a hit. "The preaching windmill" was just off the farm himself (or talked like it) and he was selling prime real estate: Paradise. Soon he had his own radio show, and was touring with the Crusade for Christ, saving souls by the dozens, or at least entertaining them, and collecting their coins. He was doing the Lord's work.

He had always had big plans. They were about to get bigger. Billy Graham had come to the Lord via Mordecai Ham, a preacher on the Southern revivalist "sawdust circuit." Ham was all fire and brimstone. He would set up his tent on the carnival grounds at the edge of town, attack the "devil's instruments" (local bootleggers and, of course, the Jews), and then call the sinners forward to be saved. Graham leapt out of his seat, into the light.

He had found his vocation. Having little desire to be a small town tent preacher, Billy enrolled in the Florida Bible Institute, where he rubbed shoulders with an older generation of more respectable revivalists. "Billy would do anything for them," his wife recalls; "literally shine their shoes." This devotion paid off, and with the right connections he made his way to Wheaton College in the Chicago suburbs. Up North, he brushed the sawdust off his knees, and started looking around for finer shoes to shine.

Billy Graham was touched by destiny three times: first by the bony finger of Ham, summoning him to the front of the tent. Secondly by the aurora borealis in Illinois, where he fell to his knees under a "Second Coming" sky, relieved at last of his lingering doubts. And thirdly by the hand of the Maker himself—William Randolph Hearst.

It was Hearst who gave him his true calling. The Crusade for Christ opened in Los Angeles the same week that the Russians tested their first atomic bomb. This fresh menace gave Graham his text: "Communism is inspired and directed by the Devil himself, who has declared war against Almighty God. Did you know that the Communists are more rampant in Los Angeles than any other city in America?"

When Hearst heard these words (through his maid, the story goes), his heart was made glad. And so, verily, he dispatched the famous two-word memo to his newspaper empire: "Puff Graham."

Puff they did. Billy Graham departed Los Angeles a national celebrity, with a holy mission. Promote the American Way of Life. It was a good fit. From the beginning he'd had a greater interest than the mere saving of individual souls. He wanted to restore fundamentalism to its rightful place in American life. The religious fervor that had illuminated (some would say darkened) the American landscape in the glory days of D. L. Moody and Billy Sunday had dimmed. A questioning, secular mood had come with the depression and war. The fires of revivalism were banked except in the South, the historic heartland of protestant Christianity. Graham's intention was to restart that fire, and if that meant sucking up to America's rulers, well, that was right and proper too.

Render unto Caesar.

Graham was henceforth Caesar's.

Hearst's tabloids lofted him like wings to Washington, D.C., the very seat of power, and Strom Thurmond introduced him to Henry Luce, who saw in this young striver what America needed, and prepared him a place on the cover of *Time*. The flashy ties were soon gone. The countrified bigotry of his forebears was set aside (it was never a good fit with the eagerly cosmopolitan Graham). Soon he was speaking to packed stadiums, and his message was Caesar's: In paradise, there are "no union dues, no labor leaders, no snakes, no disease."

But here, below: "Christianity needs a show of strength and force; we must maintain the strongest military establishment on Earth."

None of that other cheek stuff. Jesus came "not to send peace but a sword!" The military-industrial complex liked that one.

The dangers were at home as well as abroad.

Joe McCarthy's suggestion that the Fifth Amendment be suspended for leftists inspired Graham to new heights of boyish enthusiasm. "Then let's do it!" he exclaimed. Especially since he knew, personally, of "over eleven hundred social-sounding organizations in this country that are Communist or Communist-inspired."

Truman, that shifty little haberdasher, didn't like him,

but Eisenhower did. Graham made a special trip to Europe to encourage the General to run. And gave him a red [sic] Bible to cherish.

Failing to prevent Kennedy's election, Graham cheerfully played golf with him. He had abandoned redneck anti-Catholicism publicly (not always privately), seeing it as inimical to America's imperial destiny. He was not about to denounce the pope, who was after all a man of consequence.

Lyndon Johnson loved him, and why not? "Nobody could ever make Lyndon Johnson feel he was right quite like Billy Graham could," says Bill Moyers; who also describes how "there'd come this light in Billy's eyes" when Johnson discussed the bombing of North Vietnam.

As for those pesky protesters, Graham was always willing to cast the first stone. "The FBI and the president know who they are and what they are up to. Congress has no more urgent business than to pass laws with teeth in them."

Billy Graham has always remained true to his original vision, which was to restore religion to its rightful place as a pillar of American power. To do that, he recognized early on, one had to honor that power. Render to it. Become one with it.

No problem. He was with Lyndon Johnson on his last night in the White House, and he was waiting in the foyer the next morning when Nixon arrived. Lyndon was fun, but Billy Graham found his true soul mate in the gimlet-eyed little Quaker from California. "There is no American I admire more than Richard Nixon," he said. He was steadfast in his sycophancy until the very end. Even when the tapes showed that Nixon had in fact been lying all along, Graham saw no defect in character. "It was all those sleeping pills, they just let a demon power come in and play over him."

It would be wrong to suggest that Graham fell in step with the anti-Communist hysteria of the 1950s. He helped create it. It would be wrong to suggest that he went along with the atrocities of the Vietnam War. He helped sanctify them. He advised Nixon to bomb the dikes, and flew to Vietnam to encourage the troops to "skin" a Viet Cong.

And in many cases, most of them undocumented, they did.

Even My Lai didn't trouble him unduly. "We have all had our My Lais in one way or another . . . with a thoughtless word, an arrogant act, or a selfish deed."

But wait. Weren't these simply the normal, if appalling, attitudes of the Silent Majority?

Absolutely. But Billy Graham was far from silent. He spoke directly to more people than any other man before or since, and always with the same theme: heaven or hell, America or Communism. Graham assembled, instructed, and emboldened this majority.

Graham has been criticized for anti-Semitism, after the release of the Nixon tapes revealed him and Nixon grumbling privately about the Jews and their "stranglehold" on America.

But this is off the mark. Some of Graham's best friends were Jews. "They swarm about me. They don't know how I really feel about what they are doing to this country." He had long ago shucked off, along with the sawdust, the strident anti-Semitism of his revivalist forebears. His was the private, mainstream, polite kind. He would never have said such things publicly.

The same with racism. He spoke out against segregation, understanding that Southern apartheid was an embarrassment to a nation that sought world hegemony. It was no longer Caesar's plan.

He was even friendly with Martin Luther King, though he refused to attend or support the March on Washington, and often criticized the civil rights movement for going "too far and too fast." Petty bigotry was not his style. Imperial power was more to his taste. He restored Protestant fundamentalism to its central place in American life when it was in danger of being overthrown by the restless secularism of the post-war era, and by the liberatory upheavals of the 1960s. He stood guard, reminding Americans that even though, individually, they were in peril of hell, as a nation they were beyond reproach, as long as they obeyed their betters, followed orders, and quit their God damned complaining.

Render unto Caesar.

Billy Graham prepared the way for the New Right, which was only sleeping, and is now in power. He was their John the Baptist. It was he, in fact, who saved George Bush Jr. from demon rum, beginning his transformation from a drunken vicious stumbling fratboy to a sober vicious stumbling president. For that alone, he deserves a place of honor in this book.

✯ ✯ ✯

Elijah Muhammad
✴

BY DARIUS JAMES

"Bad" American? Or Messenger from a Lost/Found Episode of *THE X FILES?*

Guided by an infernal map charted by one of Italy's more inspired cartographers, the editors of the present volume have consigned the Honorable Elijah Muhammad, the divine messenger of America's melanin-enabled, to a circle of hell reserved for an unwholesome and scurvy bunch designated the "Bad American." And, as I am the kind of backward and foolish Negro Mr. Muhammad so often castigated (See: Colin Powell and Condoleezza Rice), it is my task to explain the reasons why he suffers for his sins against the Republic.

Now, of course, some might argue this job is better suited for the likes of the far more erudite (and pugnacious) Stanley Crouch. Some would even prefer the hemp-forged wit of David Chappelle. What you are going to get, however, is my own ketamine-induced psychoses. *So tough fucking luck . . . !*

Under current legislated standards (See: Patriot Act I & II), I'm not exactly what you might call a "model American." I stopped reciting the Pledge of Allegiance in the sixth grade (normally followed by a group sing-along of some antebellum-era minstrel-show aberration like "Camptown Races"). In my sophomore year of high school, I was arrested and jailed for burning a United States flag. I was an advocate of armed insurrection in the United States until staring down the barrel of a M1 rifle one night in the Andes mountains taught me the wisdom of Dr. King's pacifist's path. And I've left the U.S to discover my Communist roots in a post-Communist Europe. So who am I to point fingers?

To be honest, when I accepted this assignment, I wasn't quite convinced the deceased prophet of America's melanin-enriched deserved having his noseholes shoved into the fecal remnants of Shabazz bean-pie he deposited on the carpet of America's political and cultural landscape. Why shouldn't he be regarded as a Great American? Wasn't he acknowledged as "an outstanding citizen who was always interested in helping young people . . . especially the poor" by another Great American, Chicago's former mayor Richard Daley? Isn't that endorsement enough to chisel The Messenger's face on Mount Rushmore?

Despite Elijah Muhammad's demonization of the white race (and you have to admit, the "white race" has got a pretty sulfurous history), and a fondness for a certain nineteenth century French satire usurped by the Czar's secret police, the members of the Nation of Islam (N.O.I.) are a polite, well-groomed, and disciplined lot. With its own institutions and businesses in black communities across the United States, the N.O.I. collectively operates as a "nation" on "enemy soil" wherein "white people" have been rendered "invisible." Industrious and self-sufficient, N.O.I. members are famous for spurning pork, intoxicants, and loose women. This is certainly more than I can say for myself.

And, in addition to providing efficient set security for some of Spike Lee's dubious "entertainments," the Nation of Islam has often succeeded where America's prison system and drug-rehabilitation programs have failed. If the N.O.I., in fact, had opened a drug-rehab center in the Wall Street area of Manhattan in the 1980s, Betty Ford would've been out of business. Imagine a skinny and runny-nosed stockbroker surrounded by a group of bald and bow-tied black men chanting *"Heroin is white! So is the Devil!"* for seventy-two straight hours. Who wouldn't give up shootin' dope after an experience like that? More importantly, Mr. Muhammad created an alternative universe equal to the mytho-poetic cosmologies evoked by the likes of Sun Ra, Lee "Scratch" Perry, and George Clinton. The story of how the big-headed scientist, Mr. Yacub, for instance, created the white race by the progressive degeneration of "black germs," is far more entertaining than anything audiences endured in the CGI-laden *Matrix* trilogy—even if Laurence Fishburne is in it. Better yet are these instructions for salvation from *The Secret Rituals of the Lost/Found Nation of Islam*, as conveyed by an N.O.I. University of Islam student in 1934: *"Cut off the heads of four devils . . . and win a trip to Mecca and a button with Allah's picture on it!"*

The seventh child of a minister-sharecropper, the future Messenger of the lost/found Tribe of Shabazz was born October 7, 1897, under the name Elija Poole in Sanderville, Georgia—a state governed at the time by the mentally challenged and conically domed. Poole, of course, was the surname of his family's previous owners. The "h" in Elija was added later. As a child, he was a devoted student of the Bible, spending all his spare time with his nose buried in what he would later call "the poison book." Also, due to the ghoulish *Night of the Living Dead* zombie-like habits of Georgia's liver-gobbling white citizenry, little Elija suffered recurrent nightmares of ominously biblical proportions. This, and his biblical readings, may explain why he eventually came to believe he was the prophet who would warn his people of the coming apocalypse.

In 1923, drawn by the promises of the automobile-manufacturing industry, Elija Poole moved to Detroit, Michigan, but eventually discovered life in the midwestern city was as harsh, brutal, and racist as life in the South. And started hitting the bottle big-time. So, for many readers, it will come as a surprise to know on the night his wife, Clara, introduced him to the mysterious man who would forever change his life, W. D. Fard, the soon-to-be *honorable* Elijah Muhammad was *stone-cold drunk!* As the inebriated host swayed on his heels in the living room of his Detroit apartment, the dapper stranger extended his hand, saying: "I know you think I'm *white;* but I am not. *I'm an Asiatic black man.*"

Elija Poole could not believe his reddened eyes. Fard "looked like . . . a Caucasian with an enviable tan" but revealed he was "the Mahdi everyone was expecting two thousand years after Christ." Yes, gentle readers, it's been alleged that the founder of the Nation of Islam—God (Allah) in the flesh—was a *white* man!

When the *Los Angeles Herald-Examiner*, prompted by information provided by the FBI, printed these claims, Elijah Muhammad denied the allegations, and on the front page of *Muhammad Speaks* offered one-hundred thousand dollars for the "evidence." Master Fard's former wife, Hazel Ford (Fard went by many aliases), stepped forward with "proof," but Elijah Muhammad refused payment. If declassified FBI documents are to be believed, W. D. Fard was Wallace Dodd Fard, a New Zealand immigrant of East Indian parentage. The FBI files also alleged Fard was a convicted dope dealer. Apparently, he was busted with his boy, Edward Donaldson, a Chinese-American, with whom he kicked the gong, by two undercover narcotics officers in Los Angeles, and served a three-year sentence in San Quentin Prison. Eventually, after establishing the lost-found Nation of Islam, Fard disappeared in 1932.

Now, on the face of it, it would appear Wallace Fard was a con man of exceptional talent; and Elijah Muhammad was a dupe who, in turn, duped his followers—just as he would be suckered by Satohata Takahashi's Japanese version of the "forty acres and a mule" scam:

After we kick us some round-eyed white ass in America, we gonna give all you loyal Asiatic black people a house in Hawaii! Surf all day! Smoke good ganja all night! Be the first Black Japanese Rastafarian!

Gullibility doesn't equate with "bad." Many people believe George W. Bush is a democratically elected president. Are they bad? No, just stupid.

Muhammad's biographer, Karl Evanzz, on "circumstantial evidence" contained in "declassified" government records, is convinced W. D. Fard is also George Farr; an agitator for pro–Japanese Nationalist interests, and an initiate of Madame Blavatsky's Theosophical Society. Farr apparently acted as an advance man for Brahmin Mohni Catterjee, the East Indian mystic; an interesting bit of information in light of I. Reed's assertion, "The history of the world is the history of the war between secret societies."

In addition to being the primary source for today's addled "New Age" concepts, Ms. Blavatsky promoted the idea of six root races—mythic constructs later twisted to serve the racist ideological purposes of the Nazis. From the information gleaned in Evanzz's biography, it appears, given Mr. Fard/Farr's involvement with theosophy, Freemasonry, the Cabala, and Indian mysticism, his occult roots may go much deeper than we know. For over seventy years, the N.O.I. has revered W. D. Fard as "God (Allah) in the flesh." This idea shouldn't be literally interpreted as the maker of the cosmos come to earth in human form; rather it means an initiate who has achieved an illuminated state of godhood through the esoteric disciplines offered by various mystery schools. I suspect the "Mr. Fard" of many aliases was one such illuminated initiate. Given his status as a rogue and dope fiend, this, of course, sounds ridiculous. However, a study of the lives of mystic such as Gurdjieff, Rasputin, and Crowley show a great deal of the rogue and con man in their characters. This, too, is part of the path of initiated illumination. The question is, of what other secret occult societies was Mr. Fard a member? And for what political purpose?

Evanzz's biography also raises two interesting questions in my mind concerning Mr. Fard/Farr's black-empowerment rabble-rousing and agitation on behalf of foreign governments: Was Mr. Fard/Farr a foreign agent? Was the N.O.I. originally designed as a front for the secret service agencies of foreign interests?

There is no proof to support the idea Mr. Fard was a foreign counter-intelligence agent. There is, however, evidence for the latter. The N.O.I. first attracted the FBI's attention because of their collective refusal to participate in the war against the Japanese during World War II. Elijah Muhammad himself served time behind bars for refusing the draft (in fact, when government agents came to apprehend him, he was found rolled up inside of a carpet under his mother's bed!). Domestically, there is clearly sufficient evidence to prove the N.O.I. was manipulated by secret service agencies in the United States. The tensions created by an FBI disinformation campaign, along with Elijah Muhammad's refusal to accept the consequences of his numerous in-house infidelities, were what led to the murder of Malcolm X, which, of course, most believe was carried out on the Messenger's say-so.

As I stated, I have no proof Mr. Fard was a Secret Service agent, but there is evidence suggesting he was involved in a number of secret societies. The 1920s and 1930s were rife the world over with bizarre, politically-ambitious organizations with esoteric and nationalist content. Espionage and esoterica have quite a history—John Dees spied for Queen Elizabeth (his codename? *007*). Rasputin worked on behalf of the Czarist government. Alcister Crowley had ties to British secret service. L. Ron Hubbard was a naval intelligence agent who claimed he was responsible for busting up a "black-magic ring" (which, incidentally, included a ceremonial magician and rocket scientist who was passing along secrets to Israel). The list goes on.

Letting my imagination run further astray, let's consider the fact that W. D. Fard looked like he was born in a cave in the Caucasus mountains, yet he was able to convince Elijah Muhammad he was a black man. More remarkable, Elijah Muhammad willingly accepted the words of a man who looked exactly like the very devils he condemned. I mean, yeah, sure, plenty of miscegenated persons passed for white back in the day (probably still do). And, if I'm to believe anything I read in Skip Gates's *Transitions*, there were also plenty of white folks abducted from Europe and hornswoggled into believing they had suddenly turned into *black slaves!* The point is, W. D. Fard, unlike Elijah Muhammad, did not have a rigid, monolithic, and authoritarian identity. His identity was fluid, changeable, *transformative*. He was "Black," "White," or "Asiatic" when it suited his purpose. And he was able to persuade Elijah Muhammad to discount the evidence of his own eyes. Seems to me he had all the necessary skills for a *shapeshifting* counter-intelligence agent.

If W. D. Fard could take a drunken black man, and build a nation-wide cult of black-supremacists lasting for more than seventy years, he could do exactly the same with a drunken white man. He had the complexion for it. Who's to say W. D. Fard wasn't working the other side of the street with his head under a sheet? It's possible. Why is it that both the N.O.I. and white-nationalist cults subscribed to the same bullshit in *The Protocols of the Learned Elders of Zion*? Why is it Elijah Muhammad found so much in common with the American Nazi Party's George Rockwell? Why was he accepting funds, as Malcolm X discovered, from racist Texas billionaire H. L. Hunt? "God" working both sides of the street? Same cult, different masks? To what "divine" ends?

None of this, of course, explicitly answers why Elijah Muhammad was a "Bad" American. This is so because Elijah Muhammad wasn't an American at all. In fact, as Louis Farrakhan indicated during a 1994 press conference with the *Washington Post*, he wasn't even a citizen of this world. Why else would he say the Messenger's head floated in a numinous cloud aboard the Mothership?

PLUTOCRATS AND DESPOILERS— LAND WRECKERS AND STRIKE BREAKERS

James H. Peabody, Andrew Carnegie and Henry Frick, Henry Ford, the Owners of the Triangle Shirtwaist Factory

These are the robbers barons, exploiters of resources, both human and natural. These are the tramplers of dignity, the pigs in the counting house. These are the fatcats driven to amass huge fortunes regardless of the cost to others. America has had many of these individuals, many of whom wind up having museums, foundations, and football stadiums named after them, philanthropy often being linked to misanthropy. It is not simply people's labor that makes these pirates rich. Like Mr. Peabody's coal train, they take Paradise away. They wreck and ravage the land, and leave only the stumps and strip mines behind. Again, many names could have appeared in this section, governmental land destroyers like Reagan's secretary of the department of the interior James Watt, and Bush's Gale Norton, among them. These are the enablers for the corporate titans who pay politicians for an unregulated right-of-way, polluters and saluters like Freeport-McMoRan's Jim Bob Moffett, the scheming gold miner Robert Friedman, and the owners of every oil company you ever heard of.

James H. Peabody

BY BRUCE STUTZ

Anybody But Peabody

"I can hire one-half of the working class to kill the other half." —Jay Gould

California had gold. Colorado had iron, lead, and molyb-denum, industrial ores that required more than a mule and a pie pan to find and extract. Big digs called for big players and the in the late nineteenth century the biggest came from the East, the Guggenheims and the Rockefellers. The Guggenheims owned the vast Colorado Smelting and Refining Company. John D. Rockefeller, Sr., owned the Colorado Fuel and Iron Company and the railroad making its way to the mines.

Recent Irish, German, and Italian immigrants made up the mines' work force and the work required ten- to twelve-hour shifts at seventeen to forty cents an hour. With labor in short supply, however, the mineworkers organized. In 1893, two thousand members of fifteen local unions formed the Western Federation of Miners. Over the next ten years it grew to consolidate two hundred unions and forty thousand mine and mill workers. Union power was such that in many towns the union was the government— its members holding offices from civil courts to town sheriff. Non–union members were not welcome.

The owners could do little but watch the union movement grow. In 1898, Colorado Democrats and Populists elected Charles H. Thomas governor. Thomas supported a bill to legislate an eight-hour workday. With the support of union workers from Denver, Cripple Creek, Climax, and Telluride, the bill passed in 1899. Guggenheim, in particular, was not pleased. He was just about to combine his Colorado Smelting and Refining with the American Smelting and Refining Company to create American Smelter Trust, which would control all but two of the state's smelting operations. He challenged the eight-hour bill in court and the next year the state's Chief Justice declared that mandating the number of hours someone could work was an unconstitutional interference with the rights of citizens.

By the turn of the century, increased immigration brought Colorado a surfeit of able bodies—enough that the mine owners felt that, if they had to, they could readily replace striking union workers with non-union labor. What they needed was someone in the state government who would work with them, to back them up when they challenged the union.

The man they chose was James H. Peabody.

A nineteenth-century banker's banker—mustachioed with a handlebar thick as horsehair, burly-nosed and low-eared, his thinning hair parted down the center and slicked to either side—Peabody had made his middling fortune along with the rest of the new Western merchant class on the mine-stimulated economy. Son of a Vermont dry goods merchant who brought him and his sixteen older brothers and sisters to Colorado in 1871, James had gone from nineteen-year-old store clerk and bookkeeper to forty-year-old bank president of Canon City's new First National. He was also Canon City treasurer, secretary and treasurer of Canon City Water Works, and president of the Electric Light Company of Canon City. Along his way he served stints as county clerk, city alderman, and when he was thirty-two, the Colorado Masons had named him state grand master, the youngest in the nation. He had no patience for anarchists.

In 1901, in anticipation of the coming year's gubernatorial election, the Western Federation of Miners moved their headquarters to Denver, within spitting distance of Guggenheim's conglomerate offices. The federation then adopted the platform of the Socialist Party and began to lobby for an eight-hour constitutional amendment that would override the state court's ruling.

The Republicans and mine owners wanted a law-and-order and anti-union candidate to take on the Western Federation of Miners. They courted Peabody. He took little convincing. To shore up his support, the mine operators formed the Colorado Mine Owner's Association, and merchants, wanting a piece of Peabody and of the union-busting action, banded together as the Telluride Businessmen's Association.

Peabody won the election but so did a ballot measure that called for a constitutional amendment to declare an eight-hour workday. However, with the backing of Rockefeller, Guggenheim, and the newly formed anti-union vigilante associations known as the Denver Citizens Alliance and Citizen's Protective League, Peabody, in 1903, had his attorney general declare the wording of the new amendment unconstitutional. The declaration, they hoped, would not only end talk of an eight-hour day but also incite the unions to action, which might in turn give the governor cause to shut them down.

In April 1903 someone dynamited the transformer house of a mine that had hired scabs rather than go along with the union's eight-hour workday demand. Arrests were made. The union claimed innocence but Peabody refused the union's request to intercede on behalf of those arrested. Instead, when violence broke out in Telluride, Peabody, supposedly at the request of the local citizenry, declared "a state of insurrection and rebellion" and brought in the National Guard.

If Peabody owed the Guggenheims, Rockefellers, and the various "Citizen Alliances" before sending in the Guard, he was now totally beholden to them. With the state treasury unable to afford the cost of the military action, Peabody was left to apply to his benefactors for funds to keep the Guard out in the field.

What the National Guard accomplished over the next weeks was, as one historian put it, nothing less than a coup d'etat. The Guard moved in on the union towns, looting homes and taking miners into custody. Some were "deported," put on trains to Kansas City and New Mexico. Others were herded into "bullpens" where they languished like prisoners in Andersonville. Still others were taken out into the mountains and left without food or water. By November, thirty had been killed and Cripple Creek was under military rule.

Wrote Samuel Gompers, president of the American Federation of Labor, to the *New York Herald:* "The mine owners, under the assumed name of the Citizens' Alliance, have unceremoniously summoned the officers elected by the people and demanded their resignations, and if they either refused or hesitated, ropes with nooses at the end were flung at their feet, the alternative given them for signing their already prepared resignations or be hanged. . . . The Citizens' Alliance has declared 'Death to unionism in the Cripple Creek district. . . . Nor do they have in mind the Cripple Creek district alone, but organized labor of the entire country."

"Big" Bill Haywood, union president, knew where to lay the blame: "The governor says the constitution commands the suppression of insurrection. If he would go and hang himself the chief insurgent would be dead. He has caused to be violated every constitutional, moral, and political right that American citizens are supposed to enjoy. . . . There has been no insurrection in Colorado except that emanating from the occupant of the capitol building."

The mine operators now had the run of Colorado. New mechanical equipment, large-scale systems of dams, steam power, and hydraulic mining, which used high-pressure hoses to wash away whole hillsides, gave them the power to shed and replace workers, to deal with the physical suf fering of the miners with the same callousness they showed to the landscape they tore into.

Wrote one miner: "The men working in the smelters are even worse off . . . for, in addition to danger peculiar to their calling, it is the most unhealthy business in the world, lead-poisoning being an everyday occurrence and a dreaded source of danger."

That same lead, along with cyanide, mercury, and acid, con- taminated the high-country streams and the drinking water. The Colorado Geologic Survey reports there are more than 11,300 abandoned mines and prospecting pits just in the national forests in the state. Of those, more than one thousand five hundred are still causing environmental damage.

By the time Peabody was up for election once again, the Federation of Miners had been gutted. Tired of the violence,

Coloradoans voted Peabody out of office in 1904. He wouldn't go without a fight, however, and challenged the election results with such fervor that the legislature agreed to declare him the winner if he agreed to step down the next day and let the lieutenant governor who won the popular vote take office. He did.

Peabody's shock-and-awe approach to settling labor strife would last long into the century. In two years Peabody had created such fear among the miners and citizens of Colorado that it took another ten years before new union battles between miners and mine owners would flare. And that would come in April 1914, when John Rockefeller, Jr., taking Peabody's approach to union-busting, let the militia and his hired security murder forty striking miners in what became known as the Ludlow Massacre. It was the kind of nightmare for which the infamous Mr. Peabody paved the way.

Andrew Carnegie and Henry Frick

BY JOE CONASON

BY THE TIME the world acknowledged him as its wealthiest man, just after the turn of the last century, Andrew Carnegie desired public admiration more than all the material riches that fifty years of striving had won him. The Scottish-born steel baron wanted his name to symbolize the striving immigrant, rugged individualist, bountiful philanthropist, and visionary industrialist; he wanted only to be known for his wisdom, benevolence, kindness, and generosity, for his sincerity as a champion of democracy and labor.

To establish those images of himself in perpetuity, he was prepared to spend nearly all of the greatest fortune that the planet had ever seen on libraries, universities, charities, churches, and of course, public relations. (His personal desk had a drawer constantly replenished with favorable press clippings, labeled "Gratitude and Sweet Words.")

In today's dollars, Carnegie spent and gave away billions to establish his legacy. Yet even those vast sums could never quite buy him out of the devil's bargain he had made so many years earlier with Henry Clay Frick. Although their association would end acrimoniously, at no small financial and personal cost to both men, neither Carnegie nor Frick could escape the memory of the plutocratic cruelty and state-sanctioned violence that had secured their industrial empire.

Both Frick and Carnegie had grown up poor in western Pennsylvania before the Civil War. Both were the sons of men who had never been able to earn more than subsistence for their families, and learned as children to be ashamed of their poverty. Both were small, aggressive, willful, sharp, and hardened by adversity. Both lacked any advanced formal education, yet they rose quickly from humble clerking positions, determined to prosper in the region's developing coal-and-iron economy. They were both extraordinarily talented financial managers and businessmen, who displayed from adolescence an almost demonic devotion to the expansion of their holdings.

That exceptional willpower and talent drove Frick to create the H. C. Frick Coke Company—which manufactured the coal-based fuel used to heat blast furnaces known as coke—and earned him his first million dollars, all before his thirty-first birthday. In the meantime Carnegie, fifteen years older than Frick, had reaped his first fortune as an investor in the Pullman Sleeping Car Company. Then he had reinvested that capital in the iron and steel industry, where Carnegie Brothers introduced such historic technological advances as the Bessemer process for making steel.

It was Carnegie who first broached a business partnership, fearing that Frick's burgeoning local monopoly on the highest-quality coke would leave him at the younger man's financial mercy. They consummated their deal over lunch in 1881, during Frick's honeymoon, by an exchange of shares in their respective companies. Eventually, Frick would become chief executive the Carnegie Steel Company, with its namesake, the great magnate, as majority shareholder. Together, they enjoyed the proceeds of two decades of unprecedented industrial expansion. But for most of that period their success was disturbed by mutual frustration, suspicion, double-dealing, and feuding. Within less than two decades their partnership broke apart irreparably.

What made Frick and Carnegie come to despise each other so intensely? As businessmen, they were entirely compatible and in many respects alike. Both were able to recall and analyze the seemingly minor details of their businesses almost effortlessly; both were capable of farsighted vision as well as mundane economies; and both had the knack for buying out competitors during depressions and fashioning monopolies.

Yet although their backgrounds were not dissimilar, the personalities of Carnegie and Frick could hardly have differed more. Expansive, intuitive, and gregarious, as well as generous, Carnegie could charm the public and the press even while critics pointed to his hypocrisy. He knew a hundred ways to change the subject when his ostentatious wealth and unaccountable power raised questions.

Frick and Carnegie represented opposing strands of the capitalist ethos that when twisted together made a strong combination, like a steel cable. While Carnegie claimed to be the friend of working people, Frick never concealed his determination to subjugate them. While Carnegie sought public approval by distributing his wealth, Frick pursued private satisfactions by collecting great artworks. Carnegie constructed philosophical rationalizations for his fortune. Frick frankly understood that power needed no excuses.

Often described as "ice cold," Frick was a morbid loner whose few friends feared his occasional outbursts of volcanic anger. He disdained publicity, and kept his few charitable gestures behind a heavy veil of privacy. He displayed no interest in the social and political issues that engaged Carnegie. His only recorded comment on American public affairs was a sour quip about Theodore Roosevelt's trust-busting presidential administration. "We bought the son of a bitch," complained Frick cynically, "and then he didn't stay bought."

As he showed during strike after strike, Frick felt no compunction when he threw thousands of miners out of work, slashed their already minimal wages by half, and ordered the summary eviction of their wives and children from company housing. If he took notice of the conditions in those filthy, crowded dwellings, or the disease and danger that killed most of his workers before they reached middle age, he never said so. Indeed, he expressed no regret when the workers who had earned his millions died in hideous battles with his hired police and Pinkerton agents. His favorite tactic was to bring in black workers from Virginia to take the jobs of striking immigrants. He only wanted a free hand, as he told Carnegie on many occasions, to wage unrelenting war on the troublesome unions.

Behind the doors of his mansions, Frick led a life so tormented by personal tragedy that he almost evokes sympathy. He lost two of his four children in their early youth. For almost four years he watched helplessly as his youngest daughter Martha slowly and agonizingly sickened and finally died from internal damage that began after she accidentally swallowed a sewing pin. Then one year after Martha's death, the infant son named for Frick died mysteriously from convulsions. Rumors spread that the three-week-old boy and other members of the Frick household had been poisoned. The awful pain of these losses eventually caused his wife Adelaide to fall into permanent depression and alcoholism. Long before she died, he had lost her, too.

His great-granddaughter, Martha Frick Symington Sanger, believes that Frick's art collection represented a mourning ritual for those children. His grief was tinged with guilt, in part because his preoccupation with building his businesses and breaking the unions had caused him to neglect his family. According to her lavishly illustrated 1998 biography, *Henry Clay Frick: An Intimate Portrait*, he had delayed bringing Carnegie's surgeons to Martha until too late, affording him ample reason to feel implicated in her death. He may also have seen Martha's death as a form of punishment: "the price exacted for the fortune accumulated."

At the time of his son's death, Frick himself was still recovering from the famous attempt on his own life by

Alexander Berkman. Only days earlier, the anarchist and would-be assassin, seeking revenge for Frick's continuing outrages against the working class, had burst into his Pittsburgh offices. Shooting him twice in the neck and back, Berkman then pulled out a stiletto and stabbed the industrialist four times. Frick later told friends that he had been saved by the divine intervention of Martha, whose apparition appeared before him during the struggle with Berkman. So widely loathed was Frick that the headlines in some morning newspapers regretted his survival: "Too Bad Serves Him Right; Frick Is a Dirty Dog and Deserves to Die."

The irony of Frick's life was that he transformed himself into a cartoon plutocrat—the national symbol of industrial villainy—so Carnegie could escape the same fate. Beating down immigrant labor unrest in his coking plants at Connellsville and Morewood hardened Frick, but his reputation was made and ruined during the bloody summer and fall of 1892 at Carnegie's Homestead steel plant.

With the price of rolled steel driven down by recession, Carnegie and Frick agreed to destroy the Amalgamated Association of Iron and Steel Workers so they could slash wages, increase productivity, and speed up production. Although Carnegie regularly pretended to be his workers' friend and protector, he encouraged Frick's scheme to lock out the union and destroy it. "We . . . approve of anything you do," he wrote to Frick from the United Kingdom that summer. "We are with you to the end." For his part, Frick was pleased that the vacillating, publicity-conscious Carnegie would be out of the country during the coming confrontation.

Cutting wages and barricading the plant doors, Frick then announced that the Amalgamated simply no longer existed at Homestead. He would decide what each individual should be paid. That was too much for the union leadership, which would have willingly made other concessions until steel prices stabilized. Meanwhile, ensconced at a remote castle in Scotland, the self-proclaimed friend of labor ignored pleas from his workers to restrain Frick. Instead, he urged his tough partner to "reorganize the whole affair" assuming that the workers would abandon the union to keep their jobs.

Thousands of Homestead employees, and many more workers from around the region, rejected Frick's ultimatum. When they mounted a strike, Frick surrounded Homestead with fences and barbed wire, transforming the plant into an armed fortress. Within days, violent clashes between the Pinkerton detective force hired by Frick and the strikers had left ten men dead and many wounded. The men, women, and children of Homestead fought back against Frick's private army, and were on the verge of victory when the Pennsylvania governor sent eight thousand five hundred heavily armed National Guardsmen to suppress the strike.

Homestead was placed under martial law, with sporadic fighting continuing into autumn. After five months, the union at last surrendered, its leaders blacklisted and its members forced to return to work as supplicants. "Life worth living again!" exulted Carnegie in a cable to Frick. They again cut wages, imposed twelve-hour workdays, and eliminated hundreds of jobs.

Indeed, the victory of the steel barons at Homestead was total and ruinous to the cause of industrial labor. Unionism in the nation's most basic industries was set back for forty years, postponing progress toward a more decent society until the advent of the New Deal. The ruthlessness of Carnegie and Frick did America grave damage.

From Carnegie's solipsistic point of view, however, the truly regrettable damage was to his own reputation. Although he had egged Frick on at every step, he turned ungrateful in the ugly aftermath. He went so far as to claim that he had opposed the lockout, a lie that enraged his grim henchman. Carnegie felt sorry for himself, as he told William Gladstone in a letter about Homestead:

> This is the trial of my life. Such a foolish step—contrary to my ideals, repugnant to every feeling of my nature. Our firm offered all it could offer, even generous terms. Our other men had gratefully accepted them. They went as far as I could have wished, but the false step was made in trying to run the Homestead Works with new men. It is a test to which workingmen should not be subjected. It is expecting too much of poor men to stand by and see their work taken by others . . . The pain I suffer increases daily.

He continued to complain about the burdensome memories of Homestead for the rest of his life.

His relationship with Frick never quite recovered from that peculiar betrayal. But their final dispute involved money, not principle. In a complex dispute over the price of the coke sold by Frick's company to Carnegie Steel, each of the two barons attempted to swindle the other. Their struggle escalated, with Carnegie trying to steal Frick's stock shares, and Frick threatening to expose Carnegie in court as a greedy hypocrite. In April 1900, Carnegie bought Frick out for $30 million; a year later, Frick came back with J. P. Morgan to buy out Carnegie and form U.S. Steel. Although they ended up living only twenty blocks apart on Fifth Avenue, the two magnates never spoke again.

More than a decade after their final rupture, the aging Carnegie sent a mutual friend to Frick seeking reconciliation. "Mr. Carnegie told me to tell you that he is getting along in years," said the friend, "and that he would like to shake hands with you before he dies and let bygones be bygones." As his great-granddaughter Martha tells the story, Frick spurned the overture, declaring defiantly that he expected to "see Carnegie in hell, which is where we both are going."

Henry Ford

✷

BY JIM CALLAGHAN

THE MOST POWERFUL image of the auto king Henry Ford can be found in the 1938 photo archives: he is standing erect in a white linen suit, not looking at the camera, flanked by two of Adolf Hitler's emissaries as one of them pins a medal from the Fuehrer on his jacket.

Ford was celebrating his seventy-fifth birthday that night, as he accepted the Grand Cross of the Supreme Order of the German Eagle in Detroit from Hitler's consul. It is inconceivable that such a brilliant man—someone brimming with ideas, sometimes full of contradictions—could not understand why he was receiving such an honor or what it meant at a time when the word "appeasement" was being heard around the world.

Watching Ford supplicate himself before Hitlerite minions, it was difficult for reporters to imagine a place called
Clonakilty in County Cork, Ireland, whence his family left
after being evicted from their tenant farm because they
had no money for the rent.

The parents of Henry Ford were escaping the ravages of
the Great Irish Hunger, the period from 1845 through
1850 when one million peasants perished, some of them
left to die on the roadside foraging for grass while decaying
bodies were picked apart by wild dogs and rats in the
barren bogs. It wasn't a "famine," a word latched onto by
Queen Victoria while her ministers shipped foodstuffs out
of the country. Two million more people fled the country
and, by 1850, Ireland had lost one-third of its population.
Ford's maternal grandmother died on a "coffin ship" while
making the trip across the Atlantic Ocean, aptly called a
"bowl of bitter tears" by James Joyce.

In accepting Germany's highest civilian honor, Ford
made the final break from his origins. He came from an
oppressed class and, in just one generation, became an
oppressor himself, a fierce opponent of trade unions, a
businessman who collaborated with the Nazis, and one of
the world's most virulent Jew-haters. This trait endeared
him to Hitler, with whom he was doing business,
building trucks for the German army despite his self-
proclaimed pacifism.

Ford was in grand company in his admiration of Hitler.
Charles "Lucky" Lindbergh, who thrilled the world with
his solo trip across the Atlantic in 1927, was one of the
Fuehrer's most outspoken admirers, leading a group called
"America First," which attempted to keep the country out
of war while Hitler rampaged through Europe. Lindbergh

and Ford were close friends; FDR even thought that "Lucky Lindy" was a Nazi at heart.

If ever there was proof needed about the power of words, Ford proved himself a brilliant propagandist, long before Joseph Goebbels put his sadistic talents to work for Hitler. Using the millions in profits from selling war machines during World War I, this man who claimed to oppose all war unleashed a torrent of abuse against Jews that permeated his every business relationship and caused pain to millions of Americans.

"I would rather tear down my plants brick by brick with my own hands," he once said, "before I would let Wall Street get a hold of them." Lest one think this was the thought of an agrarian anti-big-business populist, Ford let it be known what he actually meant: he believed that Jews controlled the major banks; hence, to him, "Wall Street" was synonymous with Shylock in *The Merchant of Venice*.

But his actions were more insidious than private expressions of hatred.

Starting in 1920, Ford authorized the printing of millions of copies of a poisonous pamphlet called *The International Jew*, a sickening description of every stereotype imaginable that had appeared in his newspaper the *Dearborn Independent*. There wasn't much about Jews that escaped his attention. His friend the essayist John Burroughs wrote in his diary how upset he became while listening to Ford rant about how Jews were responsible for World War I and had caused "an outbreak of robbery and thieving all across the country." Burroughs, however, chose to remain silent and never publicly criticized his friend.

Ford used his newspaper to spread his filth around the country. In Germany, a young colonel named Adolf Hitler was an admiring reader. According to Neil Baldwin's book *Henry Ford and the Jews*, Ford car dealers were forced to sign up for subscriptions. He printed the forged *Protocols of the Elders of Zion*, which purported to describe plans by Jewish and Freemason "elders" for world dominance by ridding society of Christian teaching. Ford continued to print such rubbish even after he was told—once by a close Jewish advisor—that they were fakes.

But it wasn't just the diabolical use of words. Ford also employed in his company a man named Fritz Julius Kuhn, the leader of the German-American Bund, the most important, and most vicious, pro-Hitler organization of the 1930s. This Ford aide-de-camp spoke at a rally at the old Madison Square Garden in New York, telling the jammed arena of twenty thousand that victory for the Reich was near. This was a man who regularly dined with Ford and ran a major part of his company.

Ford was also friendly with another rabid Jew-hater: Father Charles Coughlin, pastor of the Shrine of the Little Flower in Royal Oak, Michigan, not far from Dearborn. Coughlin, who lunched monthly with Ford, started out as a working-class populist but quickly lost his way, and his nationwide radio audience listened week after week as he denounced "the money changers in the temple." Coughlin even told his listeners that *Kristallnacht* was justified because of "past events," meaning essentially that it was the Jews' own fault.

Although he was often accused of financing Coughlin, no proof was ever offered, but it doesn't take a great leap of faith to imagine that some of Ford's money found its way into the Coughlin coffers.

If there was one group of people that Ford despised more than Jews, it was members of any trade union, especially those who tried to organize his plants. "Labor unions are the worst thing that ever struck the earth," he bellowed. He believed that unions were part of a Bolshevik plot to over-throw America, and, in an all-too-common bout of para-noia, saw Jews as the real powers in their organizations.

Ford hired ex-cons and gun-wielding thugs, disguised as employees of "security companies," to keep the nascent United Auto Workers (UAW) out of his factories. He made deals with Detroit and New York mobsters, including people like Joe Adonis, a veteran of New York's Murder, Inc., to beat up his workers. Adonis and other mob killers were rewarded with Ford dealerships which they held onto, years after Ford himself died, as part of their effort to, in the words of Michael Corleone, "become completely legitimate." Ford had his agents spy on the workers, had them followed after work and, in one act that energized the idealistic organizers of the Congress of Industrial Organi-zations (CIO), sent a goon squad to waylay Walter Reuther and his comrades as they attempted to march over a bridge into the Ford River Rouge plant outside Detroit.

As much as he hated unions, Ford shocked the country and his big business friends in 1914 by giving his workers the unheard wage of five dollars per day at a time when the average American was making half that amount. Surely, part of his motivation was to keep out the unions—the radical Industrial Workers of the World were planning to organize the Ford plants—but he also believed that his workers should be able to afford the cars they were making, and in the end, it cost him nothing because the grateful (as much as one could be toiling on an assembly line for ten hours a day) workers actually produced more. Ford called it "profit sharing" and explained to the men that if production didn't increase concomitant with their fatter pay envelopes, the five dollars would be history. The day after the five dollar wage was announced, ten thousand job-seekers stormed the gates of the Ford plant, nearly causing a riot.

Ford had to be convinced by his top executive, James Couzens, who said: "When you have a team of horses and no work for it, you feed it and care for it just the same. Our workmen deserve just as good treatment as our horses." The move was unprecedented in the annals of American labor relations. As Douglas Brinkley pointed out in his book *Wheels of the World,* "up to that bold moment no business had ever nodded to the importance of labor in such a dramatic and costly way. The five dollar day marked, if any one date could, the end of the Gilded Age."

Not so fortunate were workers in Nazi death camps who received nothing close to five dollars a day for their toils twenty years later. There is ample evidence that the Ford "subsidiary" company in Germany cooperated with the Nazi regime in using slave laborers. As reported by Ken Silverstein in the *Nation* (January 24, 2000), Ford was complicit in building the Nazi war machine and collaborated with the Vichy government in France after the Nazi occupation. Ford had made it clear over a long period of time how he felt about Jews and, more dangerously, that he didn't care much about who won the war.

Ford was an iconoclast and, in many ways, far ahead of his time. He believed that cars could run on vegetables—the precursor to today's blend of corn and gasoline called ethanol—and tinkered with alternatives to the gasoline-powered Model A, which even he admitted caused too much air pollution. After the Volstead Act became law, he hatched a plan to turn breweries into alternative fuel plants using grain, which he claimed would help both the farmers and the environment. He also believed that German (not Irish) potatoes could run a car. "All the world is waiting for a substitute for gasoline," he said. He didn't think much of workers who smoked, after his close friend Thomas Alva Edison told him that smoking caused brain damage. (Edison would not even employ men who smoked the dirty weed.) Ford prohibited smoking in his offices and plants. He was a fervent believer in recycling and was close friends with George Washington Carver of the Tuskegee Institute—giving money for research—and forbade any sort of discrimination against black workers.

Busy as he was, he found time in 1918 to run for the United States Senate in Michigan, with the backing of internationalist Woodrow Wilson. He ran a quixotic Ross Perot type of campaign. (Eighty years after Ford's run, Perot coined the phrase "gotta look under the hood of that car.") He threw ideas across the transom, was a strong believer in women's suffrage, and denounced large campaign expenditures, proclaiming: "All this campaign spending is bunk. I wouldn't give a dime to a campaign committee." True to his word, he spent a miserly $336 and lost by fewer than seven thousand votes out of four hundred and thirty thousand cast.

In 1927, faced with an enormous public relations problem involving a libel suit, as well as stiff competition from other auto companies, Ford authorized a written statement apologizing to Jews for any "unintentional" pain he may have caused. Reading the statement today, it sounds like yesterday's weather report or one of those pathetic apologies issued by public officials and celebrities after they make some inane comment. He took the coward's way out by blaming his editors for the vicious attacks and claimed his hateful words over a seven-year period were "unintentional." After the "apology," he waffled on whether to close down his newspaper, saying, "I might have to go after those Jews again."

That was about the extent of Ford's atonement after years of irrational ravings against Jews. The apology was worthless, an insipid attempt to redeem whatever goodwill he thought he still had around the country; it was sort of like Andrew Carnegie or John D. Rockefeller worrying about meeting their maker with nothing to show but warehouses full of possessions and more money than they could count.

Ford died at the age of eighty-four in 1947 with his wife Clara at his bedside, in a fifty-six-room mansion called Fair Lane situated on thirteen hundred acres. It was a long journey from the poverty of his family's origins in County Cork.

In 1997, executives at the Ford Motor Company, including the founder's great-grandson, took a page from the propaganda book of the company's patriarch, and became the sole television network sponsor of *Schindler's List*.

There was no mention of the *Dearborn Independent*.

✳   ✳   ✳

The Owners of the Triangle Shirtwaist Factory

✳

BY GEOFFREY GRAY

The Shirtwaist Kings

Murderers! Merders! Assassinos! The workers of the Triangle Shirtwaist Company barked these words at their bosses in Yiddish, Italian, and an English flecked with old country tongue. It was the first day of the trial with the first snow of the winter falling that chilled December morning in 1911, a heavy sheet of white melting on city concrete. The newspaper reporters on hand counted over one hundred of the mourners, the vast majority women cloaked in black dresses.

They were the survivors and the relatives and friends and neighbors of the dead, all grieving and filled with the rage and demons only innocent death can bring.

It had been only eight months since that single match or cigarette butt had fallen into a bin of cotton scrap on the eight floor of the flagship waist and blouse factory, consuming it in virtually one gulp while 146 workers— trapped without proper exits or fire escapes, and most gruesomely, with a locked door—perished in only a matter of minutes. Over eighty workers leaped through the windows and chose the hundred feet of free fall instead of the raging flames.

The owners, Max Blanck, dapper and verbose, and Isaac Harris, his meeker partner, were both charged with manslaughter. When they arrived at the courthouse around noon, the mob of mourners, who had been there since 8:00 A.M., surrounded them, and with full throat, "howled and snatched," according to the *New York Sun*. It was an "emotional hysteria," the *Tribune* wrote. Some of the women pounded on their chests; others tore and clawed at their own hair. The rage had to come out somehow.

Members of the crowd also carried photographs and tintypes, pumping them like picket signs, perhaps in the hopes that when the Triangle owners pushed through the frenzy around them they might somehow lock eyes with a seamstress like Rosie Freedman, only eighteen years old, who had lived in a one-room tenement with four other adults and worked to save pennies for her family back in Bialystok. Or Michela Marciano, who had made after-work plans to meet her fiancé on the corner only minutes after the fire first started to rage; or Margaret Schwartz, another seamstress, who was last seen on the ninth floor of the factory on her knees, her body covered in flames, stuck in front of the locked door, shrieking.

One witness, as chronicled by author and *Washington Post* reporter David Von Drehle in his recent, elegant book on the famous disaster, *Triangle* (Atlantic/Grove, 2003), remembered her words.

"Open the door! Fire! I am lost! There is fire!"

It would be here, in these photographs, at this moment of connection between the living rich and the dead poor, that the inherent responsibilities of a boss to an employee—or simply one garment worker or boot strap immigrant to another—might have stirred whatever collective guilt was lodged in the bellies of the Triangle owners and guided them to place some form of responsibility onto themselves: an admission, a confession, an apology.

Instead, in front of the courthouse, the owners pulled

the fine-tailored cloth of their topcoats to shield their faces—maybe to hide their shame, maybe to protect themselves from the vengeful fingers and fists and taunts of the mob. When the pair finally pushed their way into the courtroom, the doors were locked behind them for their safety. Hundreds were left waiting in the corridors. Their screams, and echoes of their screams, could still be heard through the courthouse walls.

"Murderers!"

Blanck, then forty-three or forty-four, and Harris, forty-six, should have known better. They were cut from the same cloth as the union organizers who marched outside their offices for better wages and the workers who had perished in their factory. They were both born in Russia and like the many millions of other immigrants they fled that land in fear of the pogroms, landing in the dirt-caked squalor of the Lower East Side and forced to maneuver through its disease-ridden streets, a world of prostitutes, thugs, gangs, opium dens, and soup kitchens ruled by Tammany chieftains like the Big Feller, Tim Sullivan. Like roughly half of the Jewish immigrants during that period, Blanck and Harris, related to each other through marriage, worked the garment trade together during its most oppressive, smoke-choked, sweatshop years.

But they were enterprising in these dismal conditions. The only way to get ahead, the only business strategy, Blanck and Harris must have figured, was to outwork the hardest workers. More importantly, they had to outsmart the competition in simple economic terms. They had to make better, more durable shirtwaists and blouses at cheaper cost. They had to be faster and more reliable. To do this, they had to take risks.

Blanck was the natural salesman. Tall, bald, and beefy, he dressed like a Broadway showman. Flashy suits. Diamond stickpins. Sleek, silk top hats. He had thick hands, ideal for offering meaty, reaffirming handshakes to clients after cutting deals on the road, or playfully patting the back of a customer after losing a bet at the horse track. When it came to business, he handled the money.

Harris was the grunt, dealing with the production lines. He was smaller, wiry, and knew every inch of the factory floor. He was more reserved in his thinking and less generous with his words. But he could design and, most important, he could sew. Together, they were an ideal business team. They soon became known as "The Shirtwaist Kings," employing over five hundred workers on any given day at the Triangle, and still more at other factories they owned like Imperial Waist, the Diamond Waist Company in New Jersey, and the International Waist Company in Pennsylvania. With sizable profit margins, the two owners both quickly moved from their cramped tenements in the East Village to the Upper West Side, where they lived in townhouses around the corner from each other. They had servants and limousines and personal chauffeurs. And yet, when hundreds of their workers marched outside the Triangle only two years before the fire, shouting union chants and demanding better wages and safer working conditions, the owners saw little reason to offer more than what they had received when they first arrived on these shining shores.

"There was a blind spot in their frame of mind," says Von Drehle, "a generational attitude that kept Mr. Blanck and Mr. Harris from making their factory safer. They figured, 'Well, we had it much worse, they have it pretty good. So why change?' "

It was true, the Triangle factory was clean and organized, in some respects. But put in a sprinkler system? It would have been too much of an investment, even though, as Von Drehle's research shows, many of the New England factories during the period had been installing affordable sprinkler systems since the 1880's. Besides, sprinklers are only worthwhile investments if a factory owner is afraid of fire. For Blanck and Harris, fire was a potential business asset, an option in hard times. If the blouses didn't sell in a particular year, or if the fashion designers in Paris chose to change their styles and the factory in New York was overstocked, Blanck and Harris could choose to set fire to their own stock. That way the unsold blouses would burn and disappear along with any losses. Then, as they'd done four separate times before (according to Van Drehle), Blanck and Harris could collect on insurance. Policies were expensive, but still a profit could be turned. It was easy money.

Arson was endemic in the New York garment industry at the time. But most of these supposedly mysterious fires flashed in the early dawn hours or throughout the night, when the factory was empty. Fire—containable, harmless, insurance-motivated fire—was expected from factory owners like Blanck and Harris. But they never planned on a fire that could not be controlled. What would transpire over those few early spring hours in 1911 would have its share of heroes—Issac Harris himself would lead many to safety—and villians. It would not be forgotten.

During the trial, which lasted three weeks and produced testimony from 155 witnesses, Max D. Steur, the famed and crafty attorney representing the Triangle owners, made fair mention of Harris's heroics. But Steur (rhymes with foyer) also looked to establish a more compelling fact to jurors: Blanck and Harris were victims of the fire, as well. They were honest businessmen, trying to make a honest living in a cutthroat business. As everyone was aware, there was a lot of competition in the garment world, workers could be fractious, irresponsible. To punish men like Blanck and Harris, who had, through the sweat of their own brow, provided jobs and a reason to live for the rabble of the Lower East Side, would not only be unduly harsh, but un-American on top of it.

Steur was considered the city's preeminent trial attorney. He was ace counsel to Tammany Hall. Steur's retainers were extraordinarily high, and, of course, to be paid before trial. "I can't think until I have the money," he once told a client. Of Steur, the *New Yorker* had written, "He is the spirit of partisanship, ruthless, mechanical, passionately cold. And morality is quite outside the matter."

Steur's strategy in the Triangle case was not necessarily to prove the innocence of his clients. His design was to cast a nimbus of doubt around the motives behind the prosecution's seemingly airtight case. His argument was this: To convict Blank and Harris of first and second degree manslaughter, prosecutors would have to prove that the factory owners had specifically known, on *the same day of the fire*, about the allegedly locked door on the factory's ninth floor, on the Washington Street side of the factory.

It was common knowledge in the factory that the Washington Street doors were locked toward the end of the work day because the Triangle owners wanted all their workers to leave through one exit, on the Greene Street side, to face a daily bag inspection. Workers had been known to pocket blouses and sewing supplies.

The prosecution was represented by the imposing and mustached Charles Bostwick, a longtime Republican and former law professor. He called on the ninth floor workers, who recounted in cinematic language their daring tales of escape. He pressed them to tell jurors what had happened when they tried to pry open the now crucial lock at the Washington Street door.

"I took hold of the handle and I turned it and I pulled it," said Mary Bucelli. "I couldn't open it."

"I tried it one way and the other," said Ida Nelson.

"I tried to turn the handle and it would not bend. It was locked," said Lillian Weiner.

To illustrate the greed of the factory owners, Bostwick asked Harris how much money they had saved annually by locking the Washington Street door. "Ten dollars or fifteen dollars or twelve dollars or eight dollars," Harris said. "Something like that."

That answer made the end of 146 lives look pretty cheap.

Undeterred, Steur kept pitching. He resisted the Yiddish interpreters to force the Triangle workers to answer his questions in a less effective, broken English. (Poor language skills, after all, might presume poor intelligence.) Charging that many of the witnesses had been coached, Steur also hammered away on the specific details that made the testimony so compelling. At the bottom of his argument was a blatant appeal to the uneasiness with which many New Yorkers regarded the seemingly endless waves of immigrants. Poor immigrants, anyway. In the end, whose word was the jury going to take, that of respectable businesspeople like Blanck and Harris, or these lumpen, ragged complainers?

After less than two hours of deliberation, they acquitted Blanck and Harris. To escape an explosion of fury in the courtroom, the Shirtwaist Kings were ushered into the small chamber and allowed to leave through a small exit typically reserved for prisoners. A limousine was waiting, but when they stepped into the early evening light they could hear the screams of the chasing mob. They ducked into a subway station. They were free men running for their lives. The workers' screams continued.

They still do.

"Murderers!"

COLLEGE OF LETTERS AND
SCIENCE: CULTURE CRIMINALS—
DISMAYING IDEAS,
DISMAYING MINDS

Anthony Comstock, Ezra Pound, John B. Watson, Frederick Taylor, Walter Winchell, Edward Teller, Colonel Tom Parker

A mind is a terrible thing to waste. These are the defilers of the national mentality, the assaulters of consciousness, the spreaders of ideas that range from the stupid to the pernicious (although this is often the same thing). Man's heroic search for the secrets of the universe, enthralling when articulated by such geniuses as Albert Einstein or Orson Welles, become a nightmare in the hands of someone like Edward Teller, who thought only of the bigger bomb, or Ezra Pound, the poet who sang the Nazis' song. Elvis might have been a national treasure, but if it had been up to Colonel Tom (and it pretty much was), all we'd have would be reruns of Clambake. The twisting of the meme is no less a crime than a robbery at gunpoint. Increasingly, American culture is the world's culture. For all the junk we turn out, we have the unchallenged capacity to generate sublime, universally accepted ideas. This is a great responsibility. Here are the culture criminals who have done their best to default on that task.

Anthony Comstock

BY STU LEVITAN

WITH A FEDERAL badge and private funding, Anthony Comstock did more to stop the distribution of information and items relating to sex, love, and family planning than any other American in our history. Serving simultaneously as inspector for the United States Post Office and secretary/chief special agent of the New York Society for the Suppression of Vice from 1873 to his death in 1915, Comstock made almost thirty-six hundred arrests, seized more than a hundred tons of books and photos, destroyed countless condoms, and drove no fewer than fifteen people to suicide. Legal principles arising from his prosecutions and persecutions shaped American jurisprudence into the 1970's, and language from the Comstock Act was incorporated into the Communications Decency Act of 1996.

"The story of Mr. Comstock's life is supernatural from beginning to end," his admiring biographer, Charles Trumbull, wrote in 1913. Heywood Broun would later write of "the wonder of Comstock's life" (in a biography that was the first selection of the Literary Guild of America). How else to describe the man after whom both an act and an attitude are named, the man who was the moving spirit behind a century of sexual repression, censorship, and assaults on reproduction rights?

Anthony Comstock was stout and forceful, able to use

girth and muscle in the battle against vice, and brave enough to do so. A pious and honest man, he relied on trickery and entrapment, and delighted in the pain and suffering of the "infidels and liberals" who opposed him. Truculent and tactless, a bull-headed bully, he was, at least in his early years, a great success at publicity and public relations.

If Comstock had limited his efforts to shutting down corrupt lotteries, medical quacks, and gambling dens (activities which showcased his courage and financial integrity), he might have been considered a noble reformer. If he had undertaken only to suppress truly obscene material, he might have gone down as a prude, but one who did no lasting damage. Instead, he attacked not just the obscene and the corrupt, but the political (particularly the feminist) as well. It was then that he did true and lasting damage, both to individuals and society.

Comstock's nature was evident early on. Born into a large and successful New Canaan, Connecticut, family in 1844, Comstock was eighteen when he killed a rabid mastiff hound; then he broke into and destroyed the dog-owner's illegal bar.

When an elder brother died at Gettysburg the next year, Comstock joined the Union Army in non-combat status in Florida, signing up as an agent of the Christian Commission and unofficial chaplain. After the war, Comstock found work as a clerk in New York City, where life was vulgar and the Young Men's Christian Association was fighting for moral purity. In 1868, shortly after attending a Y lecture on the perils of obscenity, Comstock started filing citizen complaints against downtown smut-peddlers. Utilizing a comprehensive state law enacted that year with the

Y's support, he also went after gambling joints and saloons for violating the Sunday-closing law.

He had found his calling.

He also found patrons who would underwrite his efforts—the financiers and industrialists behind the New York Y such as Morris Ketchum Jesup, J. Pierpont Morgan, and Samuel Colgate. And then he found a foe who would catapult him to prominence he would never completely lose.

Victoria Woodhull, the first woman to address a committee of Congress and the 1872 presidential nominee of the Equal Rights Party, and her sister, Tennessee Claflin, ran a Wall Street brokerage and published a weekly radical tabloid (the first paper in America to publish *The Communist Manifesto*). Both the brokerage and weekly were subsidized by Woodhull's lover, Cornelius Vanderbilt.

In a bizarre attempt to advance her free-love views, Woodhull published a scandalous attack exposing the adulterous hypocrisy of the Reverend Henry Ward Beecher. That November 2, 1872, issue also recounted how businessman Luther Challis had deflowered a young maiden and triumphantly displayed her virginal blood on his finger.

Comstock, the outraged citizen, had the sisters arrested on federal obscenity charges. They were found not guilty the following summer after the judge ruled a recent recodification did not cover newspapers. Before this, however, anticipating this flaw in the law, Jesup had already sent Comstock to Washington to seek a stronger federal statute.

He had high-level help—his bill was drafted by United States Supreme Court Justice William Strong, who, as president of the National Reform Association, had strenuously advocated a constitutional amendment declaring "Lord Jesus Christ as the Ruler among the nations, and His Will, revealed in Holy Scriptures, as of supreme authority." With Congress distracted by the Crédit Mobilier scandal, Comstock got his measure adopted with less than an hour's debate in the waning moments before adjournment. President Grant signed the bill the following day, March 3, 1873. In addition to greatly expanding federal power over content of the mails, it also created the position of an unpaid special agent in the post office, authorized to seize proscribed material and arrest those sending it. Everyone understood that Comstock would be named to the special agent post, which he was on March 6, the day before his twenty-ninth birthday. Ten days later the New York Y abolished its interim anti-vice committee and created the New York Society for the Suppression of Vice, which provided Comstock with financial and other support for the next forty-two years.

The 1872 federal postal code forbade "obscene . . . vulgar and indecent" publications, but made no mention of condoms ("rubber goods"), advertisements for abortion, or information about contraception. The 1873 "Act for the Suppression of Trade in, and Circulation of, Obscene Literature and Articles of Immoral Use," commonly called "The Comstock Act," did, as would the twenty-four "Little Comstock" state laws to follow. For this John Ashcroft precursor, the Golden Age had just begun.

Comstock was not filled with compassion for those he went after. When "Madame Restell," an elderly Cockney midwife-turned-abortionist slit her throat in her Manhattan mansion the night before her trial in early 1878 (she had already failed in her attempt to bribe Comstock, who had used his customary tactics of deceit and entrapment to get her to provide proscribed "abortion pills," whereupon he arrested her), the agent was unapologetic: "A bloody ending to a bloody life," was Comstock's only comment about how he "forever stopped her pre-natal murders." He made no mention of the matter in his 1883 book, *Traps for the Young.*

During the prime of his career, Comstock was both hated and feared. Later, thanks to a series of stunning missteps centering on fine art and the theater, that fear turned to contempt and ridicule. Proclaiming a "Morals, not Art or Literature" campaign, Comstock, acting in the service of the Society for the Suppression of Vice, declared, "If we must have 'works of art' that are shocking to modesty or offensive to decency," they should be restricted to art galleries and not "disseminated indiscriminately before the public." So, too, with "rare and classical works" of literature with offensive matter; "restricted, perhaps, for the student or literary man," but not in general circulation. Books banned under the Comstock Law included classics such as *Lysistrata* and the *Decameron*, as well as modern works by Joyce, Wilde, Lawrence, Steinbeck, and Faulkner. "Do not forget that *lust breeds crime*," Comstock wrote. "I believe that there is a devil. Vile books and papers are branding-irons heated in the fires of hell, and used by Satan to sear the highest life of the soul."

Comstock was adept at spotting indecency, even where others might not. An 1888 *Life* cartoon has him arresting an artist, who protests that only the head of the bathing woman is visible. "Don't you suppose I can imagine what is under the water?" Comstock replies. In 1905, when Comstock tried to ban the New York production of George

Bernard Shaw's *Mrs. Warren's Profession* (already banned in England due to its sympathetic discussion of the economic causes of prostitution), the playwright railed against what he called "comstockery." Comstock, who had never heard of Shaw prior to the imbroglio, called the playwright an "Irish smut dealer," and warned against his other "filthy productions." Naturally, the producers seized on the controversy to raise prices, and the play became a hit—especially after Comstock lost his suit to shut the play down. The following August, more comstockery in action, as the sixty-two-year-old agent raided the offices of the Art Students League because its publication contained reproductions and drawings of nudes; he arrested a young female bookkeeper (the only employee present) and maintained the prosecution until the copies had been destroyed.

"Let Anthony's Punishment Fit the Crime," a *Life* cartoon scoffed in September, showing a sweating Comstock both sketching a full nude and posing that way for others. The magazine stayed on the attack two weeks later, showing St. Peter blocking Anthony at the pearly gates: "No, Anthony, no. We may have things here you would object to."

Comstock's zealotry again backfired in 1913, in his campaign against *September Morn*, a painting of a young nude woman standing demurely in a quiet lake ringed by cloud-capped mountains. Dime lithographs of the Paul Chabas painting were moving slowly when publicist Harry Reichenbach installed a blow-up of the work in an art shop window, hired a gaggle of young boys to gawk—and then called Comstock to complain. Comstock eventually took the bait, visited the scene, and ordered the picture's removal. When the proprietor refused, Comstock went to court; the publicity put the painting on the front page and in the Metropolitan Museum of Art.

Comstock waged his final crusade against Margaret Sanger, the birth control pioneer and comrade of such radicals as Emma Goldman and "Big Bill" Haywood. After Comstock secured a Post Office ruling that the Socialist newspaper *The Call* could not be mailed if it contained Sanger's series *What Every Girl Should Know*, Sanger made birth control a matter of free speech in the monthly *The Woman Rebel.* (Motto: "Working Women, build up within yourselves a conscious fighting character against all things which enslave you.") Calling for open defiance of the Comstock Laws, she wrote that nothing "could ever frighten the capitalist class so much as the universal practice of the prevention of conception." Sanger also made another personal point: "Comstockery must die!" she wrote.

The initial issue, in March 1914, was suppressed, and five following issues were suppressed and confiscated. A federal grand jury issued three indictments against Sanger covering twelve counts, including obscenity charges for articles discussing family planning or The Birth Control League. Aghast at Sanger's attitude ("Can they not use self-control? Or must they sink to the level of the beasts?" he asked rhetorically in a 1915 interview in *Harper's* magazine) Comstock successfully restricted Sanger's efforts to the clandestine distribution of pamphlets.

After a series of postponements, Sanger fled to London on a Canadian passport that November. Deprived of his targeted messenger, Comstock still sought suppression of the message. The next month he sent his assistant to wheedle Sanger's husband, William, into providing a copy of her birth control tract, *Family Limitation*. Indicted for distribution of the "obscene" pamphlet, Sanger was convicted and sent to jail.

The excitement of the stormy trial proved too much for the aging Comstock, and a lingering bout with pneumonia took a turn for the worse. Upon his death on September 20, 1915, the *New York Times* eulogized him as "a thoroughly honest man who through a long life, for the scantiest of material rewards, devoted his courage and energy to the protection of society from a detestable and dangerous group of enemies."

Ezra Pound

BY JOHN PALATTELLA

EZRA POUND WAS a poet who never tired of playing at being someone else. His early poems and translations are a bundle of borrowed personae, images, and tones. In his essays Pound sometimes concealed himself behind noms de plume, such as Hiram Janus, B. H. Dias, and William Atheling. During his London years, when he was the self-appointed promoter of literary modernism and the source of a torrent of essays, manifestos, and correspondence, Pound's moniker was E.P. As E.P. his biggest find was T .S. Eliot, whose work he tirelessly promoted and edited. (We owe to Pound the version of *The Waste Land* that we read today.) Like Eliot, Pound was from the Midwest, and he coined nicknames for Eliot and himself that sentimentalized their American roots. Eliot was Possum, Pound was Brer Rabbit.

Despite his affection for personae and masks, Pound ended up leading a life haunted by his family name. *Pound:* a place of confinement for criminals and animals. On May 26, 1945, the poet was detained in northwest Italy by the United States Army and charged with treason for talks he had broadcast over Fascist Italian radio from 1940 to 1943. Pound was interrogated at a military detention training center near Pisa, and he told his wife Dorothy that the tent he occupied there had a "mappin terrace" where he could stroll and enjoy the fresh air. Pound was likening himself to a caged animal: The phrase "mappin terrace" alludes to a stone terrace for roaming bears at the London Zoo, the construction of which had been funded by the jewelry company Mappin & Webb in the early twentieth century.

Pound: a unit of measure, money. When Pound took to the airwaves of Rome Radio, he usually discussed, in a cryptic, rambling, and didactic manner, the moral bankruptcy of international finance and the virtues of an alternative monetary system, General C. H. Douglas's program of Social Credit, which Pound had backed since 1918. The problem was not the international money supply, Pound claimed, but the powerful financiers who, with the blessings of governments, manipulated it for personal gain. Like many Jeffersonians, Pound considered financiers to be the natural enemies of democracy.

Pound: pound of flesh, a harsh debt. In the poet's radio talks financiers were always Jews. "I think it is time the American United States citizen studied Mr. Morgenthau's treasury reports, whether or not he is out in front proclaiming the coming of Zion," Pound told his audience in April 1943. In his radio talks, as in his poems, letters, and essays, Pound describes Jews as clannish and conniving, and upbraids them for charging interest and thereby siphoning money off national resources. Not only are financiers Jews, but all Jews are Shylocks.

Pound was not just an economic and political anti-Semite. He was also obsessed with racial purity (he complained to friends that he looked Jewish) and he cultivated theories about the deleterious effects of circumcision on the personal character of male Jews. "It must do something, after all these years and years, where the most sensible nerves in the body are, rubbing them off, over and over again," Pound told Charles Olson during one of the visits the younger poet paid to him at St. Elizabeth's Hospital in Washington, D.C., where, after being found insane and unfit to stand trial for treason in 1946, Pound was incarcerated for twelve years. The poet formerly known as Brer Rabbit had become Case Number 58,102. It's doubtful that Pound was legally insane (there is ample evidence that he understood the case against him), so his theory about circumcision should not be interpreted as a symptom of insanity. In fact, Pound had pressed the same theory on William Carlos Williams in 1936, telling his friend by letter that "Jews having been circumcised for centuries/it must have had some effect on the character." As Eliot Weinberger has explained, Pound's theories about circumcision complemented his theories about economics: "Jews, then, with their numb or diseased genitals, were incapable of imagination, and could only employ their evident intelligence in life-denying manipulations of power, mainly the control of money, the most lifeless thing of all."

In 1948, the Library of Congress awarded Pound the Bollingen Prize for his *Pisan Cantos*, which he had written during his detention in Pisa. (*The Pisan Cantos* is the sixth section of Pound's unfinished mammoth poem *The Cantos.*) Karl Shapiro was on the Bollingen committee, and he opposed giving the award to Pound on the grounds that his "political and moral philosophy ultimately vitiates the poetry and lowers its standards as a literary work." Though principled and tactful, Shapiro's condemnation is too narrow. What ultimately corrupted Pound's poetry and thought was the combination of his anti-Semitism and megalomania. After all, it was not anti-Semitism but Pound's mania for absolutes that rendered much of *The Cantos* into heaps of citations, allusions, ideograms, abbreviations, and hieroglyphics. Those heaps are the signature of Pound the crank—or, as Gertrude Stein acidly remarked, "the village explainer." And it was Pound's delusions of power that prompted him to attribute Mussolini's downfall to his failure to use Pound's translation of Confucius as a model for reforming his fascist government. Similarly, after arriving in Washington, D.C., for his arraignment, Pound informed the Associated Press that he wanted to learn Georgian so he could negotiate the terms of the postwar peace with Stalin on behalf of the United States. The White House never took him up on the offer.

In August 1943, shortly after hearing on the radio that he had been indicted for treason, Pound wrote a letter to United States Attorney General Francis Biddle defending his radio talks. In his letter Pound claimed he was not guilty of treason since he had neither argued against the Second World War nor urged U.S. troops to revolt. Rather, he had railed against a global system of finance that "creates one war after another." Pound concluded his letter by stating that "a war between the United States and Italy is monstrous and should not have occurred. . . . Someone must take account of these things. And having taken account must act on his knowledge; admitting that his knowledge is partial and his judgment subject to error."

Yes, someone must take account of these things, and the test of Pound's own accounting—his sense of humility—is *The Pisan Cantos*. The culmination of the volume, if not *The Cantos* as a whole, is "Canto 81," the seventh of The *Pisan Cantos'* eleven poems, in which the imprisoned Pound consoles himself by recalling artists who embody a certain "nobility of mind." After cataloging the achievements of these artists, Pound tries to elect himself to their company by reckoning with the severe errors of judgment that had landed him in Pisa.

Thou art a beaten dog beneath the hail,
A swollen magpie in a fitful sun,
Half black half white
Nor knowst'ou wing from tail
Pull down thy vanity
    How mean thy hates
Fostered in falsity
    Pull down thy vanity,
Rathe to destroy, niggard in charity,
Pull down thy vanity,
    I say pull down.

But to have done instead of not doing
    that is not vanity

After alluding to another noble mind Pound delivers the concluding lines:

> To have gathered from the air a live tradition
> or from a fine old eye the unconquered flame
> That is not vanity.
> Here error is all in the not done,
> all in the diffidence that faltered . . .

Reading "Canto 81" one feels neither anger nor pity but shock. Pound admits his errors of moral judgment but then recants, implying that the greater error would have been not doing anything for fear of committing an error of moral judgment: "Here error is all in the not done." Error, in other words, lies in not accepting that error can be a consequence of any action. This observation is true but also shrewdly tactical. Late in his life Pound called his anti-Semitism a mistake and dismissed it as a "suburban prejudice." But "the tone of that repentance is all wrong," William Gass has written, "suggesting that Pound had made some unpleasant error on his tax forms which turned out to have unpleasant consequences." The same is true of "Canto 81," in which Pound is blinded by his dazzling lyricism. What concerns Pound most is how an admission of moral error, rather than being an opportunity for the necessary and painstaking reevaluation of specific ideas and beliefs, is merely an occasion for donning the penitent's mask. After such humility, what forgiveness?

Throughout his life Pound made his stage the political platform of poetic romanticism. The two main planks of that platform are that the poet is an unacknowledged legislator of the world, the holder of a secret supreme power, and that the world would be a fine place if people only read the right books—or, better yet, if the world's political leaders invited poets like Pound to lecture them about the right books. Anyone searching for a reason to pull down that platform need look no further than the books and vanity of Ezra Pound.

John B. Watson
⁂

BY MARK JACOBSON

SOMEWHERE NEAR BALTIMORE, Maryland, sometime in the early to middle 1920's, a young boy known as Little Albert grew up intensely afraid of white-colored objects. We do not know the breadth of Little Albert's whiteness phobia. Possibly he ran in terror upon seeing pieces of chalk, blank pages in a book, a glass of milk. Falling snow might have sent him into fits. We do, however, know he harbored deep fears of white mice and men with cottony beards. We know this because there are photos of the little boy shrieking in terror as a man dressed as Santa Claus looms over him.

The man in the Santa beard was John Broadus Watson, widely regarded as the father of behavioral psychology. In the early days of the twentieth century, as the first winds of European psychoanalysis began to reach these shores, Watson—a former frat-boy hell raiser and son of a Greenville, South Carolina Ku Klux Klan sympathizer—who became the head of the fledgling psychology department at Johns Hopkins, was considered America's answer to Sigmund Freud. Declaring psychology to a be "a purely objective branch of natural science" in which "introspection forms no essential part," Watson denied the mysterioso of the id and super-ego (he called Freud's approach "voodooism"). Instead, Watson, who once supposed that consciousness perhaps stemmed not from the brain but the larynx, trumpeted an extreme nature/nurture vision which posited humankind as a race of programmable machine-like beings, tabulae rasae to be molded by science into a utopian planned society.

"Give me a dozen healthy infants, well-formed, and my own specified world to bring them up in and I'll guarantee to take any one at random and train him to become any type of specialist I might select—doctor, lawyer, artist, merchant-chief, and, yes, even beggarman and thief, regardless of his talents, penchants, tendencies, abilities, vocations, and race of his ancestors," Watson wrote as an addenda to his ground-breaking 1913 manifesto, *Psychology as the Behaviorist Views It*, a manuscript which would have a profound influence on latter-day behaviorists such as B. F. Skinner.

Little Albert, taken from a foundling home before his first birthday, was one of those "healthy, well-formed" infants. Now in the care of the famous Dr. Watson, who, at thirty-six, would become the youngest president of the American Psychological Association, Little Albert was shown a live rat, a rabbit, a dog, and a monkey. The menagerie elicited no fear in the child. The boy was, however, easily upset when Watson and his assistant Rosalie Rayner struck a steel bar with a hammer. When the loud clanging was accompanied by the presentation of the white rat, the boy soon began to associate the two. After seven such pairings Little Albert now began to cry at the mere sight of the rat, even when the noise was not present. Similar experiments were conducted with a white rabbit, dog, fur coat, and eventually the Santa Claus mask. On the occasions when Albert would not cry when seeing the rat, Watson and Rayner placed the animal on the child's chest. After this, Watson recorded, Albert "first began to fret and then covered his eyes with both hands." Eventually the whiteness alone would upset the boy.

Watson hoped to one day "gain experimental control over the whole range of emotional reactions" but his work was soon derailed as he fell prey to his own outsized libido. He was discovered in a passionate tryst with his grad student assistant Raynor. This led to a messy divorce from his wife Mary Ickes (sister of Harold Ickes, who became FDR's secretary of the interior and aunt of Clinton operative Harold Ickes, Jr.). Proprieties being what they were (the previous head of Psychology at Johns Hopkins, James Mark Baldwin, had been dismissed after being caught in a brothel), Watson's appointment, and his academic career, were terminated. His lab was shut down, his work discontinued. Alas, this also included the Little Albert experiments. The boy, now nearing age two, was returned to the foundling home. Watson never bothered to de-condition Little Albert from his fear of all things white, if such a reversal was actually possible, setting up what would surely be one of the more harrowing existences of the scientific age. But we will never know the boy's traumas, as he was never heard from again.

Watson made no public comments regarding Little Albert's fate, but the psychologist was undeterred. "I shall never be satisfied until I have a laboratory in which I can bring up children from birth to three or four years of age under constant observation," he wrote in a June 1920 letter to Johns Hopkins University President Frank J. Goodnow.

Watson may have been chased from the ivory tower, but he would soon find himself operating in the much larger, and infinitely more far-reaching, laboratory of social control. He became a vice president at the J. Walter Thompson advertising agency, where he would apply his behavioral techniques to the selling of products like Yuban Coffee, Pebeco toothpaste, Johnson & Johnson's baby powder, and Pond's cold cream. As the foremost name in American psychology, Watson was a prize catch for Stanley Resor's firm. The investment (Watson was now making four times as much as he did in academia) was a wise one, as the behaviorist first articulated many tenets that remain staples of the advertising business even today. To ensure a reaction from the consumer, Watson told advertisers, "you must tell him something that will tie him up with fear, something that will stir up a mild rage, that will call out an affectionate or love response, or strike at a deep psychological or habit need."

Pioneering the use of the celebrity endorsement, Watson induced the Queen of Rumania and the Queen of Spain to do testimonials about the beneficial effects of Pond's Extra Cold Cream on royal skin. No fan of long-winded ads, Watson advocated campaigns that "dispense with rational copy almost entirely." Reason was "useless" to the ad man when compared to the pull of the emotions. Watson demonstrated this premise most graphically in his campaigns for Odorono, the deodorant semi-memorialized in a song from *The Who Sell Out* album *("Couldn't face another show, no/her deodorant had let her down/she should have used Odorono").* Taking an active role in both the development and marketing of the product, Watson recognized the market potential of heightening paranoias concerning body odor and halitosis. The idea may seem commonplace now, but Watson was the first to recognize the selling principle that if an ad man could create fear or doubt in the mind of the potential buyer, then it would be a simple matter to sell the consumer a product to combat the apprehension.

Watson may have stumbled in his attempt to create a race of fully cued Little Alberts, but he did his utmost to help program an entire culture. In many ways we have all become his children, a possibility the behaviorist may have been attempting to solidify when, employing the power of his still-puissant scientific reputation, he authored the best-selling and exceedingly bizarre 1928 book, *The Psychological Care of the Infant and Child.* Declaring a radical Platonic jihad against family life, which he claimed undermined a child's individuality and independence, Watson suggested toilet training in the first few months of life and inveighed against "the mawkish and sentimental coddling of children."

"Never hug and kiss them," Watson infamously wrote, "never let them sit on your lap. If you must, kiss them once on the forehead when they say good night. Shake hands with them in the morning." It sounds like some tired British comedy sketch, but the book sold widely, more or less inventing a whole genre of self-help tomes and sending many more liberal thinkers into despair. "Watsonism has become gospel and catechism in the nurseries and drawing rooms of America," bemoaned famous educator and philosopher Mortimer Adler in

1928, certain that the ultimate Orwellian future was upon us. Indeed, it was the spread of the behaviorist child-rearing regimen that was part of the original impetus for Benjamin Spock to write his infinitely more rational book, *Baby and Child Care*, which would quickly eclipse Watson's.

For all his advice (he wrote a number of essays against the institution of marriage) Watson experienced much sadness while raising own children. The eldest of the two sons from his marriage to Rosalie Raynor committed suicide, and the family history is rife with unhappy tales. In her memoir, *Breaking the Silence*, actress Mariette Hartley (whose greatest success would come, ironically, in a series of TV commercials) delves into the roots of her family's various addictions, including her mother's and her own, pinning much of it on her grandfather, John B. Watson, whom she reviles as a "difficult man" for several pages.

Watson would soon slip into semi-obscurity, his early contributions to behaviorism usually reduced to a couple of lines in Psychology 101 textbooks, his remarkable role in the scientific crossover to advertising barely mentioned in an era when billions are spent on "market research" every year. Facelessly commuting from his Connecticut home to Madison Avenue until late in his sixties, Watson occasionally expressed remorse over missed opportunities.

Quoted in 1936, he said: "I sometimes think I regret that I could not have a group of infant farms where I could have brought up thirty pure-blooded Negroes on one, thirty pure-blooded Anglo-Saxons on another, and thirty Chinese on a third—all under similar conditions. Some day it will be done, but by a younger man." He eventually passed away in rural Woodbury, Connecticut, after years of attempting to invent a more efficient home barbeque.

Frederick Taylor

⚹

BY ART KLEINER

FREDERICK TAYLOR, AN extremely ambitious, nineteenth-century man, had the common trait of many highly destructive people: He solved a problem and created a worse one. The problem he solved was the downright inconsistent efficiency and effectiveness of industrial society. Simply put, factories weren't well-ordered machines. They creaked and collapsed; they foundered; and the people in them had the all-too-human habit of thinking for themselves. Frederick Taylor solved all that.

As the first management consultant of the industrial era (working originally for steel companies in the New York–to–Philadelphia corridor), he was a self-proclaimed champion of efficiency. He applied an engineer's mindset to human work. He studied people on the factory shop floor. He found the most efficient specimens. He forced everyone else to work the way they worked. He paid them a bit more, and fired those who couldn't keep the pace.

The famous Taylor story was his encounter with a muscular German ironworker named "Schmidt" (or so Taylor called him in his memoir, though his real name was Henry Noll.) He could load metal bars onto railroad cars faster and work longer at it, day after day, than anyone else. So

Taylor took him aside, offered to pay him more ("You'll be a high-priced man," Taylor said), and gradually weeded out the workforce until he only had others like Noll onboard. This is often told as a story about efficiency; teaching other workmen to work like Noll. But it's really a story about treating people as interchangeable parts; those who could keep Noll's pace could also keep their jobs.

There are three premises behind "scientific management," as Taylor called his approach. The first is the idea that work is best thought of in terms of discrete component parts; that when you measure these component parts separately, you can push everyone to work, nearly all the time, at the speed that only the best achieved before. The second is the idea that only carefully trained experts can innovate. Workers, whether in the factory or the office, are too accustomed to their ingrained, inferior ways of working, thinking, talking. The first Taylorists, trained by the master himself, would show up in factories with stopwatches, hovering behind workers, trying to shave a few minutes off their time by finding more efficient ways for them to stand and move. Those who could perform fastest got paid a bit better. The rest got fired. The third premise was that people, like machines, can be fixed when they go bad. Anyone could adapt to the "one best way of working." Anyone could bend to meet the pace. If you didn't fit, you weren't trying hard enough. And if you managed to reshape yourself into the prevailing mode, then never mind the cost, the stress, the alcoholism, the destruction of your personal life, and the waste of your spirit and thought.

For this approach to organizing work made factories far more profitable, and more consistent, than the nineteenth-century craft ateliers that it replaced. This was, in fact, the great bargain of the industrial age. Taylor saw mechanization in a way that we take for granted today, but that few others could see in the late 1800s: as a path to wealth, a vehicle for widespread economic growth. If you could get people to make more goods per dollar, then everywhere people could buy goods at cheaper prices. You might mechanize work, but in the process you could democratize consumption.

"Everyone who is controlled by a stopwatch has unquestionably the same disagreeable feeling," said one early advocate, quoted in Robert Kanigel's masterful biography of Taylor, *The One Best Way*. That was the feeling of being a machine: "in possession of no initiative. [But] is it not better to work eight or nine hours and resign [oneself] . . . and earn one third more?" Not only did you earn more, but in a world dominated by Taylorist factories, you could buy a lot more. The plethora of stuff—of junk, really—that we live with and take for granted is a legacy of Taylor's ideas.

That's not the problem with Taylorism. (Even if living in a junked up world is a nightmare at times, it's a better nightmare to live in than a world where stuff is difficult to make and expensive to buy.) Even the horrific twentieth-century legacy of Nazi concentration camps and Stalinist gulags (both of which adopted Taylorist methods to torture and genocide) are not the worst problem. The worst is that we've outgrown Taylorism, and yet we can't shake free of it.

As it happens, it's been proven over the past forty to fifty years that much more effective and profitable ways exist to set up and run factories (and other enterprises). The work of quality experts W. Edwards Deming and Joseph Juran (and their many colleagues and followers), the financial literacy movement, the Toyota production system, and the socio-technical approach to organizing work—the most profitable approaches—all represent definitive contradictions of Taylor's theory. The quality theory says: Raising everyone's awareness, and inviting them to join in the quest for continual improvement (while continually improving their own knowledge of production and quality) is the only effective, sustainable way to run an enterprise these days, and the most successful companies practice this as much as they can. Indeed, the contempt for Taylorism couldn't be stronger in the most sophisticated management circles. When I first began writing about management, I interviewed Joseph Juran, and naively asked him if he was an "efficiency expert."

"No," he said, "that would be like calling a lawyer a shyster."

But Taylorism persists. Even those who know the difference in theory fall prey to it in practice. In factories, schools, offices, and even ordinary associating groups, there's always some appointed boss who runs roughshod over the minds and hearts of the other people in the room. Petty tyrants everywhere still pull rank and abuse their underlings and call it being "scientific." And the rest of us accept it. At some deep, reptilian level of the human heart, we seem to think that's a better way to live. Why does it go on? Because (and this *is* a dirty little secret, perhaps the dirtiest little secret of industrial society), Taylorism is addictive. Followers get used to being followers: Not having to think much, doing what they're told, not worrying about the future of the enterprise or their own place in the system. And bosses grow accustomed to being treated like omniscient experts, with everyone conspiring to guess their priorities and give them credit for all the solutions.

Even workers learned to accept it. From the beginning, labor unions were Taylor's biggest enemies. Workers in a Taylor-designed system felt drained and worn at the end of the day, no good for anything but collapse. And they *hated* the fact that someone, hired by management, was watching them in the name of control. But over time, they came to accept the Faustian bargain: entering the middle class, at the expense of having to think much. One could argue that the demise of unions as a political force had a lot to do with their acceptance of this bargain.

Being a boss or follower in a Taylorist system is so addictive, despite the pain, that after a few years of operating this way it's hard for people to imagine working any other way. Our capacity to stop being machines atrophies. And thus Taylorism spreads: beyond factories to offices, government agencies, volunteer organizations, schools, and ultimately to families. (Taylorism in schools is perhaps its most pernicious influence. What is attention deficit disorder but the inability to conform to a Taylorist schedule? What is Ritalin but a Taylorist solution to the ADD problem?) We who work in Taylor's shadow will chafe, we'll scratch, we'll fight the system in our minds—and then we'll reinforce and replicate it everywhere we go.

As Frederick Taylor, apparently, did in his own life. Biographer Robert Kanigel portrays him as a machine-like person himself: fastidious, argumentative, energetic, idealistic, and repetitively brilliant. (Like the machine tools he trained with as an apprentice, he was also highly temperamental.) He pursued his quest with humorless determination, in a way that transcended every other aspect of his life. He came from an aristocratic background, but drove himself to understand the industrial factory floor, even to the point of foregoing college for apprenticeship. He slept a few hours per night, drove his workers to grim neuroses and his wife to neurasthenia. (She was a girlish optimist until they married, then gradually became a moody invalid, and then suddenly reverted to girlish optimism after he died.)

In the end, Taylor left a question for all of us: Are we ready to trust people enough to move beyond his "one best way"? Is the culture ready to leave Taylorism behind? I used to think so, but I have to admit, after twenty years of writing about management, that if I had to place a bet on the battle between the Taylorist machine and the effective human being, odds would go to the machine.

Walter Winchell
✴

BY JOHN HOMANS

WALTER WINCHELL'S CHIEF character flaw, the one from which all the others sprung, was that he needed to be THISCLOSE to the hind ends of the powerful. And once he'd stationed himself there, he invited everyone else in for a peek, raising the curtain (like Joel Grey in *Cabaret*) to "Mr. and Mrs. North and South America, from border to border and coast to coast, and all the ships at sea," as his famous intro went.

There's an argument to be made that Winchell was a

democratizing, egalitarian force. Indeed, Winchell's life is a parable of American social mobility. A mediocrity as a vaudevillian, he reinvented himself as the most powerful of gossip columnists, creator and destroyer of reputations, and then as the leading member of the fourth estate, war counselor to presidents. His inheritance from vaudeville seems to have been the importance of publicity, and a deep shamelessness, coupled with the knowledge that at bottom, people's motivations were simple, crude, prurient, human.

When he first built his column at William Randolph Hearst's *Mirror*, the nascent publicity business was beginning to boom. As with the latter-day Sidney Falco who would do anything to get his crummy retainers in good with Winchell-like Burt Lancaster in *The Sweet Smell of Success*, a vast crop of press agents strove to get space for their clients in the column with hilarious ingenuity born of desperation. Winchell ran his empire like a tinpot dictator—those who crossed him ended up on his Drop Dead list, the kind of banishment he knew could ruin a career—but that wasn't his problem. He was "like a shark with little fish all around him," said one press agent, which doesn't get far enough. He had a deep streak of sadism. He was hard, vindictive, unsentimental. He would ruin you for a spilled drink. He despised his legions of sycophants, even as he depended on them, and they despised him, too, even as they fawned over him. Finally, even the celebrities were merely there to provide him with material. They knew, and he knew, that they didn't exist if he didn't write about them. Somehow, however, he knew the same about himself: the relationship was symbiotic, circular, vicious.

As a journalist, he was not exactly a dishonest broker, but his value system was such that maintaining power was his first priority. Second was coddling his sources. Accuracy and principle were perfectly acceptable, if they happened not to conflict with his higher values. His feuds were often wonderful sport. And he was often on the right side. In his glory years, he was a devout Roosevelt man. (His mash notes to FDR are treacly and mortifying. It's hard to believe an adult could write them.) But of course, since Roosevelt was president, and Winchell loved power, this made perfect sense. His feud with William Randolph Hearst pushed him close to defecting, but then, as he reflected, "What if I lose my column? Then's I'm no different than the loudmouth in the bar."

As World War II loomed, Winchell pushed his way into the elite of serious journalism. He didn't care about boundaries, or credentials. Journalism's mandarin class, ever sensitive to assaults on their own power, rebelled. How could a mere Broadway publicist comment on the most serious of world affairs? So high culture's bouncer went to work. *The New Yorker*—in a six-parter, the longest published up to that time—eviscerated Winchell's journalistic practices and fulminated at vast length on his cultural power. Harold Ross came to regret it, since Winchell wasted no opportunity in the next few years to fire back, but it provided the focal point for the anger many felt at Winchell's cultural power. He spent the rest of his life getting thrown out of his own club.

His affair with the American elite was too hot not to cool down. Put on the spot when Josephine Baker was denied service in the Stork, he sided neither with his old friend and patron Sherman Billingsley, nor with Baker's civil rights message, but instead tried to weasel out and defend himself. Winchell was anything but surefooted when principle was involved. He lashed out at Baker with unsourced accusations of Communist ties. The tactic linked him to Joseph McCarthy, who was on the rise at the time, though the connection was more metaphorical than anything else—both were in possession of secret information from unnamed sources, both were in the business of ruining people.

At the end of his life, Winchell became the emblem of the *schadenfreude* culture he helped invent. Where once he'd been the emcee at the great American carnival, he became a sideshow, a snarling old forest animal in a cage, and tormenting him became something of a national rite of passage. Ed Sullivan, long an enemy, savaged him over the Josephine Baker incident. Later, Jack Paar poked at Winchell relentlessly on *The Tonight Show*, knowing he no longer had the strength to fight back.

Winchell was haunted by the shadow of his power, and his rage was all the greater because he had seen it coming. "Nothing recedes like success," was one of his kitschy aphorisms. His lifelong paranoia was proven right, which is another way of saying he understood what he'd built—he knew it would destroy him. He was disposable—the great American has-been.

Nonetheless the machine that he built is still running. It is hard to imagine the endless assembly line of the P.R. world with its lemming-like pushers of books, films, and third-rate "personalities" without Winchell. In his sour, crotchety way, he is the father of every celebrity rag clogging the newsstand shelves and grandfather to E! television and its attendant promo culture choke. He rewrote the Machiavellian equation for the media age: Power = fame. If a Broadway publicist could advise presidents, is it that great a leap to someone like Arnold Schwarzenegger (or Ronald Reagan for that matter) becoming governor of California? In light of the events of the past fifty years, nothing seems too far-fetched, if you've got a big enough mouthpiece. Not, of course, that any of this could be considered contrary to the American dream of upward mobility. Yet even Winchell understood that the process made both groups, celebrities and public, gawkers and gawked at, coarser, angrier, more desperate. Winchell turned fame from an uncanny flower to a weed. By commodifying it, he removed its mystery.

"Stars," as the *Us* magazine slogan has it, "they're just like us." A small man, and he brought everyone down to his level. God knows, many needed to be brought down a peg. But, inarguably, he made the world less interesting. Which, for a journalist, isn't a good thing.

Edward Teller

BY MARK JACOBSON

TERRY SOUTHERN, AUTHOR of the screenplay for *Dr. Strangelove*, often corrected the surmised assumption that he based the title character of his film on Henry Kissinger. Peter Sellers's immortal performance might have borne "a quite remarkable and a bit scary" resemblance to Nixon's secretary of state, Southern said, but in 1961, when he wrote the film along with director Stanley Kubrick, Kissinger was "not known to me." What Southern was going for was the creation of a character who possessed an "ultra-hyper-super detached 'logic' that allowed one to speak in terms of mega-deaths." In 1961, outside of the ex-Nazi rocket maker Werner Von Braun, there was only one man who maintained such intimate relations with what would be called The Doomsday Machine. This was Edward Teller, the real Dr. Strangelove.

Like Strangelove, the bushy-browed, Budapest-born Teller, one of the prominent Manhattan Project scientists who came together in the New Mexico desert to create the atomic bomb, always dreamed of a still bigger bang, a more apocalyptic moment. The night before the fateful test of the device affectionately referred to as "the gadget," the Los Alamos scientists, unsure of exactly what they had fashioned, organized a pool to guess the size of explosion which would open the door to the Atomic Age. J. Robert Oppenheimer, the metaphysically minded head of the Project, fearful that the bomb would be a dud, modestly ventured the blast would equal three hundred tons of TNT. Hans Bethe, German immigrant theoretician, was more expansive, supposing the bomb yield at eight thousand tons of TNT. I.I. Rabi predicted eighteen thousand tons (which would turn out to be the correct figure). Teller, however, foresaw by far the largest cataclysm, forty-five thousand tons, more than twice the size of the next highest guess. According to Bethe, who would come distrust and loathe his ambitious colleague, "Edward always wanted something big."

Indeed, even before the first A-bomb was dropped from the bay doors of the B-29 *Enola Gay* and fell on Hiroshima, instantly killing upward of one hundred thousand people, Edward Teller, once an insular boy who did not speak until he was five, leading his parents to believe he might be retarded (and who spent most of his life walking about on a prosthetic foot following a childhood streetcar accident in Budapest) was mobilizing his considerable intellect and single-minded obsession to get his own way to make an unthinkably larger bomb.

"The Super," Teller called it, a hydrogen bomb, a thermonuclear device one hundred times more powerful than the parcel of doom dropped on Hiroshima. Teller first became smitten with the idea for the H-bomb as early as 1941 after several conversations with Enrico Fermi, leading the famous Italian physicist to say, "in my acquaintance, you are the only monomaniac with several manias." The fusion of hydrogen nuclei would generate a reaction far more powerful than the fission-based prototypes, Teller contended, making no secret of these feelings at Los Alamos. As Oppenheimer and the others raced to produce the fission bomb, Teller was often a resentful and uncooperative presence, sometimes loudly playing Beethoven late into the night, much to the chagrin of his fitfully sleeping colleagues. After the shocking results of Hiroshima and Nagasaki left many of the scientists questioning their role in the creation of so terrible a weapon, Teller continued to campaign for the Super, eventually leaving Los Alamos over what he perceived as excessive foot-dragging on construction of the bigger bomb.

It was Cold War hysteria that allowed Teller, a most consummate of Cold Warriors, to achieve his goals. With phrases like "the missile gap" and "space race" still in the addled future, gathering national fear was already cresting when the Soviets exploded an A-bomb of their own in 1949. The fervor only ratcheted upward with the revelation that Karl Fuchs, a key Manhattan Project scientist, had acted as a Soviet spy. General Curtis LeMay, who would later achieve undying fame for his Vietnam-era threat to bomb the North Vietnamese "back to the stone-age," suggested the United States launch preventive warfare on seventy Soviet cities, a plan that called for the simultaneous deployment of 133 nuclear bombs. President Truman, who ordered the use of the bomb on the beaten Japanese, found LeMay's approach extreme, but turned an approving ear to Teller's incessant lobbying on behalf of the Super. In what would be one of the first of numerous dire exhortations to bulk up the defense budget, Teller, famous among the Los Alamos scientists as a consummate chess player, told the president and the various generals with whom he would enter into a decades long codependent relationship, "If the Russians demonstrate a Super before we possess one, our situation will be hopeless."

After some needed adjustment to Teller's scheme (his original bomb design had proved unworkable—a shortcoming he blamed on the recalcitrance and lack of imagination of his former Los Alamos confederates) the first fusion bomb, code named "Mike," fifty times more destructive than the Hiroshima gadget, was exploded in July of 1952 over Eniwetok Atoll. The remote South Pacific island was obliterated from the face of the earth, the first time humanity had demonstrated the ability to alter the planetary map with such alacrity. Film of the explosion was later used for the Doomsday Machine ending of *Dr. Strangelove*. At the time, the Mike test was pronounced a total success, a personal vindication for Teller and his Super campaign, leading, of course, to much more testing, and the battle of megatonic one-upsmanship between the United States and the Soviet Union.

It wasn't until sometime later that major defects in the atmospheric testing scheme cropped up. Researchers determined that of the 11,650 people involved in the Mike test, all but 408 had received unsafe amounts of radiation. This was something of a monkey wrench to Teller, who often underplayed the long-term effects of bomb fallout, touting nuclear weaponry as "safe." To demonstrate his contempt for what he considered unreasonable concern for the ill effects of radiation, Teller brought a bottle of tanning lotion with him while viewing the original New Mexico blast. For him it might as well have been a day at the beach, albeit under the rays of a man-made sun.

Firmly ensconced as the chief alchemist of the military-industrial complex, the Strategic Air Command's favorite immigrant/sorcerer/Jewish genius, Teller, the savvy assimilationist, moved to consolidate his power zone. Tired of battling for hegemony at Los Alamos, he became head of the rival, weapons-friendly Lawrence Livermore Lab in northern California. But it was Teller's eager sandbagging of his former boss, Oppenheimer, during the height of the McCarthy period that earned him enduring opprobrium from the majority of his fellow atomic scientists. In 1953, the Atomic Energy Commission, citing Oppenheimer's alleged "long-term associations with the Communist Party" (his wife and brother had been Party members) and his continuing opposition to the development of the H-bomb advocated by Teller, suspended the scientist's security clearance.

In the acrimonious hearing that followed, during which the FBI wiretapped Oppenheimer's conversations with his lawyer, Teller, once more acting in his adopted role as the lone patriot amongst the suspiciously accented and motivated eggheads, delivered the decisive testimony. Allowing that he did not think Oppenheimer (who, after all, was a native-born citizen and had worked day and night to produce the atomic bomb in the service of the United States) would "knowingly" hurt the nation, Teller testified that "in a great number of cases I have seen Dr. Oppenheimer act . . . in a way which for me was exceedingly hard to understand. . . . To this extent I feel that I would like to see the vital interests of this country in hands which I understand better, and therefore trust more." After this "expert" corroboration/justification of the commission's charges, Oppenheimer's clearance was revoked permanently, effectively removing all functional moral opposition to the weapons program advocated by Teller and his fellow Cold Warriors.

With the Test Ban treaty in 1963 and the Strategic Arms Limitation Talks of the 1970s—both of which he opposed—Teller, aside from being regularly called out by rebellious Berkeley students who assembled in front of his house to accuse him of being "a war criminal," appeared to recede from public life. Actually he was engaged in what he described in his memoirs as a "vitally important work": the first draft of what would come to be called the Strategic Defense Initiative, or "Star Wars." Displaying much political clairvoyance, Teller first presented his idea for the space-based missile shield to Reagan at the Livermore Lab back in the middle sixties, soon after the Great Communicator was elected Governor of California. "What we told the Governor was not simple," Teller later recalled. "It was clear to me that this was all new to him, but when the briefing was finished, I knew he had listened."

After Reagan's election as president, which Teller called "a miracle for our country," the old atom blaster was back in the saddle, once again the true blue American John

Wayne of nuclear scientists, influencing policy and drafting billion-dollar plans to fight the Soviet Union in outer space, if need be. With the downscaling of the project under the first President Bush, Teller, decrying Gorbachev's perestroika policy as "an illusion," refused to give up, revising his original defense plan to include "brilliant pebbles," 100-pound armed satellite devices that could be deployed at the bargain price of only $1 million per issue. Nothing if not persistent, before his death at age ninety-five in 2003, Teller expressed a degree of vindication in the fact that the newly souped-up military-industrial complex run by the current Bush presidency was again interested in his original Star Wars plan as a potential measure to fight the worldwide terrorist threat.

What are we to make of a man like Edward Teller, master of brinksmanship, who some might describe as the canniest of mad scientists? According to Teller himself, he was always a man of peace, not war. In response to a statement signed by many nuclear scientists and physicists refusing to continue to work on the "production, testing, or stockpiling of atomic weapons," Teller dutifully informed a Senate Foreign Relations Committee hearing on Disarmament of the pacifist, lily-livered, naïveté of his former colleagues' position. "I choose the profession of a scientist because I am in love with science," said Teller, ever the hardnosed "realist." "I would not willingly or eagerly do anything else. . . . I don't like weapons. I would love to have peace. But for peace we need weapons and I do not think my views are distorted. I believe I am contributing to a peaceful world."

Perhaps there is truth in that idea. As Teller never tired of reminding his detractors, millions died in world wars before the invention of atomic weapons, and despite all the fear generated by the presence of the bomb, no world wars had been fought since. But is it worth all the fear? And what can be said of those who willfully exploited that fear?

Leaving Hungary not too many steps in front of the Nazi holocaust, Edward Teller came to live in the world where he embodied what Terry Southern would call "the ultra-hyper-super detached 'logic' that allowed one to speak in terms of mega-deaths." It is probably only by the skin of our teeth that we have escaped being cast in whatever repressed nightmares haunted Teller's sleep. Like the author of the Book of Revelations, he was a man given to visions, none of which anyone in their right mind would care to behold. Years after the first atomic explosion, Teller was asked what he thought of his vanquished colleague Oppenheimer's initial response to seeing the looming mushroom cloud. Quoting Lord Shiva from the Bhagavad-Gita, Oppenheimer summed up the awe and horror of humanity's new ability to commit mass suicide: "I am become Death, the destroyer of worlds." For Oppenheimer there was an awesome regret in his famous statement, as if all his labors had turned him into one more Dr. Frankenstein, creator of something terribly unholy. But as for Teller, he was "very impressed" by his former boss's quote. "For me," he said, "it was much to the point."

✳   ✳   ✳

Danny Goldberg

Colonel Tom Parker
✯

BY DANNY GOLDBERG

THE ROLE OF a personal manager in the music business is the source of many legends. A manager is supposed to negotiate the best economic deals for a client, give advice about career decisions, and often function as the voice of the artist to the outside world, as well as control the access of outsiders.

There are managers who have worked selflessly for singers only to be dumped at the moment of success as depicted in Woody Allen's film *Broadway Danny Rose*. There are managers who quietly do their work for decades, and there are flamboyant characters who have entered the stage of popular culture themselves.

In the documentary about Bob Dylan *Don't Look Back*, Dylan's manager Albert Grossman comes across as a manipulative genius, at times nasty and condescending to others, a bit obsequious to Dylan, but always fiercely protective of his client. Another indelible image from the 1960s is that of the Beatles in stunned mourning as they returned from an Indian visit to the Maharishi and learned of the death of their manager Brian Epstein.

Epstein and Grossman worked for geniuses whose music echoed around the world for decades. They had, in addition to their responsibility to their clients, a responsibility to history, which, by all accounts, they handled appropriately.

There is, however, a dark side in the world of managers. There are those who abuse the trust of their clients, who present them with false choices and inaccurate information and who instead of serving their clients' interests, ruthlessly exploit them and sometimes trick them out of their money or steal it outright.

There has probably never been a more destructive and villainous manager than Andre Van Juijk, a man who was suspected of murder in his native Holland, entered the United States illegally, and never became a naturalized United States citizen. He quickly entered the world of carnivals and later became a manager of musical performers. By the time he met the artist who would make him famous, he was only known by the American name he had given himself: Colonel Tom Parker.

When Parker first began managing Elvis Presley in 1955, the very idea of calling a rock and roll singer an "artist" would have been laughable. It is certainly understandable that in those early years, Parker would have been focused on cashing in as quickly as possible both for his own sake and, arguably, for the sake of Presley who came from a poor Southern family bedeviled by debts.

Almost immediately, however, Elvis became one of the biggest money-making entertainers of all time. The first of his televised appearances on *The Ed Sullivan Show* was seen by 82 percent of American television households. According to the definitive book *The Colonel*, by Alanna Nash, Elvis's per-night fee for concerts immediately rose from five hundred dollars a night to twenty-five thousand dollars, and his merchandising grossed $22 million within a year.

For the remaining twenty-one years of Elvis Presley's life, his career was marred by Parker's small-minded, self-interested decisions. Parker constructed Presley's contracts so that he, alone, made most of the decisions, and when Elvis complained, Parker usually was able to construct manipulative scenarios that made the great singer despairingly back down.

The most famous anomaly of Presley's career is the fact that, despite a huge worldwide following, he never toured outside of the United States. This decision had nothing to do with Elvis but was because Parker feared that, because of his own illegal status, he would not be allowed back in the United States, and he didn't want Elvis touring anywhere without him playing the role of gatekeeper.

Under the cynical assumption that Elvis records would sell the same amount regardless of the material, Parker made sure that, for most of Elvis's career, the singer only recorded songs in which either Parker or his cronies had a copyright interest. He institutionalized this by creating a music publishing company to hold these assets, of which Parker himself owned 40 percent while Presley only owned 15 percent. One of the rare occasions on which another person gained access to Presley was when producer Chips Moman recorded "Suspicious Minds" and refused to give up any of the copyright interest. RCA Records prevailed over Parker's objections and the song went on to become Presley's last number one hit. Despite the success, Parker made sure that Presley never again worked with Moman in the last seven years of his life lest he risk losing control again.

Similarly, it was no accident that Presley made a depressing series of Hollywood formula movies, such as *Clambake*. This, despite the fact that he had aspirations to be a serious actor and deeply admired artistic films such as *Rebel Without a Cause*, from which he could recite entire scenes. Early in Presley's career, Parker told 20th Century

Fox's Buddy Adler, "There's no sense in sending me a script because I can't read. The only thing I'm interested in is how much you're gonna pay me."

A typical example of missed opportunities was the remake of *A Star Is Born*. Barbra Streisand offered Elvis the co-starring role, which the Colonel managed to kill, despite Elvis's enthusiasm, by demanding impossible terms. Parker would later claim that Presley himself insisted that he scuttle the *Star Is Born* deal because he was too insecure to attempt the role. Indeed, no one knows what goes on behind closed doors between a manager and a client. There are times when it is a manager's responsibility to be the "bad guy" for such decisions. At other times a conscientious manager needs to push a performer to do things that would be good for him.

The pattern, over years, of Elvis's business is such that no such glib explanation can remove from the Colonel the stench of crass self-dealing. By all accounts, the Colonel did everything to ruthlessly quash any creative growth on Elvis's part, and to reduce his career to an endless recapitulation of a highly merchandisable cartoon version of his early celebrity.

Even by the standards of the 1950s, Parker's economic relationship with Presley was aggressive. He started with a 25 percent commission (management commissions are typically 15 to 20 percent), and later raised it to 50 percent. That didn't include numerous reported side deals that gave Parker money off the top in exchange for "delivering" Elvis. For example, when Parker negotiated the sale of early Elvis masters to RCA for $10.5 million, he received $6 million and Elvis only $4.5 million.

By the 1970s, Parker had developed a pathological

gambling problem which put him in debt for millions of dollars in Las Vegas, leading to an astounding 837 casino performances by Elvis Presley from 1969 to 1976, mostly at the rate of two shows a night. Late in Elvis's life, Parker created a merchandising company called Boxcar in which, again, he had 40 percent of the stock compared to 1 percent for Elvis.

Perhaps the most sickening incident from the canon of Elvis books is the way that Parker sneeringly discouraged Elvis's interest in spirituality which could, perhaps, have been the sole strategy that might have inspired Presley to stop abusing drugs during his later years. The Colonel accused Presley of being on a "religious kick." Larry Geller, the friend of Presley's who was his link to Eastern spirituality, found his home broken into shortly after Parker's harangue. The only items missing were books and tapes from the Self Realization Fellowship that had elicited Elvis's interest. According to Nash's book, Geller believes that only Parker would have engineered the crime, and Geller soon found himself unable to make contact with Elvis.

Although this kind of behavior would have been immoral regardless of who Parker's client was, it is vital to remember that this is Elvis Presley we're talking about: Elvis—the master singer who helped invent rock and roll, whose stunning voice could have lasted for decades, whose early screen charisma rivaled that of Brando and Dean, whose cultural genius changed Western concepts of male sexuality, who opened the pop door for black music. With his unique charismatic energy and talent, Elvis could very possibly have reinvented himself with any kind of decent encouragement. There are few more depressing contrasts in American cultural history than the juxtaposition of photos of the early, inspirational Elvis and the later, bloated caricature he became.

Other than Peter Shaffer's depiction of Salieri's jealous torment of Mozart in *Amadeus*, it is hard to think of any other so conscious a debasement of genius as that of Parker to Presley. The great songwriter Jerry Lieber said Elvis "was trapped by his dependency on the Colonel. He worshipped him as maker and savior but despised him because he was never able to take control over his own life."

Of course, Elvis is ultimately responsible for much of the tragedy of his own life, but also deserves the glory of the great music and energy he left behind. But Colonel Parker, instead of making things better for Elvis, made them worse. He abused his trust, squandered his opportunity, and disgraced his profession. His sole legacy is as an example of what not to be.

BUMP IN THE NIGHT— CROOKS AND CRIMINALS

Lee Christmas and Machine Gun Guy Molony, Morris Levy, Frankie Carbo, Charles Manson, OJ Simpson

The title of this section speaks for itself. These are people whose philosophy might be summed up as "I kill, therefore I am." Using either six-gun or fountain pen (mostly heavy artillery), some of these individuals killed things besides people, e.g., hopes, dreams, the pursuit of happiness. Then there are the murderous madmen like Charles Manson. In the context of this indictment, Manson serves as a stand-in for America's seemingly endless roster of serial killers: Ted Bundy, John Wayne Gacy, Jeffrey Dahmer, and the like. The inclusion here of Frankie Carbo and Morris Levy, two gangsters of perhaps less repute than other tabloid creatures (like Al Capone, Santo Trafficante, Frank Costello, Jesse James, and a whole slew of Westies and Purple Gangs) only goes to show how deep the roster of bad men runs in the U.S. of A.

Lee Christmas and Machine Gun Guy Molony
✵
BY LUCIUS SHEPARD

I FIRST WAS made aware of Lee Christmas on coming upon a photograph in an obscure travel book that depicted a slight, boyish-looking blond man standing amid palm trees, wearing a comic-opera military uniform with out-sized epaulets, topped off by a wide-brimmed hat bearing an ostrich plume, and accessorized by a belted sword with an ornate grip. The caption beneath the photograph read: "Lee Christmas on the beach at La Ceiba." Several lines of text referred to him as a soldier of fortune who, during the early portion of the twentieth century, assisted the rise to power of the United Fruit Company in Central America. United Fruit, called *El Pulpo* (The Octopus) by Latin Americans due to its grasping, acquisitive nature, domi-nated the political reality of Honduras and acted as an oppressive force throughout the southern portion of the hemisphere for the better part of a century. Indeed, the most notorious president of the company, Samuel Zemurray, aka "The Banana Man," was—with the help of Christmas and his associate, Machine Gun Guy Molony— instrumental in overthrowing a number of governments that tried to institute land reform, the last of these being the leftist administration of Jacobo Arbenz in Guatemala during the early 1950s. United Fruit's power over Central

America and portions of South America was so extensive that at one point, for instance, they owned 42 percent of all land in Guatemala, paid no taxes or import duties, and controlled that country's other two largest enterprises, International Railways of Central America and Empress Electrica. It's impossible to calculate the number of lives extinguished as a direct result of their repressive policies in dealing with agrarian reform—a conservative estimate would put the toll in the tens of thousands, but that total rises dramatically if one adds in the hundreds of thousands slaughtered and disappeared by the various dictators propped up by the company. The Guatemalan regime of Colonel Castillo Armas alone was responsible for one thosand forty thousand people killed and another forty-five thousand disappeared. The United Fruit logo, Chiquita Banana, became the symbol of United States oppression throughout Latin America.

Captivated by the photograph of Christmas, especially by a quality in his pose that struck me as self-deprecating, I did some research and learned that he had been a railroad engineer in Louisiana who had fallen asleep at the wheel and wrecked his train. Unable to get work, abandoned by his family, he traveled to Honduras where he found employment with a small fruit company, driving trains on a narrow gauge railway between San Pedro Sula and Puerto Cortez. In 1897, a Guatemalan-sponsored revolution took Puerto Cortez with thirteen men and commandeered Christmas's train. Offered a choice between joining the revolution or being executed, he taught his captors how to armor the flatcars with the scrap iron left along the tracks, and thus protected, they gained control of the entire north coast of the country in less than a week. For his service, having in that brief time secured a reputation for extreme heroism and a disdainful attitude toward physical danger, Christmas was awarded the rank of captain. When the revolution was defeated, he fled to Guatemala. There, the government entrusted him with funds and sent him to New Orleans to buy guns for a new revolution, but Christmas spent the money gambling and whoring. In 1898, under an amnesty, he returned to Honduras and was employed by the president, Terencio Sierra, who had hired a small army of thugs with the idea of forestalling the election process and maintaining his power—he believed that Christmas's charismatic presence would serve to keep them in line. But Christmas, whom Sierra elevated to the rank of colonel and made head of the National Police, had developed a relationship with Sierra's political rival, Manuel Bonilla, himself an ally—if not a pawn—of various men involved with United Fruit. In 1903, Christmas swung the National Police over to Bonilla's side and marched on Tegucigalpa, seizing control of the city after laying siege to it with Krupps guns, thus earning the rank of general under Bonilla.

Christmas spent much of the next few years courting his third wife, though still married to his second; he was eventually to marry a fourth, and fathered innumerable illegitimate children. In 1906, a Nicaraguan-sponsored revolution ousted Bonilla. He and Christmas sought refuge in Guatemala, where Christmas became the chief of the Guatemalan secret police—his charisma remained a currency he could trade on—but all the while he sought to reinstate Bonilla as president in Honduras. In 1910, Christmas returned to Honduras at the head of an armed expedition financed by Samuel Zemurray. Accompanying him was Guy Molony, a young machine gunner who stood six-and-a-half-feet tall and had fought in the Boer Wars when he was sixteen. The force captured the Bay Islands and then La Ceiba, where they did battle against a garrison led by one General Carillo who rode into battle on a white mule and carried a golden sword and, like Christmas, was rumored to be unkillable. This rumor proved to be untrue. Six weeks later, the country had fallen and Bonilla was on his way to becoming president again. Shortly thereafter, the Honduran congress approved a concession that ceded Zemurray an enormous tract of land and waived his obligation to pay taxes, thereby ushering in fruit company domination of the country.

In 1976, I interviewed a great many people in Honduras regarding Christmas and Molony. One, Fred Welcomes, was a Bay Island fisherman, then in his nineties, blinded by cataracts, who had fought alongside Christmas at the Battle of La Ceiba. He explained that Christmas had recruited the blacks of the islands because they were better marksman in those days than were the defenders of La Ceiba.

"Dat de case no longer," he said. "De Sponnish have since learned de use of weapons."

The shanty in which I interviewed Welcomes was lit by a kerosene lamp, and in that light his cataracts showed thick and shiny, like raw silver nuggets. His appearance and the lantern gave the scene the air of a ghost story, and this idea was amplified when, in a raspy, windy voice, he gave me a word-for-word account of Christmas's speech to his troops prior to the Battle of La Ceiba.

"Lee gathered us on de dock," he said. "And he walk up and down in front of us and say, 'Boys, you done break your mothers' hearts, but you no be breaking mine. We gonna come down on de Sponnish like a buzzard on a sick steer.'"

Welcomes and others told me of incidents during which

Christmas, already wounded, walked directly into enemy fire and how, when captured, he would laugh at threats of execution. I came to understand that this behavior, the self-deprecation I had sensed in him, the ridiculous uniform, these were to a large degree the product of a Lord Jim complex. He believed he had ruined his life in the States and as a result he placed scant value on it and perceived his victories to be something of a joke. He sought an American redemption, one that was never forthcoming—when he offered his services to the Wilson administration prior to World War I, the offer was summarily rejected. I suspect that his loyalty to Bonilla was at least in part due to his hope that by pleasing Bonilla's masters, he might repair his stateside reputation. Molony's brand of heroism was if anything more extreme than Christmas's. He once blew up an armory atop which he was standing in order to prevent it from falling into counter-revolutionary hands. Yet his motives were, apparently, less redemptive than mercenary. Though he returned to New Orleans often, at one point serving there as chief of police, he remained active in Central American politics throughout the 1950s, assisting Zemurray in various aggressions. I've seen a photograph of Molony taken in the mid-fifties shaking hands with Vice President Richard Nixon at the Tegucigalpa airport—an immense Bull Connorish figure clad in chinos and a slouch hat. He died in 1972 at the age of eighty-nine, prosperous, fat, and unrepentant, after a lifetime of violent accomplishment.

Flying over Honduras you cross vast stretches in which you see nothing below except bananas, and whenever I look down on these plantations, I imagine the dozens of back-fence wars fought to sustain them, and I think of the two men who orchestrated many of those wars and made others possible: Molony, the implacable giant armed with a gas cylinder–powered machine gun, engaged in creating the new century, and Christmas, the charismatic womanizer with his good looks, his ostrich plume and fancy sword, unable to escape the shame of the century just past. Carrying themselves like colonialist versions of Butch Cassidy and Sundance, oppositional personalities joined in a strange dynamic by the forces of manifest destiny and business—if, indeed, those forces were ever separate; they seem more colorful fictions than neglected historical figures. And because they are so neglected, because no mention whatsoever is made of them in Honduran history books and little recorded elsewhere, we are forced to conjecture as to the bloody intimacy of their relationship and the character they brought to their semi-patriotic miscreance. Doubtless they joked and whored together as they toppled governments and thwarted coups, but we're unable to determine if the true weight and measure of their work became clear to them, if they ever understood that what must have seemed at the beginning an adventure was in fact the inception of a remorseless political enterprise.

We only know for certain that they were friends. In 1922, following Manuel Bonilla's death and a series of businesss reversals, Christmas wired Molony for money and received $100 for a ticket back to New Orleans. There he lobbied the fruit companies for a job, but was deemed too old to function as once he had and found no takers. In December of that year, while still in New Orleans, he fell ill and died. Guy Molony paid for his funeral.

✳   ✳   ✳

Morris Levy

BY JAMES MARSHALL

Between Rock 'n' Roll and a Hard Place

In a business so notoriously sleazy as the record biz, the legacy of Morris Levy still inspires fear and awe in those who where unfortunate enough to be on the losing end of the deal. Morris Levy stood above all others in his blatant disregard for the contractual obligations a record company has towards its artists and for the artists themselves.

There is no chapter on Morris "Moishe" Levy in *Rolling Stone's Illustrated History of Rock 'n' Roll*, or any other book that purports to tell the "history" of rock 'n' roll. This is both sad and typical, as the history of rock's birth is shrouded by much misinformation and colored by many lies. It is in the vested interest of those who stand to profit from these myths to keep alive a storyline that could be easily stuffed into an episode of *Happy Days*. But we know better. Moishe Levy, gangster and creep, a longtime associate of New York's Genovese Mafia family, was probably the single most important early "businessman" in the shaping of the music that would come to be perhaps the dominant cultural force of the second half of the twentieth century.

Levy controlled many independent record companies, including Roulette, Gone, Gee, End, and Rama (for which many of the famous early rock stars like Buddy Holly recorded). He was also the owner of song publishing consortiums, numerous nightclubs (including the famous Birdland), and a ranch in upstate New York called Sunnyview

Farms, valued at $15 million. In addition to being manager of rock's best known early deejay (and payola victim), Alan Freed, Levy was also a songwriter of some note, at least if you believe the songwriter credits which used to appear below the giant hole of the 45 rpm records. Even if he likely couldn't carry a tune and never read a note of music in his life, Morris's greatest hits are "California Sun," "I'm Not a Juvenile Delinquent," "Ya Ya," "Hey Let's Twist," and many others. As for Levy's supposed writing partners, the true authors of these classic songs, let's just say they understood the wisdom of sharing their credit line (and royalties, of course) with Morris. Despite the music industry's perpetual whitewashing (he is usually called, euphemistically, "a Runyonesque character"), all this mayhem and much, much more is part of the vicious legend of Morris, a Sephardic Jew who referred to himself as a "Turk" and was once dubbed "the Octopus" by no less an authority on marine life than *Variety*.

Moishe was born on August 27, 1927, in the Bronx, New York. Among little Morris's boyhood chums were names destined to spice up many a *New York Daily News* Gangland column: Vincent "The Chin" Gigante and Tommy "Three Fingers Brown" Eboli. An early self-starter, Moishe was expelled from school in grade six, supposedly for assaulting a teacher with an axe handle. Barely into his teens, Levy headed south to Broadway, a mere subway ride away, where as a young teen he began working in the photography darkrooms that many nightclubs ran on premises. A quick study, Morris soon graduated to club photographer, then to the lucrative coat checkroom at such colorful nightspots as the Ubangi Club, Toby's, the Embers, Topsy's Chicken Roost, and the Village Inn. Using this

experience as a jumping off place, the ambitious young
Levy soon found himself knee-deep in the show biz underground, that sketchy zone where brass knuckles sometimes
overlap with true art. In his early twenties, he acquired a
controlling interest the Fifty-second Street landmark Birdland, a club most people associate with the great Charlie
Parker, from whom the club got its name. Levy obtained
the place from noted jazz buff Joe "The Wop" Cataldo,
who'd held it in partnership with Morris Gurlack,
although the duo were, in reality, fronting for Frankie
Carbo, the gangster who ruled the boxing world for
decades, and John "Johnny Bathbeach" Oddo, a Columbo
capo. Eventually, Levy would become the owner of record
of many other joints: the Royal Roost, the Roundtable, Bop
City, and the Blue Note, or, in other words, several of the
leading jazz clubs in one of the music's most creative times,
even if Morris probably was more familiar with names like
Dominick Ciaffone and Gaetano Vastola than Lester
Young or Thelonious Monk. (For fans, the character of
Hesh Rabkin on the television show *The Sopranos* is a com-
posite of Levy and Vastola.)

The nightclub biz can be a tough way to make a living
as Levy was reminded in January of 1959 when his brother
Irving was stabbed to death in front of Birdland by a
hoodlum whose prostitute wife he had eighty-six'd from
the premises. By the early fifties Levy was already looking
to branch out. Realizing that song publishing was the most
lucrative part of the record business (and that copyrights
don't talk back), Levy soon hired jazz pianist George
Shearing to write a theme song for Birdland. "Lullaby of
Birdland" became the first in an immense, and immensely
profitable, publishing empire with Big Seven music as its

flagship. Acquiring copyrights everywhere and every way, Levy soon bought and stole his way to a catalogue that would eventually include over thirty-two thousand tunes.

Never tone deaf to a good deal, Levy also got into the record biz proper via the aegis of George Goldner, a key, if largely forgotten, rock 'n' roll *auteur*. A man blessed with "an ear," that is, an uncanny ability to find and/or mold a hit record, Goldner discovered and often produced such talents as the Crows, the Harptones, Frankie Lyman & the Teenagers, and many more. A true fifties bon vivant, Goldner, a sharp dresser and noted dancer, combined his superlative talent-scout skills with a spectacular gift of gab which was easily the equal of any Hansons' drug store comic, raising the art of free-associative bullshit a notch every time he opened his yap. Unfortunately, Goldner was beset by a nasty gambling habit. George would start a new label, get some hits, and when the distributors paid up he'd hit the racetrack and lose the whole mess. Shark that he was, Levy missed no step in quickly taking advantage of his prospective partner's major weakness. Moishe was always there to bail Goldner out of a tight spot, usually in return for many of the master tapes and the publishing rights that Goldner had so shrewdly conned the song-writers out of, often adding his own name to the writing credits. Levy would then substitute his own name for Goldner's; hence Levy is today listed as the writer of "Why Do Fools Fall in Love?" although, should you find an early pressing of the disc, you would find Goldner's name in the writer's credit. Asked under oath at a hearing into unfair music industry practices about his many songwriting credits, Morris said, "You know, I don't sit down at a piano and write a song like some guys. . . ."

One of rock 'n' roll's saddest and most enduring tales is that of Frankie Lyman & the Teenagers. They came together in 1955 in Harlem's Sugar Hill when members of a disbanded group called the Earth Angels came across twelve-year-old Frankie Lyman (whose initial reaction was, "What! Me sing with Puerto Ricans? Those guys can't sing."). When they did get together they soon auditioned by serenading Richard Barrett, George Goldner's A&R man, from the sidewalk of 161st Street under the window of Barrett's Harlem apartment. Barrett took the kids downtown and their first hit, "Why Do Fools Fall in Love?" was recorded and issued on Gee in 1956. "Fools," which grew out of a poem called "Why Do Birds Sing So Gay," by Teenager Herman Santiago's girlfriend, would become one of the most valuable copyrights in rock history, especially later on when Diana Ross took it on a chart run up to number six in 1981. For two decades lawsuits flew, decisions were handed down, but in the end, Levy walked away with the cake. The Teenagers got nothing. Frankie Lyman died in 1967 inside his grandmother's bathroom with a spike in his arm at age twenty-eight. Puberty had killed his career, but for a brief moment, he was the original Stevie Wonder, a thirteen-year-old star, and a natural. When he died, he left four widows to fight it out over an estate worth less than nothing. Morris Levy had sucked all the money from it.

Probably to prove he didn't really need Goldner, Levy opened the Roulette label in 1956, issuing discs by his jazz favorites like Count Basie and Pearl Bailey as well as white rockabilly from Buddy Knox, Jimmy Bowen, Joanne Campbell, and Ronnie Hawkins. Later he would hit pay dirt in the early sixties with Joey Dee and the Starlighters (of "Peppermint Twist" fame) then again with garage-band-turned-pop-icons Tommy James & the Shondells.

What made Morris Levy such an exceptional bad guy in the era of "whatever the market will stand" capitalism was his singular disdain for his artists and, more to the point, paying them. Having put up the capital for recording, manufacturing, and marketing, Levy considered the end product to be his personal property. "Royalties? Ya' want royalty, go to England," Levy was quoted as saying. In one famous conversation with Goldner, Levy bragged about winning a bidding war for the services of a particularly hot artist by giving him an unheard of (for the time) royalty rate of 18 percent. When Goldner asked him how he could afford to pay such a high dividend, Levy replied simply, "I ain't gonna pay him." Through all this mendacity, Levy retained his supporters. The folks at the United Jewish Appeal sure loved him; as a staunch supporter of Israel and top fundraiser, he was once named their Man of the Year.

As mentioned, it is impossible to write a true history of pop music without Levy, who in 1955 tried to trademark the term "rock and roll," claiming it was his invention and anyone using it should pay a royalty. Levy's founding-father status is further cemented by his relationship with Alan Freed, the disc jockey from Cleveland who, once installed at New York's WINS, held court for rock 'n' roll's glory years from 1956 through 1959.

Around this time Levy was able to put together what he boasted was "the best payola system in the United States." Payola, that is, paying disc jockeys for airplay, was not yet illegal. Levy began sending out rock 'n' roll package tours across America. Then Levy would hire the top deejays in each locale, to emcee the shows and also cut them in for a piece of the door. In this manner he would be guaranteed airplay for his discs. The shows themselves were no small potatoes. Freed's 1956 Christmas Rock and Roll Ball at the Brooklyn Paramount grossed $107, 000.

Levy remained a force in the music business for several years, as witnessed by his strange encounter with John Lennon during the latter phase of the Beatle's career. According to legend, Levy, who held copyrights to many of the Chuck Berry hits, called Lennon on the phone to demonstrate the similarity between Berry's song "You Can't Catch Me" and John's *White Album* tune "Come Together" (the two songs share a line in the lyric). Aware of Morris's notoriety, Lennon was amused to hear from the old gangster, but this soon dissipated, as Levy began threatening the former Beatle with a plagiarism suit. Mortified by this idea, Lennon agreed to sit down at the Roundtable, where after some more tough guy talk from Levy, John not only agreed to record three songs in the Big Seven catalog on his next LP (which would be *Rock and Roll,* his collection of classic cover tunes, mostly produced by a then-sociopathic Phil Spector), but also to give Levy the LP to sell via direct TV marketing under the misguided idea that his label, Capitol Records, did not own such rights. After Spector kidnapped the master tapes, replacement sessions were held at Levy's upstate New York ranch (supposedly where Yoko got wind of how much money was to be made in cattle breeding). An LP of covers called *Roots* (not the same performances found on *Rock and Roll*) was issued in 1974 on Levy's Adam III label; he began selling it via cheesy late-night TV spots. Capitol, of course, had the record pulled, lawsuits went back and forth for years. Lennon, for his part, always professed a begrudging admiration for Moishe. Go forth and figure.

The FBI had been watching Levy for a long time, at one time bugging his Brill Building office with a hidden camera. Yet Morris continued to do business. In 1975, he took a cop's eye out in a brawl and walked without a day in jail. His ties to the Genovese Family were blatant. One Levy company, Promo Records, sold half of its stock to mobster Three Fingers Eboli and kept him on the payroll for a grand a week. The girlfriend of Vincent "The Chin" Gigante, boss of the Genovese family, lived in Levy's Upper East Side brownstone. The Feds finally caught up with Moishe in 1988 following a record deal gone wrong. Levy and the aforementioned Corky Vastola had formed a company called Scorpio Music that bought and sold cut outs (discontinued records sold at a discount price) from MCA Records. They offered sixty-six tractor-trailers worth of goods to one John LaMonte. When he refused to pay for the discs, Vastola broke his jaw with one punch. Unfortunately for the gangsters, the feds were watching and made their case stick, with Levy eventually sentenced to eight years in the can. By 1990, raising money for his appeal, Moishe sold out—Roulette, Big Seven, everything but the ranch—a deal which brought in between $55 million and $70 million dollars. In the end, Levy wouldn't need the money: he died in 1991 of liver cancer, in the middle of his appeal. At least this is the official word; many close to him swear that Morris, following a long-time dream, is still alive, in Australia, raising horses.

Then again, there are a lot of stories about Morris Levy, who, for many, qualifies as a walking urban legend. No doubt Shep Sheppard (the Heartbeats, and Shep & the Limelites), who was found in a ditch on the side of a Long Island road with a bullet in his head, took a few good tales to his grave. Probably, he just wanted his royalties, like everyone else.

Frankie Carbo

BY STUART MARQUES

LOTS OF GANGSTERS killed more men than Frankie Carbo, but he was in many ways as bad as the worst of them because he killed dreams. As a hit man, "Mr. Gray" executed mobsters like Harry "Big Greenie" Greenberg and Bugsy Siegel. As a ruthless fight fixer and shadow manager, he controlled boxing officials like Jim Norris, and slapped around talented fighters like Johnny Saxton. He crushed the dreams of pugs he controlled, like Sonny Liston, and those he couldn't, like Al "Bummy" Davis. He smashed the hopes of kids who oozed sweat pounding the heavy bag in gyms from Brooklyn to Los Angeles. He betrayed every fighter who pissed blood from taking too many kidney punches in bouts they couldn't win.

Frankie Carbo was not the first man to fix fights or ruthlessly control boxers, but he refined it to a level of high art carried on today by his bastard children, Bob Arum and Don King. He is the personification of every corrupt fight manager or promoter in movies across the years, from Alex Baxter as "Little Boy" in *The Set-Up*, to Rod Steiger as "Nick Benko" in *The Harder They Fall*, to Jackie Gleason as "Maish Rennick" in *Requiem for a Heavyweight.* Paul John Carbo came off the streets of the Lower East Side, which produced the likes of Meyer Lansky and Rocky Graziano, and grew up in The Bronx, the New York City borough that would shape Jake LaMotta. Born in 1904, he became a petty thief by the time he was twelve, when he notched his first arrest. His first big pinch, one of at least seventeen, was for assault and grand larceny when he was eighteen. His first known murder, one of at least a half-dozen, came at the age of twenty, when he killed another crook in a dispute over a stolen taxicab. In what would become a pattern, he fled to avoid arrest, but was soon busted in Philadelphia and shipped back to New York. He was convicted of manslaughter and packed off to Sing Sing, where he honed his skills and made new, murderous alliances.

When he got out in 1930, he fell in with the Brooklyn-based Murder Inc., as a hit man for hire. Working under mob butcher Albert Anastasia, he was part of a stable of sullen, ruthless killers that included Abe "Kid Twist" Reles, Allie "Tick Tock" Tannenbaum, and Louis "Lepke" Buchalter, the only organized crime boss to end up in the electric chair. Carbo was accused of five murders, the most notorious coming on Thanksgiving Day, 1939, when Carbo, Lepke, Bugsy Siegel, "Mendy" Weiss, Tannenbaum, and Reles took part in the shooting death of Big Greenie Greenberg in Los Angeles. Greenberg, who had become a fugitive, was marked for death because he had sent a threatening message to Lepke that he would become a rat unless the mob took care of him financially. Tick Tock and Reles, who soon became rats themselves, fingered Carbo. Tannenbaum said he saw Mr. Fury shoot Greenie five times, and Reles put him at the scene. But Reles took a swan dive out of Coney Island's Half-Moon Hotel—with or without help from Carbo and Anastasia. A jury then acquitted Carbo of Greenie's murder because they were unwilling to convict solely on Tannenbaum's word.

Five years later, Carbo was tapped to whack Bugsy Siegel for stealing $2 million from the mob while erecting the first fancy casino in Las Vegas. "Bugsy had built the Flamingo out in Vegas," veteran investigator Jack Bonomi told author David Remnick some years later. "But he made the mistake of welshing on his creditors. You're not supposed to do that. So they gave the contract to Meyer Lansky to collect or kill Bugsy. Frank Carbo got the call." Siegel was famously rubbed out as he sat on a sumptuous couch in a house he shared with his mistress, Virginia Hill. Police let photographers into the house to snap pictures of Carbo's bloody handiwork. Along the way, Carbo, a rugged five-foot-eight-inch-tall, one hundred eighty-pound guy with a high-pitched voice, steel-gray hair, a two-inch scar on his thumb, and ice where his heart should have been, worked his way up from mob hit man to the "underworld boxing czar"; from man-killer to dream-killer. He accomplished this by muscling commissioners, promoters, and managers for a piece, or total control, of fighters. His turf was mostly middleweights, but he dabbled in all divisions and, directly or through front men like Blinky Palermo, Herman "Hymie The Mink" Wallman, Gabe Genovese, and International Boxing Club Commissioner James Norris, had pieces of, or control over, such fighters as Johnny Saxton, Carmen Basilio, Virgil Atkins, Davey Moore, Paul Pender, Kid Gavilan, and Sonny Liston.

This enabled him and his cronies to decide who fought whom and who won. Fighters were forced to take a dive and judges were bribed to vote for, or against, Carbo's boxer. He bet twenty thousand dollars and made a bundle when Jake "Bad Breath" LaMotta took a dive against Billy Fox in 1947 to get a title shot against middleweight champion Marcel Cerdan. In 1953, legendary fight manager Ray Arcel made the unfortunate mistake of trying to promote a series of televised fights for ABC, to challenge *Gillette's Friday Night Fights*, controlled by Carbo's puppets, Norris and the IBC. After one show at Boston Garden, Arcel was jumped and beaten over the head with a lead pipe. He suffered a fractured skull and concussion and lay in a coma before making a somewhat miraculous recovery. Arcel never fingered his assailants, believed to have been Carbo's henchmen, but the attack drove Arcel out of boxing for twenty years. A few years later, Carbo pressured a Los Angeles promoter named Jackie Leonard for 50 percent of welterweight champion Don Jordan for himself and Palermo so they could "make a buck." Leonard was ordered to fly to Miami, where he met with Carbo, Palermo, and Gabe Genovese, a cousin of mob boss Vito Genovese. The strong-arm extended back to Los Angeles, where Carbo and L.A.'s mob boss, Louis Dragna, tried to intimidate Leonard. Carbo and local hit man Joe Sica made follow-up visits, making direct threats to Leonard and thinly veiled ones to Jordan's manager, Don Nesseth.

In 1956, Gabe Genovese, acting at Carbo's behest, extorted ten thousand dollars from a Syracuse promoter to arrange a fight between Carmen Basilio and Johnny Saxton, whom Palermo managed. The fight took place at the Onondaga County War Memorial on September 12, 1956. Basilio won. Basilio's managers, John DeJohn and Joe Netro, paid Genovese about sixty thousand dollars between 1955 and 1958 to arrange fights. Netro admitted as much to U. S. Senate investigators. Asked if he made the payments to Genovese because of his connection to Carbo, Netro replied: "Well, if I said no . . . I would be lying to you. We wanted to get him [Basilio] the best possible matches." Basilio also testified. Asked his opinion of Carbo and Genovese, the tough old fighter said: "There are ladies present here and in all respect to them I have to contain my inner feelings. But I just do not have any respect for those fellows and they do not belong in boxing."

Years later, Basilio told a reporter from the *Syracuse Post-Standard:* "He [Carbo] was the boss of boxing. If he said two guys had to fight, they fought." Though he specialized in middleweights, Carbo went after all good fighters, regardless of weight. His biggest catch was the sullen Sonny Liston, who learned to fight on the street and to box in prison. Liston was a leg-breaker for small-time hoods in St. Louis and later for Carbo and Palermo. He came under control of Carbo and a series of shadow managers who carved him up into more pieces than seemed humanly possible, so he sometimes came out of his fights penniless. Carbo's reign over boxing stretched from 1930 to the 1960s, even while he was in jail. The law started closing in on him in 1958, when a New York grand jury indicted him on charges of being a shadow manager and matchmaker.

When the charges hit, Carbo did what he had always done; he fled. But it turned out he feared his mob rivals even more. In May of 1959, New Jersey state police got a tip he was hiding out in the home of a mobster in Haddon Township in southern New Jersey. Three troopers went to the front of the house and three to the rear. When cops knocked on the door, Mr. Gray bolted out the back and started running. One of the men at the back, a detective sergeant named William Kreps, shouted "Halt!" and a relieved Carbo stopped.

"I thought it was a rubout," he blurted with relief. He was taken in shackles to New York, where he pleaded guilty to three counts of undercover managing and matchmaking and was sentenced to two years on Rikers Island. The law enforcement vise quickly tightened. In 1959, a federal grand jury in Los Angeles indicted him for trying to shake down Don Jordan's manager and promoters, and he was sentenced to twenty-five years. He spent some of it in Alcatraz and the rest in a joint near Seattle. Palermo went to Leavenworth, but somehow managed to return to the fringes of boxing in the early 1980s, after he got out. Once, on the eve of a big fight at Bally's Park Place casino, he was repeatedly paged for telephone calls. Don Jordan was quoted years later as saying he was "like a slave" to the mob. "When they disowned me, I said, 'You're no friends. You're dogs. Now you're my enemies.' "

"They said, 'Talk and you die.' "

New York police detective Frank Marrone told a United States Senate subcommittee in 1960. Carbo controlled boxing for more than thirty years. "There wasn't anyone over him," Marrone said. "There wasn't a professional fighter he didn't control or have a piece of." One of Carbo's jailed front men, Irving Mishel, refused to tell Senate investigators about Carbo because, he said, he had been "threatened with violence" in prison, even though Carbo was in a different jail at the time.

The senators pleaded and offered protection but the pudgy Mishel repeatedly shook his head "no," and took the Fifth. Carbo remained in prison until 1974, when he was released early due to ill health. He finally met his maker in 1976, in a nursing home in Miami Beach. He got off easier than the fighters he controlled or tried to muscle in on. Bummy Davis, who stood up to Carbo and Reles, paid for it by never getting a big-money fight or a title shot. He died in 1945 at the age of twenty-five, shot on the streets of Brownsville while trying to stop a holdup. Johnny Saxton ended up broken and mad in a New Jersey psychiatric hospital for the criminally insane. And Sonny Liston was nearly destitute when he was found dead in his Las Vegas home, surrounded by a syringe, bags of heroin, and controversy over whether the overdose was accidental or murder. Liston's tombstone in Paradise Memorial Gardens in Vegas reads, "Charles A. 'Sonny' Liston, 1932–1970. A Man."

Frankie Carbo's should read, "Paul John 'Frankie' Carbo, 1904–1976. Dream Killer."

Charles Manson

BY LEGS MCNEIL

Misunderstood Madman

For almost forty years now, the accepted motive behind the so-called crime of the century—the slaughter of pregnant movie star Sharon Tate and six others during two nights of murder in August 1969—has been attributed to Charles Manson and his philosophy of "Helter Skelter," i.e., a race war fueled by enormous intakes of psychedelic drugs that Manson supposedly believed would incite the biblical prophecy of Armageddon.

In order to get convictions against Manson and his followers, who were known as the Family, for the obscenely gruesome murders (one victim was stabbed seventy-five times, another forty-five times), L.A. County District Attorney Vincent Bugliosi, whose book *Helter Skelter* became a vastly successful best seller, had no choice but to convince the jury that Manson acted to facilitate his insane race theories. Nothing else in the case made sense. Nothing of value was stolen and the victims appeared to have been chosen at random. Bugliosi's best—and most sensational—bet was to play the hippie madman card, painting Manson as a messianic cult leader who believed himself to be Christ and the Devil rolled up into one, a truly demonic figure who held absolute power over his minions.

In Bugliosi's telling, Manson sent his followers out to commit the Tate/LaBianca murders as a how-to demonstration that would show blacks how to start a race war that would eventually leave Charlie and the Family in power. It was Bugliosi's conjecture that since Manson supposedly believed blacks were inferior, they would not know how to assert their power after they won the war, leaving them no chance but to turn to Charlie and his followers, who would emerge from their Death Valley hiding place and assume control.

This had to be the wackiest "I Want to Rule the World" formula in human history. Except that the jury bought it, we bought it, and even Charles Manson bought it, since the madness and grandiosity of the Helter Skelter scenario transformed the charismatic ex-con into Satan incarnate, a concept Charlie kind of fancied.

The truth, however, is somewhat more mundane. The motives for the Tate/LaBianca murders were revenge, trampled ambition, and fallout from a drug deal gone wrong. At the core of it, Charlie Manson was just another sixties wannabe, one more guitar strummer with an out-sized notion of his own talent and the belief that if he played his cards right he could become a rock star, as famous as Elvis or anyone else. Unbelievably, it almost happened, with Beach Boy Dennis Wilson's help. Manson was on the verge of a recording career when he shot a black drug dealer named Bernard Crowe, thereby losing his peace-and-love credibility. Once Wilson's businesspeople found out Charlie wasn't Jesus, they booted Manson out on his ass, thereby ending his shot at the big-time, at least through conventional means.

No doubt the Beach Boy brain trust had reason to worry about their major investment, what with Brian being nutty, and Dennis, the wild one of the brood, allowing Manson to live at his mansion on Sunset Boulevard for weeks at time long before the famous crimes occurred. Indeed, it was through Dennis Wilson that Manson met many of the people who would become followers and would actually commit the Tate/LaBianca murders. Yet Bugliosi never bothered to call Wilson to the stand during the spectacular eleven-month trial. If Charlie was simply a would-be rocker, even a rejected one, that made him a little too human, the last thing Bugliosi wanted, because this wasn't the kind of case any prosecutor could lose and keep his career afloat. As it was, Bugliosi was on safe ground. In Manson, he was dealing with severely damaged goods, a lifetime criminal, an inmate whose sensibility had been shaped from the first by the American Justice system. Or, as noted counter-culture critic and historian Paul Krassner put it, "Charles Manson is America's Frankenstein

Monster, a logical product of the prison system—racist, paranoid, and violent."

Charles Manson has said of his upbringing, "My father is the jailhouse. My father is your system." Born "no name Maddox," according to his birth certificate, on November 12, 1934, he was the illegitimate son of a "loose" sixteen-year-old girl named Kathleen Maddox, who later married an older man, William Manson, from whom Charlie got his name, a moniker which would enter the national consciousness as a bigger-than-life, *Friday the 13th*-style boogeyman, and, later as a transgender shock-rock figure. In 1939, Kathleen Maddox and her brother, Luther, held up a gas station and got five years in the West Virginia State Penitentiary. From then on Charlie lived with his aunt and uncle until Kathleen was released in 1942. After winning back custody of her child, Kathleen soon gave up on him and sent the young Manson to live at a foster home. No regular home was available, so the court sent him to the Gibault School for Boys in Terre Haute, Indiana. It would be the first stop in what would become a pattern of incarceration that would last until he was released from McNeil Island prison in 1967 at age thirty-two, after serving seventeen years, more than half his life, behind bars.

Had it been any other time, Manson might have continued his noirish journey in relative anonymity. But it wasn't any normal time. It was the Summer of Love, a particularly American episode in which even a career criminal could arrive in San Francisco's Haight Ashbury, assemble a small tribe of reject/runaway hippie girls, and drive down the California coast to Los Angeles in a converted school bus preaching a highly personalized message of peace and love.

As former District Attorney Vincent Bugliosi even admitted, "I don't think Charlie and the Family were thinking about murder when they were in Topanga Canyon. Like the rest of the hippies, they were thinking about making love, making music, and taking drugs. Murder was the last thing on their minds."

Charlie and the Family were accepted, tolerated, and even welcomed and worshipped in Topanga Canyon, the rock star–infested hills where they came to settle for a time. Neil Young has been quoted as saying, "A lot of pretty well-known musicians around L.A. knew Manson, though they'd probably deny it now. The girls were always around too. They'd be there right on the couch with me, singing a song. And Charlie'd talk to me all the while about how he'd been in jail so much there was no longer any difference about being 'in' or 'out' of jail."

"Yeah, Neil Young gave me a motorcycle," Charlie recalled in an interview after his imprisonment. "I hung out with all them people, that was my neighborhood. Jimi Hendrix lived three doors from Dennis Wilson, and Elvis lived two blocks away. He ran me out of his yard once. I got mad at him; I was going to throw some rocks at him. Mostly because I thought he was an idiot, an egotistical, fucking punk."

According to many, Charlie had an "okay" voice, as "folkie" as the next. But mostly it was his mysterious ability to attract large numbers of women that caught the eye of many Topanga rockers, including Dennis Wilson. Gregg Jakobson, one of the Beach Boys Brothers' Records talent scouts and producers, remembers Dennis calling him one day and saying, "Hey Gregg, you should have been down here. Some guy pulled up in a big black bus and he's got about thirty girls." John Phillips, Mamas and Papas frontman, remembers Dennis calling and telling him, "This guy Charlie's here with all these great looking chicks. He has all these chicks hanging out like servants. You can come over and fuck any of them you want. It's a great party."

Brian Wilson, Dennis's bizarre genius of a brother, remembers, "Dennis supplied the Beach Boys' *20/20* album with the oddest cut, 'Never Learn Not to Love.' He's credited as writer, but the song owed itself to his strange new friend. It was originally titled 'Cease to Exist.' Dennis liked it. He pushed to record it as a favor to the vagabond musician he called the Wizard. At the time, the Wizard was trying to persuade Dennis to quit the Beach Boys and take up with his Family."

"Dennis Wilson wanted to live with us," Family member Sandra Goode recollects. "He was going to just drop everything and come and be with us whether it was living in a tent, or whatever. And his brothers basically said, 'You know, you're bound by contract, and if you renege we're gonna have you committed. We're gonna get psychiatric testimony that you've flipped your lid.' "

Partly due to their association with Dennis Wilson, the Family attracted new members, forcing Charlie to find a new and larger home. They relocated to the Spahn Movie Ranch, a rundown riding stable once used to film western movies and television shows, located on the northern rim of the San Fernando Valley. It was there, after excessive listening to the Beatles' *White Album*, that Charlie began refining his "Helter Skelter" vision for the acid/apocalyptic future, a concept Vincent Bugliosi would help make famous, a lot more famous than John Lennon ever intended.

Despite Charlie's vivid imagery, according to most Family members, no one actually took these prospective events literally. Instead, they preferred to spend their days "Magical Mystery Touring," playacting different fantasy roles while taking drugs, fornicating, and indulging in Charlie's nightly sing-alongs. It was around this time that Terry Melcher, a music producer and one of Doris Day's sons, came into the picture.

"When Gregg Jakobson and I arrived at the ranch," Melcher says, "Manson was sitting in a chair in front of a defunct saloon on a simulated Western street. He was sound asleep. Gregg woke him and he led us along a path where there was a rope hanging from a tree. He said to grab hold of the rope, which swung us across a gully to a low place where there were about forty people sitting in a circle around a campfire site. Of these, five or six were men, and all the rest were girls. There were tents pitched all around. Several of the girls were holding babies. Gregg had urged me to come because he thought the setup was interesting on a kind of cultural level as well as musical. He thought it might make a television special."

Melcher's girlfriend of the time, the movie star Candice Bergen, remembers, "One night Terry went out with one of the Beach Boys and came back talking enthusiastically about the commune they'd visited—an abandoned ranch where a group of kids ran naked. He talked about these 'soft, simple girls' sitting naked around with this Christ-like guy, all singing sweetly together. 'Why can't they sing dressed?' I snapped. He asked politely if I would like to come out and see the ranch. It was a rhetorical question: we both knew I'd hate it and they would hate me, so I sulked and said no thanks. Anyway, by then I'd heard enough about Charlie Manson and his minstrels. But Terry was intrigued by this man, by his apparent spirituality and lack of materialism. He admired the naturalness of their life on the ranch, the simplicity, the closeness."

Though Terry Melcher did his best to separate himself from the Manson Family after the murders, Candice Bergen and others confirm his infatuation with Charlie and the Family as being the "real thing" in a town built on glimmer and glitz. Melcher's interest piqued Manson's. In the weird frisson of the 1960s, Charlie Manson, who would become the national demon, was depending on the son of Doris Day, America's squeaky clean heroine, to make him a star.

It might have happened, too—stranger things have—if it wasn't for the entry of the aforementioned Bernard (Lottsapoppa) Crowe, a local L.A. pot dealer. Trying to score a bundle for his growing family, Manson got in a dispute with Lottsapoppa, an argument that would end with Charlie shooting the dealer. Fleeing the scene, Manson, apparently buying into at least some of his developing race war scenario, began telling everyone, "I just offed a Black Panther." (In reality, Crowe had nothing to do with the Panthers, except maybe to sell them pot.)

Word of the shooting soon got out, cooling Terry Melcher and Dennis Wilson on the idea of Charlie Manson as a potential Beach Boy opening act. Manson's peace-and-love façade was crumbling fast. After buying two thousand hits of bad mescaline from the Family's long-time acid dealer, Gary Hinman, Charlie resold the drugs to the Straight Satans Motorcycle Club, who proceeded to freak out, en masse. In retaliation, the Straight Satans arrived in full force at Spahn's Ranch threatening to burn the place to the ground if Manson and part-time Family member Bobby Beausoleil (star of Kenneth Anger's unseen film *Lucifer Rising*) didn't get their money back. Beausoleil, notably hotheaded, attempted to resolve the matter by tying the dealer Hinman to a tree and, along with Family members Mary Brunner and Susan Atkins, torturing him for two days. Not to be outdone, Manson was soon on the scene, slashing off Hinman's ear with a sword. Eventually Beausoleil killed Hinman by stabbing him twice in the heart.

Despite its gory detail, the Hinman killing did not stray from Manson's established M.O.: certainly he was a con-man, a stealer of credit cards and cars, pimper of women, but when it came to killing, this was strictly in the line of business and according to some demented sense of under-world honor. Hinman had cheated a supposed friend so he deserved to die. As Manson never tired to preaching to his Family of nubiles, "Your word is your bond and your bond is your word."

Of course, the Tate/LaBianca murders would move everything to a whole other level. According to most reports, this is what happened: thinking he was already involved in two murders, Charlie went looking for Dennis Wilson and Terry Melcher for money so he could move the Family to Barker Ranch in Death Valley and hide out from the cops. He arrived at 10050 Cielo Drive but was rudely informed by the owner of the house, Rudy Altobelli, that Terry Melcher no longer lived there. Altobelli would later tell this reporter he had known Charlie Manson and seen him around the house (he'd denied knowing Manson at the trial). In fact, Manson girls Susan Atkins and Catherine Share were regular users of the pool at the house at 10050

Cielo Drive long before the murders, a fact confirmed by Terry Melcher to Vincent Bugliosi when he was updating his book a few years ago.

This brings us to one of the main questions that continues to haunt observers about the Manson case to this day. The police have always assumed Manson never knew who really lived in the mansion on Cielo Drive. But none of that makes sense. After all, Charlie was tapped in. He knew what cooked. He wasn't one to knock on the wrong door. What would Charlie Manson be doing hanging around the Sharon Tate and Roman Polanski home after Terry Melcher and Candice Bergen moved out? The reason for Manson's appearance at the house could pertain to the ongoing sex parties that were alleged to have occurred on a regular basis at 10050 Cielo Drive. According to many sources, a number of pornographic tapes featuring Sharon Tate were seized at the crime scene, supposedly showing Yul Brynner, as well as a bunch of other Hollywood luminaries, engaging in orgies. These tapes were conveniently destroyed. Other speculation centers on murder victims Wojiciech (Vojtek) Frykowski, and his girlfriend, coffee heiress Abigail Folger. Allegedly, Frykowski was badgering Folger into investing in a huge MDA (an illegal hallucinogenic drug) deal that she was trying to weasel out of through her psychiatrist. Sex parties and drug deals: now that sounds like something Charlie Manson, career criminal, faux-Christ/Casanova figure, might take more than a passing interest in.

Still, how do you jump from shakedowns and drug killings to something like what happened on that August weekend in 1969? The answer might lie in Manson's developing relationship with the notorious Leda Amun Ra. More commonly known as "Leda The Witch," Amum Ra was well known in the Hollywood hipster underground. *Esquire* magazine even did a lead feature on her in their 1968 issue with the dire headline, "Evil Lurks in California. Lee Marvin is Afraid." According to a secret Manson manuscript—call it a missing Manson Codex, if you want—recovered by this reporter, Charlie met with Leda Amun Ra in June of 1969, two months before the Tate/LaBianca murders, and the two discussed their different philosophies.

Most likely written by Family member Sandra Goode, the document, over one thousand pages in length, describes Leda Amun Ra as "a witch. . . . A self-made witch. She was thirty-three but could easily pass for twenty-two. She is not a regular witch, but an 'acid witch.' She was awakened to the Devil's cause by means of the drug." Describing how Leda "made her own rules to practicing witchcraft," the document says "she often stated that the young generation was destined to become hers." It goes on to tell how Leda, who lived in a castle-like structure in the Hollywood Hills, supposedly concentrated on "starlets or young actors in Hollywood, and sometimes they were members of rock groups, who dealt in underground music." Many of these people had been to her satanic parties. Apparently this attracted the attention of one more outsider with larger designs on the wild drug land of Hollywood, Charles Manson.

"Charles Manson's interest in witchcraft led him to a meeting with Leda Amun Ra," the recovered Manson document asserts, describing their get-together. "Charlie arrived at the Castle and Leda met him wearing a full-length flowing gown of black silk. Around her neck she wore a Christfigure upside down on a cross.

"I've heard of you," Leda told him.

"I've heard lots about you, too," Charlie replied.

"That philosophy of yours is wrong, you know," Leda said.

"Why?" Charlie asked.

"I'll show you," Leda said. At this point Leda led Charlie into her swank bedroom. They argued about how special people "know" that they are "chosen," and if they are "chosen" they must act for the right reasons. Leda told Charlie he was doing it all for the wrong reasons, i.e., not for Satan.

"You don't really believe in what you say you do, you just do it," Leda told Charlie.

"How do you know that?"

Leda looked at Charlie and said, "Because a freak can read another freak's mind."

"Why do you say that I don't believe what I say I do?" Charlie asked.

"Because, what is it that you really believe in? Killing, right?"

"Right," Charlie answered her.

Leda then tried to convert Charlie to Satanism, which didn't go over real big, but at the end, she invited him to one of her parties the next Wednesday at 11:00 P.M. Charlie accepted and this section of the manuscript ends on this chilling, if contradictory, note: "Charlie left Leda's temple and drove slowly back to the ranch. That night, he knifed an old man and scratched out a note that read 'girl out in the woods behind the bunkhouse—for the sake of the devil....'"

The manuscript goes on to quote Manson talking about various Hollywood houses Leda hipped him to. "I don't know much about the history of the place, but long before we arrived there, it had been a party house, a freak-out pad, and, for some, a hide-out. One of the girls quickly dubbed it the 'Spiral Staircase.' Its isolated location served a lot of purposes for a lot of different people and, like the lady who owned the place, some far-out, spaced-out, weird people were frequent visitors there.

"The day we first drove up, we were innocent children in comparison to some of those we saw in our visits there," Charlie continued. "In looking back, I think I can honestly say that our philosophy—fun and games, love and sex, peaceful friendship for everyone—began changing into the madness that eventually engulfed us in that house. It was kind of a 'House of Transition.' . . . People with beautiful faces or charming personalities, people who made great contributions to society came there in the middle of the night, to indulge in what they preached against by day. There were nationally respected celebrities, a prominent sports figure or two, some of the influential and the wealthy, and on occasion, some who wore the cloth and preached the word of God. It was a strange house, but one to learn in; a place where mental sickness and mass confusion were the best that one could expect. . . .

"Planting fear in their people is the way a lot of leaders keep control. Love and doing our own thing was what held us together and that's the way I wanted everything to be, but at a later date, the things I was exposed to at the Staircase may have come back to me . . . if outsiders moved in so easily for sex. They could just as easily start maneuvering some of the girls into heavier shit—like chains, whips, blood-drinking, animal death, and even human sacrifice. It was a hard-core multiple-devil worshipping bunch of people who passed through the doors of the 'Spiral Staircase.' "

There is no specific mention of 10050 Cielo Drive in Manson's ruminations, but the implication is clear. Could it be that Charlie Manson, America's homemade Frankenstein Monster, killed out of outrage at Hollywood society's decadence? Vincent Bugliosi played up the crazed "Helter Skelter" scenario like a pop culture maestro: he knew it would work. It was what people wanted to hear: the idea that, in the end, Charlie Manson and his thrill kill kult would turn out to be the true final result of the counterculture and its obvious excesses. (It is more than coincidence that the Manson killings and Woodstock happened within days of each other.) There was a kind of cold comfort there for the silent majority and their corrupt Nixonian pieties.

For Manson's part, he might have been a fall guy, but he was a very willing fall guy, soaking up whatever wacko tripe came down the pike during those loopy times, twisting it to fit his own maniacal self-vision. This is one more reason to hate Charlie, because in a real way he let down the culture he claimed to defend—not only by killing at least thirty people as some kind of drug-addled paranoiac justification for not becoming a star. But also for wanting to be a star to begin with. In his sick way he was just one more hanger-on, pissed at being excluded by the "Beautiful People." Manson was articulate, charismatic, and a leader—but he allowed himself to believe the hype, the hippie hype, the gangster hype, the celebrity hype, and the devil hype. America needed a Frankenstein monster to explain away a sick society, and there was Charlie, playing the role better than Boris Karloff ever could.

People say, "Well, Charlie is just crazy."

But I wonder. Maybe Charlie, still playing his assigned role, only acts crazy when Geraldo shows up. But watch the BBC documentary on Manson and you'll see he's not as nutty as he pretends. Even his prosecutor, Vincent Bugliosi, said that before Charlie moved to the Spahn Ranch (and he had his meeting with Leda the Witch, too) "Charlie wasn't interested in murder, he was just interested in making love, music, and taking drugs, like thousands of other hippies."

The only thing he did of any consequence was to kill the sixties by mixing speed, LSD, and belladonna, and sending a bunch of hippie zombies to do something "witchy" at the Tate/LaBianca houses. That's the trouble with Frankensteins on speed, LSD, and belladonna—they tend to leave something "witchy" behind.

OJ Simpson

BY LUCIUS SHEPARD

WHEN PEOPLE ARE deprived of power, life loses meaning and death acquires a certain glamour. They've known this in Mexico for some time—photographs of the anonymous and mutilated dead occupy the front pages of the twenty-four daily newspapers in Mexico City, often mounted side-by-side with shots of half-naked actresses and pop stars. "*Notas rojas*," they call it. Red news.

I've been in Mexican homes in which the photograph of a family member's bloody remains has been snipped from a newspaper to serve as the centerpiece of a shrine. It's as if the violated flesh has been deemed a truer emblem of a loved one's memory than the smile of a confirmation photo or the purposeful, forward-looking pose of a graduation shot. As if violent death conferred a peak celebrity upon the deceased.

The media style in our own country hasn't entirely descended to that level, nor have our sensibilities concerning our friends and family been so degraded. Yet as the people of the United States and their government grow more separate in their fundamental aims, as the corporate mind continues to cast its enormous stupefying spell over the public will, and the gap widens between the powerful and the powerless, it's becoming evident that American values are heading in a similar direction. This appears to be an inevitable decline, the natural issue of history and not the product of a single cause.

However, there was a moment a decade ago, in the midst of a New York Knicks playoff game, when the architecture of this decline was made clear, when it proudly announced itself, when the tarp was pulled off the new model of both our media and our culture, and millions of televison screens showed a white Bronco cruising slowly along the L.A. freeway to the accompaniment of endless, uninformative chatter. From that seminal event followed the nine-month gestation of a trial, and from the trial emerged the first official icon of the media-sponsored reality: Orenthal James Simpson. OJ.

We watch him now in TV clips, stumbling drunkenly, arthritically, across putting greens; we notice him glaring with unalloyed belligerence from the covers of tabloids as we stand in check-out lines, his torso thickened, features coarsened. It seems impossible that he once hurdled through airports and, with a fluid shift of his hips, a jab step, left linebackers grasping at air. The failure of the body is something we're accustomed to seeing with athletes, but what we have come to perceive in OJ Simpson is a deeper failure, one less often brought to public view—the decaying of a spirit, a leprosy of the soul. In truth, the man was never remotely akin to the healthy, good-humored image he presented, and yet that his decay may be merely apparent does not concern us. We insist that we are observing a process of corruption, an affliction engendered by drugs and privilege, metastasized by a horrid crime. We hold to this belief because it nourishes our notions of justice and order.

The times are such that under normal circumstances two murders—only two—should not qualify a man as a great villain, especially when his culpability for those crimes has not been secured by verdict. In a world in which the concept of cause and effect has been diluted, guilt and innocence have become relative values. Blame once laid squarely at the feet of criminals is frequently ascribed to drugs, chromosomes, sugar, childhood abuse, etc., and thus some may be inclined to temper our judgment of OJ. However animalistic and abhorrent his crime, however premeditated, it was nonetheless a crime of passionate obsession and, by contrast to the crimes of kings and countries, a small thing. Though we love to loathe and are fascinated by the bloody-handed among us, we understand that the true villains of our age, of every age, have cleaner hands than common killers. But the grossness of OJ's purported act, the butchery of his ex-wife and a man he may have presumed to be her lover, disgusts us not only because it was vile; it was an unseemly betrayal of celebrity, of our contract with celebrity. It ratified our right to revile him as though his villainy were Hitler-esque. He was for a time and may remain the most hated man in America. He is damnable by our consensus wish if not by law or reason. We abjure him, we cast him out.

The legacy of all murders and murderers is families gutted by grief and loss, their bond eaten away as if by a cancer, but the murders of Ron Goldman and Nicole Brown Simpson served also to expose and accelerate a process of decay—much like the one we perceive in OJ—in the national character. When they were slain, the age of celebrity was already upon us, the trends that have squeezed our culture into its current distorted shape already flowing. The event that was contrived of the Simpson murders, the media circus surrounding the trial and its controversial verdict, imparted a powerful impulse to those trends and channeled them full-speed into the cultural mainstream. Thus the most pernicious legacy of those deaths and OJ's involvement in them may well prove to be Court TV; the elevation of punditry to an occupation; the reduction of political and social analysis into an idiotic point-counterpoint during which people with opposing views shrill at one another; all these elements and much else effecting a conspiracy of noise that drowns out rational discourse, dumbing down its audience and transforming the news into a marketing device designed to sell cheapness of every sort, a shallow variety show that produces war coverage in the form of a mini-series complete with glorioso theme music and titles such as "The Road to Freedom," and is increasingly concerned with OJs and Michael Jacksons and Bennifers and the like.

Though OJ's notoriety has dimmed, supplanted in the

news by a host of fresh celebrity felons, he continues on occasion to stumble into view, mumbling bellicose threats or making some swaggering denial. No one pays much attention. By ignoring him, we damn him further. Whatever he carries within him of that night when a young man and a beautiful woman were slaughtered, left like yesterday's catch amid drying spills of blood, the expensive silence and the silk black air, the screams, the sexual stabbing and the sickly hot rush of life . . . those memories and the memories of what led to that night are the poison he must swallow every day, and we notice with some satisfaction that it looks to be taking a toll. The cult of celebrity, in essence, holds a mirror to our souls and so there seems something Dorian Grayish about these intermittent sightings. This unconvicted murderer, this villain emeritus secure in his bubble of legally guaranteed wealth, immune to punishment . . . he might be a living portrait kept in the nation's attic that registers the measure of our own decay, the toll taken by having allowed ourselves to become, as has he, pampered and protected, enfeebled and self-absorbed, the victims of a dissolute process.

Our fascination with OJ and his criminal peers is, then, the poison we swallow, that we have been directed to swallow, and we're greedy for it now. We demand new victims, new perpetrators. When no worthwhile celebrities present themselves for our ritual vilification, we welcome the elevation of a Scott Peterson, say, to celebrity status. We need such people to feel good about our own victimization. In conversation, we refer to them by their Christian names as if they are friends who have betrayed an intimacy. The time we pass despising them could be better spent, but like OJ we have been debased by an obsession, we have given ourselves over to a sickness that is threatening to define us.

It's as a kind of cultural criminal, then, that OJ Simpson is of significance. As an Orwellian figure erected by the media to provide a suitable target for our daily Two-Minute Hate. The blood on his hands does not truly concern us. Nor do his denials, his doubtlessly thuddingly dull mental life, his night sweats and visions, his druggy pleasures, his existential pains. Only his image has meaning, and eventually, that image will come to represent not evil or an act of violence, but a period of time at the end of the twentieth century, a wasted, dispirited decade when death acquired a certain glamour, when a number of intellectual choices were taken away from us and palliatives applied to ease the transition, when the momentum of history overbore the community of hope, shortly before the real trouble began.

THE NINTH CIRCLE—
WORST OF THE WORST

J. Edgar Hoover, Joseph McCarthy,
Roy Cohn, Richard M. Nixon,
Henry Kissinger, George W. Bush

*It is a testament to American democracy that this country
has not produced a genocidal mass killer on the unthink-
able level of Adolf Hitler, Joseph Stalin, or Pol Pot. We
have not avoided our Milosevics by accident. The Constitution and, we would hope, the refusal of the hybrid
assemblage of this country to stand for such large-scale
murderers, protects us, if not the Native Americans. This
doesn't mean that* within the context of American history *we are without our first-class monsters. The body
count incurred on Richard Nixon's watch (with the help
of his key henchman, Henry Kissinger)—the crimes of
Vietnam, Cambodia, Laos, Chile, and other spots around
the globe—may not reach Hitlerian proportions but
cannot be considered acceptable by any civilized standard. The foremost quality of all the occupants of the
Ninth Circle, the hottest of hells, is that the loathsome
residents can all be said to be truly un-American, due to
their wanton disregard for the freedoms that Americans
depend on and cherish.*

*A note on George W. Bush: Although something of a
rookie in comparison with the veteran evildoers here, he is
placed in this mendacious company on the (de)merits of his
behavior in office through his first term. Few presidential*

acts can be more troubling than the pressing of a policy of preventative war, especially when that war (and much else in his repellent administration) has been based on lies and gross misrepresentation. His potential for heinous behavior appears unlimited.

J. Edgar Hoover

BY PATRICIA BOSWORTH

I **NEVER MET** J. Edgar Hoover, the devious little squash-nosed director of the FBI, but I felt as if I had because I heard so much about him when I was growing up. He and my father had many dealings with one another during the Cold War hysteria—that time in America of witch hunts and loyalty oaths—when anti-Communism let loose a wave of political oppression that seems almost incomprehensible today.

My father's name was Bartley C. Crum. In 1947 he'd been one of six lawyers defending the Hollywood Ten (screenwriters and directors accused of putting anti-American propaganda into their films). My father was also one of the vice presidents of the Lawyers Guild when the Guild took off on Hoover's gigantic anti-Communist purge. Untold numbers of alleged subversives were identified through wire-tapping, informers, and guilt by association. My father kept pointing out that all this Red Baiting was inconsistent with American ideals.

In case you've forgotten, J. Edgar Hoover (the master crime fighter) had been obsessed with the "evils" of Communism ever since he headed the Palmer Raids back in 1919 and helped deport thousands of dissident aliens (Emma Goldman among them) because he believed they were "enemies of our country"—Communists threatened "the American way of life."

"These men and women are plotting against America," he wrote, "working out smears, seeking to discredit free government, planning for revolution." In 1919, Hoover linked American Communists to the revolutions sweeping Europe. During the 1940s, he believed American Communists were responsible for the theft of atomic secrets and the infiltration of the government. By 1947, Hoover had become the supreme leader of the American anti-Communism right. He helped Richard Nixon send alleged Russian spy Alger Hiss to prison in 1948, and in 1949, he worked behind the scenes with Roy Cohn to convict Julius and Ethel Rosenberg of passing atomic bomb secrets to the Soviets. The Rosenbergs were subsequently executed after a sensational trial. Hoover always equated Communism with treason.

Meanwhile our phones were being tapped as my father helped the other lawyers for the Ten gather evidence to establish that the purpose of HUAC was not to investigate un-American activities but to penalize the likes of screenwriters Dalton Trumbo and John Howard Lawson because Committee members such as Richard Nixon thought they were "political criminals."

And when my father began handling loyalty cases pro bono (mostly teachers and government workers), he was followed by FBI agents wherever he went—Washington, Chicago, New York, Hollywood, San Francisco. The surveillance increased in 1951 after the movie star Rita Hayworth became his client and he suddenly had to deal with the FBI, too, which was ironic since the FBI was still harassing him. While Rita was married to Orson Welles she had lent her name to all sorts of left wing causes, and Hoover had a big fat file on her marked "X" (meaning security risk).

Things really got rough when Hoover started pressuring my father to name names. By 1952 this had become a ritual—to name names of "alleged Communists"—they might be friends, colleagues, even people you barely knew, but you had to name someone to prove your patriotism. It was a debasing ritual, but Hoover's purpose was even more sinister—to make it seem as if a vast and dangerous conspiracy was being revealed, when in fact it wasn't against the law to be a Communist in America.

Hoover wouldn't let up harassing my father, and his business suffered because his more conservative clients disapproved of his continued defense of subversives. Agents dropped by his law office every week to try and change his mind. They promised he'd get more clients if he'd just name some names, but he refused and instead made a fiery speech on the radio in which he condemned Hoover's peculiar brand of Americanism. He was especially critical of HUAC's terrorizing and pillorying of its opponents. At the time, Hoover had joined HUAC and Senator Joseph McCarthy and Roy Cohn in an ugly smear campaign about how the State Department was "riddled with Commies." Not long after my father made that radio speech Hoover put him on the Security Index; that meant he was labeled a dangerous subversive and in case of an emergency he could be sent to a concentration camp.

During the spring of 1953 our phones went crazy ringing off the hook or going dead. Sometimes I'd be talking to a friend and there'd be an ominous click on the line. My mother was furious because she couldn't even make an appointment with her hairdresser. As for my father, he was often forced to run to a pay phone on the corner if he needed to make a personal call.

In desperation he hired a private detective to find out where the wire taps were in our apartment. The detective's name was Guy; he'd served briefly as Rita Hayworth's bodyguard and my father trusted him. Guy was a former FBI agent who now worked out of a small agency in the Empire State Building. He maintained he'd done everything in his time—made illegal break-ins, tailed Lee Mortimer of *Confidential* magazine, and he'd also been in the CIA as a secret agent during World War II for "Wild Bill" Donovan. "Bill and Hoover despised each other," he said. I was home from boarding school that April so my father took me along when he and Guy met for lunch.

When we arrived at the Drake Hotel restaurant the foyer appeared empty. The maître d' said our guest hadn't shown up yet, but suddenly Guy materialized from behind a potted palm. He explained that that was part of his ability as a spy—an undercover agent—to seem to be invisible. He said he'd been watching us look for him. "I can melt into the walls of a room," but he added, "Don't ask me how." Up close he was a nondescript, balding fellow, middle-aged, rather blurred features. He wore a rumpled suit. But his voice was rich and soothing, and slightly accented. He spoke many languages, he said.

Throughout the lunch Guy drank tequilas and gossiped about Hoover. "He stutters and he likes dogs and he goes to the same restaurant every day for lunch—Harvey's in Washington. He always carries a bottle of his own salad dressing with him." He was invariably accompanied by his live-in companion, Clyde Tolson, whom he called "Slugger." (Tolson supposedly addressed Hoover as "Edna" in private.) Nobody was ever allowed to join them for lunch. Once when some famous super-agent tried to sit with them, Hoover got so angry at the familiarity he fired the agent that afternoon. "If Hoover liked you, you could do no wrong," Guy said. If he didn't you were in trouble. He had a hate on for Melvin Purvis, the agent who shot Dillinger, because Mel got so much publicity and Hoover wanted all the credit.

"Hoover demanded unconditional loyalty from his agents and we gave it to him," Guy went on. "He ran the Bureau like a well-oiled machine. So many rules and regulations, you had to adhere to 'em too. But that was also part of being an agent; that and believing that the FBI was doing a superb job of enforcing the law in America, upholding our morals and protecting America from undesirables, including ethnics and 'moral rats.'"

Hoover could be very touchy. You had to flatter him a lot. Guy said he used to write him flowery letters from the field praising his speeches and telling him how great he was. "I never ever criticized the FBI even if the FBI was fucking up because Hoover thought he *was* the FBI," Guy said.

What was the source of Hoover's power? My father wanted to know. His secrecy, Guy answered, his savage treatment of his enemies, and his supreme confidence in himself. Hoover had been head of the FBI a long time, since 1924, and by the 1950s he had dirt on everybody in high-ranking positions—damaging, shameful stuff about people's behavior. All that information was in Hoover's files—millions and millions of files—a lot of them labeled CELEBRITY, or IMPORTANT PEOPLE. These were stashed in Hoover's private office where he used to mull over them in the dead of night.

When pressed, Guy admitted that much of the information in the files was not accurate; a lot of it was either misleading or downright lies. But the agents and informers who spread the half truths and distortions never admitted they'd collected erroneous data. They were too afraid of Hoover's anger.

As we were finishing lunch, my father asked Guy the question he'd wanted to ask him all along. What proof, if any, did Hoover have that he was a member of the Communist Party?

Guy answered as if reciting from a file: "In-the-opinion-of-the-department-there-is-evidence-Bart-Crum-has-a-prolonged-adherence-to-the Communist-Party."

"What evidence for Christ sake?"

"It has been alleged that you are a Communist."

"But what allegations?"

"Well, didn't you raise money for a movie about the Spanish Civil War with Ernest Hemingway back in 1937? Weren't you publisher of *PM?* Didn't you know Paul Robeson and work with him on the Committee to End Lynching? Didn't you advise Haakan Chevalier? Weren't you close to Harry Bridges?"

"Yeah to all that but it doesn't make me a Communist!"

The discussion went on for a while longer but it was obvious Guy could shed no light on what dirt Hoover had on my father. Late that afternoon Guy came back to our apartment with us and tried to find the wire taps. He prowled around the living room peering into flower vases and under lampshades. I watched as he took our telephones apart but he could find nothing, and then he couldn't reassemble our phones.

The following week my father's passport was taken away by federal agents and then he was called down to Washington to "answer some questions." It was implied that if they were answered the way Hoover wanted he would get his passport back and his name would be cleared.

The "inquisition" took place in a sparsely furnished Justice Department office. My father said he felt very angry during the proceedings and so nervous he almost peed in his pants.

He was questioned about every phase of his life. Born in Sacramento in 1900 to a family of ranchers, baptized a Catholic, still practicing, once considered becoming a priest, graduated from Bolt Hall law school at Berkeley in 1924, first job as a lawyer in John Francis Neylan's firm in San Francisco, became part of William Randolph Hearst's legal counsel in 1929.

The main point Hoover wanted to clarify was whether it was true my father had become Bill Schneiderman's lawyer in 1943 when Schneiderman was president of the American Communist Party.

No, it was not true. Carol King had been Schneiderman's lawyer. My father had been advising Wendell Willkie who, along with King, defended Schneiderman when he was being threatened with deportation proceedings. They took the case all the way up to the Supreme Court and won.

Afterward, our family was assured the "inquisition" had gone smoothly. But years later I discovered my father had informed—named the names of two Communist lawyer colleagues—members of the party who'd been named time and time again. He'd proved his patriotism to Hoover. He never revealed the terrible pressures, financial and otherwise, that forced him to name names.

Lewis Nichols, Hoover's right hand man (the PR wizard who'd promoted the G-man image for the FBI), supposedly told my father, off the record, that he thought his persecution had been a bit excessive, and besides, he'd learned his lesson. He had run into Nichols in Washington in 1958 after he'd begun working for Robert Kennedy when Kennedy was trying to document the corruption within the Teamsters union for the Crime Commission.

As a matter of fact my father often ate lunch at Harvey's. He'd run into Nichols there and he'd seen J. Edgar Hoover, too, seated with Clyde Tolson. He'd passed their table and paused for an instant, and that's when he realized that Hoover smelt of perfume; he stunk like a whore doused with cheap drugstore perfume.

My father worked hard for the Crime Commission. To show his appreciation, Robert Kennedy slipped him one of the FBI files to peruse. When he started to read it he burst out laughing; all it contained were pages and pages of inane taped phone conversations that I'd had with my boyfriends when I was a teenager in San Francisco.

Joseph McCarthy

BY DENIS WOYCHUK

JOSEPH MCCARTHY RUINED my father's life. Or at least this is what I've come to believe, after all these years. It has been a puzzle, often based on circumstantial evidence and what I admit to be a subjective reading of the parental record. But I am convinced it is true.

You see, my father was never much of a talker, and although he could speak and understand almost four languages—Russian, Polish, Ukrainian, and some English

—he hardly ever spoke to me in any of them. Mostly he told me to shut up. "Stop yammering like an old woman," he'd say to me when I was six years old and prattling on about something or other, as small children will. "Men don't talk. They just sit." Still, as I grew to manhood, dribs and drabs of information came to me, and from those little packets of "facts," along with my own observations and conversations with my mother and others, I know that McCarthy, a man I never met other than in my childhood nightmares, where he appeared as a large, indistinct, yet hideously frightening boogeyman, cast a shadow over the lives of my family in the Land of Opportunity.

How little I understood about the role of the junior Senator from the state of Wisconsin (Where was Wisconsin? Near Philadelphia, or Montana?) in the dissolution of what I imagined to be normality back in the days when I was growing up in our nice-enough Brooklyn neighborhood. I couldn't have guessed that this fat man on television waving pieces of paper on which he claimed were written names of dozens of "Communists" was actually messing up my life. What I did know was that even in our lower middle-class circle of immigrant families, we were poorer than most. Money was always a problem. A good deal of this owed to the fact that my father was not working much, and when he did, it was at a far lower level than his talents or erudition appeared to merit. There were a lot of boys in the neighborhood whose fathers seemed far dumber than my dad, less cultured and more proletarian in the lumpen sense of the word. Yet these boys had things I didn't. They went to private summer camp when I didn't. They got to brag about what swell schools they were likely to attend, when I didn't. I suppose

I knew it had something to do with my father, that he'd turned bitter and begun to resent us, his family, for whom he could not provide.

But the real blow fell when he left us. I was about twelve, and from what I've been able to glean from self-analysis, I must have blamed myself for driving him away, even if I had no clue whatsoever what was going on in his head. On the other hand, my father's departure was also kind of a relief since he'd been so quick with the strap. It was confusing. I missed him, on one hand; on the other, with him gone, I got hit less.

He moved to the Lower East Side and after a long absence, he began to come around every few months to suggest that maybe I'd like to live with him in his little tenement apartment on Avenue C. Even then that struck me as an insane choice: leave my friends, my school, and my mom for a hardscrabble existence as the soft new kid in a tough, drug-infested neighborhood. But I had lingering guilt/loyalty issues about my father. I knew he was frustrated and angry and I was his only joy. The resultant pressure was enormous. Ultimately I decided it had been hard enough finding my place in Brooklyn and I wasn't ready to start over. I started avoiding him. Eventually he stopped coming around.

After that maybe I saw him every year or so, occasionally skipping one here or there. I went to see him one winter when I was in college. By now he lived with an old Polish lady on East Tenth Street near Second Avenue, and the neighborhood stank of garbage. When I climbed the three floors to his apartment and rang the bell, he answered on the first ring. He seemed to be smaller and he was glowing. "Come in, let's have a drink." His iron-gray hair had by now turned white but he still wore it in a crew cut. He had on a big bulky sweater and a stocking filled with garlic was draped around his neck. "It's for my cold," he said. Inside on the wall was a two-foot-tall cross, Jesus in white plastic glued to the wooden crucifix. "This is *her* room," he said. "She's getting close to death. I sleep in the back."

We went into his room—a sparsely furnished cubby with only a bed, a dresser, and a bottle that said "Vodka" on the label but was filled with red liquid. "Let's celebrate," he said and he took the bottle I'd brought him, put it away in the bottom drawer, and from his own bottle he poured out two red drinks. "But don't get into the habit." And then we drank: vodka with cranberry juice.

Once we settled in, I told him about my summer job as a mop-up night porter with Local 32B because I knew he'd like that. Then I told him I wanted to become a teacher.

"Don't be stupid!" he spat. "What you want that for? Stupid! Stupid! You think you so smart but you end up with nothing. Learn a trade, something you can use. Plumber. Carpenter. Or even a cook; people always have to eat. But teacher? A woman's job. It makes me ashamed. Join the Navy and learn something you can use. Don't end up in a slum on the Lower East Side." He could have ended the sentence by saying "like me," but that would have been redundant.

Still, it was a good thing to be there then, with my father, this strange, distant man who carried around the burden of a secret, which had ruined his life. Until then, a lot of what I knew about my father was the sort of bare bones biography one might read in a short encyclopedia entry, if any encyclopedia bothered to detail the existence of people like Dad.

My father was born in the Ukraine in 1911 to a family of peasants of the Greco-Catholic faith. World War I began in 1914 and was still raging when the Russian Revolution of 1917 made conditions in the Ukraine even worse. In the famine that followed the fighting, my father lost his mother; without someone to care for them, his two brothers starved to death. My father grew up fatherless, motherless, destined for bitterness. His step-uncle took him in and he worked as a shepherd and slept with the sheep. In winter months he carried a charred board that he snatched from the fire; when his rag-wrapped feet began to freeze, he'd throw the board down on the frozen earth and jump on it to thaw them.

He left Europe in 1929 and came to America just in time for the depression, but for him it was as though he had finally joined the carnival of life: there was always a restaurant job washing dishes, and people, people everywhere, and all of them still had to eat. Work was the reason he had come to this country and even during these "hard times," he always found work—even if it was only working jobs that other people didn't want. He was young and happy then in the land of the free and home of the brave but he wanted to move up, and somehow, within a few years he got himself hooked up with the Merchant Marines. I don't know how. When World War II started, he was a welder in a shipyard in Baltimore.

It was after the war that he made his mistake. He was caught selling issues of the *Daily Worker* (key word: *worker*) outside the shipyard. Asked about it, he said while he liked the paper, and had respect for many of ideals of the Bolsheviks, he nonetheless knew people like him would always be at the mercy of a leader like Stalin. He sold the *Daily Worker* in accord with a good, solid American work ethic: for the pocket money. This did not, however, stop someone from writing his name down. My father never knew who fingered him or who gave his name to which bureaucrat, who put it in which file, where it came to the attention of whomever. But from that time on, he was suspect.

Suddenly unemployable, he retreated to the sweatshops of New York, where a thousand tiny factories pumped out new clothes for the nation, but FBI agents tracked him down. They would visit his place of employ and tell his boss that if he were still on the payroll in two weeks' time, they would have to examine the company's books. Then the boss, following the familiar and cowardly pattern of so many Americans during this peculiar, sad period of our history, would take my father aside with a sad grin and tell him, "Look, I can't afford the risk," and my father would lose his sweatshop job pressing pants for minimum wage. Eventually, my father would get another sweatshop job, but sooner or later the FBI would come calling and Daddy was back on the streets.

Now why was it, in this brave, free land of ours that a man could lose his livelihood on mere accusation, without a conviction, without even a trial? What was it that made a generous good-hearted people give up their fellow man, surrender to fear, and do so with a sense of relief that it was he, not they, who was facing ruin? My father never exactly knew, or at least he never talked about it. Thinking about it now, he often grumbled about J. Edgar Hoover, the House

Un-American Activities Committee and several other Nixonian Commie fighters. But in his mind they had all merged into the central figure of the time: McCarthy.

This is when McCarthy began to stalk my dreams. Someone was destroying our lives and we didn't believe in the Devil, so it became the bulbous shouter from Wisconsin. This ghost-goblin haunting the poorly tuned in black-and-white TV: the repository of everything evil.

"McCarthy," my father said to me that day in his Lower East Side hovel, spitting the name like a curse. "McCarthy." It was McCarthy who had crushed his dreams, McCarthy who had brought him to this intolerable station.

Over the years, I have read my share about McCarthy, listened to the many complaints about the man. I understand how he made paranoia a basis for self-preservation, how he turned free speech into an act of subversion, the way he justified persecution and slander under the rubric of patriotism. Due to his machinations, the notion of American rights disappeared overnight. Accusation without evidence became a means to destroy livelihoods and thereby lives. Our culture began to eat its workers. I've read all this and believe it.

But for me, this is not a dry argument. McCarthy isn't just someone to invoke every time you don't like the way a politician does things, the way people are sometimes careless tossing around Hitler's name. It is personal. I see it through the admittedly subjective and perhaps diminished prism of my father's life in this country. A fat man holding pieces of paper with names of so-called Communists, who weren't Communists at all—sometimes there were no names on the paper at all—created a cowardly political climate in which others could not keep a job. And for want of a job, a family was lost.

I never quite knew about this, and even if I had, I don't know how I might have helped my father. There were opportunities, I know now. I recall one such forty-five-year-old occasion. It was before he left us, when we used to take walks, just the two of us. We went to Prospect Park, near my house in Brooklyn. He didn't talk at all, and we sat down on a bench together in silence. I was starting to get restless when all of a sudden I saw this kid from school, a kid who was always on my case, a bully. I sat tight because I knew that if I got up we'd just have to fight. This kid turned out to be with his father, someone who knew my father.

"Sasha, you godless Bolshevik," called the man to my father, "how're you feeding your family these days?"

"You got work?" As it turned out, my father had worked for the man, someone who might pass for a petty capitalist overlord in the rubric of the *Daily Worker*.

"Oh, I don't know. Maybe. Maybe not. Let's go to the pavilion for a beer and I'll see if I can't come up with something."

So in they went, and his boy gave me an evil smirk. Didn't say anything. Chucked pebbles at me. I sat on the ground, closed my eyes, felt the sting. Soon enough my dad came out, beer in hand, with this kid's old man. The kid's father was smiling; mine was stone.

"Hey Billy," the man called to his son. "I got a bet here with Sasha that my boy can lick his boy."

And Billy was on me like a cat. But soon enough, I got up, kicked him in the stomach, knocked him down. My stone-faced old man didn't seem to be rooting for me. "No kicking," he said.

And Billy was there again, clawing, spitting, raging. I tried boxing, but he just came in. I got in another kick, knocked him down again. At this point my father interceded, took me aside. Eyes shut, he whispered: "Don't kick. Now you must let him knock you down."

"Daddy!"

"Let him."

And Billy was back, windmilling. I meant to put up my hands, but he caught me, just under the right eye. I went down. There didn't seem to be much point in getting up. So I cried. It was clear to me, then, the nature of the "bet" my father made with Billy's father. Like Charlie in *On the Waterfront*, he sold me out, set me up to get beaten and humiliated. His humiliation became mine. The truth is I don't even know if my father got whatever job the man claimed he'd get after I was beaten up. My father, possibly out of shame, wouldn't even look at me then. After that, I didn't see him for a long, long time.

You might imagine this to be irrational, but I blame McCarthy for that too. It was McCarthy and his brethren who put my father into such desperate straits that he was willing to use me like a pit bull. It didn't matter if I'd managed to kick that kid's butt or not. My father, and by extension our family, was already lost.

Now, you might dispute all this, and wonder why my little saga of life under McCarthyism matters much in the scope of all the other miserable things this man did during his brief but bilious reign as America's Grand Inquisitor. Certainly McCarthy ruined the lives of other, possibly grander personages than my father. It is possible that my father could have called upon other resources, dug deep within himself to overcome the oppressive failure he encountered. You might even say that he was psyched out by McCarthy, that McCarthy and the sway he held over many frightened, paranoid, immigrant-hating people in this country was at least partially in my father's head.

You might think that. But to be sure, the existence of Joseph McCarthy and the sleazy ethic he imbued didn't do my father any good, especially when all Dad wanted to be was a good American.

There is something of a happy ending to all this, since my father has managed to survive. He just turned ninety-two and lives in Miami. Whether due to many years of drinking, or simply old age, his thinking and memory are not so clear. This has its upside. Each year, along with his memory, he loses some of his bitterness. Recently, when I visited him at the adult home where he lives, he couldn't even remember being blacklisted. His memory of life as a workingman without work has passed from him as have recollections of visits from the FBI. The name McCarthy, which used to elicit a torrent of cursing, draws a bemused blank. Each year he is a little purer, a little closer to heaven, forgetting as he sits in the warm Miami sun while McCarthy, dead at age forty-eight from a nerve disorder exacerbated by alcohol abuse, rots in the dirt. So maybe there is a God, after all.

Roy Cohn
✳
BY TOM GOGOLA

I'VE BEEN FASCINATED with Roy Cohn since the early 1980s, when I was a suburban teenager out in the tri-state hinterlands possessed of a reactionary anti-Communist streak and an unfortunate appreciation for the go-team politics of Ronald Reagan. Despite those long-discarded tendencies and allegiances, I actually got to know the bold-face Cohn before I knew about his anti-Commie activities in the McCarthy and J. Edgar Hoover eras. As a delivery boy for the *Daily News* and an avid newspaper reader, and a potential future lawyer, I saw Cohn as, if not a hero, at least a person to be looked up to, to emulate, even: Who knew you could be a lawyer and a celebrity too!? This Cohn I learned about not from the news pages but the gossip pages, Liz Smith and Suzy, Page Six, and Cindy Adams. To me, he was all about glitz and access and power and fun. He was suave and sharp, and seemed to be everywhere at once, all the time—a rich and famous lawyer to the rich and famous.

If there were hints of a darker Cohn lurking behind those jaunty blurbs about power lunches and book parties and birthday bashes at Sardi's, they were lost on me. So of course when he died in 1986 of AIDS-related cancer I was shocked and mortified and freaked out. I had absolutely no idea that he was gay, that he was as hated as he was by many of those with whom he shared gossip-column inches, or that he had earned said hatred through the pinko putsches of the anti-Communist witch-hunt era.

The fearsome Cohn died, the gloves came off, and there was nobody to stem the tide of bitter glee that attended his death in some circles. Nicholas Von Hoffman's startling biography came out and I greedily read it. HBO did a teleproduction of his life starring James Woods, and I lapped it up. By then I was in college; all my teenage right-wing posturing went up in smoke, in the manner pre-scribed by Cheech and Chong, and before long I was dipping, and then diving, into the history of the American left. I bring this up because I've long been laboring under the assumption that everybody on the left must know who Roy Cohn was. Not true. As I was working on this piece, I engaged a Jewish Communist friend on the subject, and despite his being proudly bathed in the blood of Bolshevism, Cohn's name elicited from him a blank look and shrugging shoulders.

But even with all the facts at my disposal, I've never been able to hate Cohn with the same viscerality with which he is hated by those on the left who grew up with the blacklists and HUAC and book-burnings. It is a generational thing, mostly, and also because no one really gave a goddamn in the eighties if you were a self-described Communist; it just meant more gravy from the supply-side train for them, and too bad for you, Retrograde Red. The formerly dead-serious consequences of such a proclamation were totally lost on that generation, and by then, Cohn had, while not disavowing his previous anti-Communism, which he never did, aligned himself with Disco Duck and his pink-tinged excesses and *in flagrante* exhibitions. 'Twas a muddle indeed, and no surprise that cognitive dissonance would strike me after his death. But the lessons from the McCarthy era are obviously in play in the present anti-terror era, with its abridgements of liberty, the onslaught of Patriot Acts, and the rest of it. We are clearly in an age where the lessons of Santayana's repeating-history aphorism must be learned, all over again.

There are a couple of tropes worth considering when it comes to puzzling out the paradoxes embodied by Roy Cohn. The first is the temptation to proclaim him as one of those people that history would need to have invented had he not been the real deal. This argument falls apart for the simple reason that what demented imagination could possibly have come up with a figure like Cohn? The fiction that has been written with Cohn in a starring role—most notably Tony Kushner's elegiac and masterful *Angels in America*—does not stray from the facts of Cohn's life even as it is fictionalized. If anything, these are delicious, if not necessarily nutritious, cold-dishing revenge fugues, and proof that you couldn't make this shit up if you tried.

Indeed, there are no figures on the contemporary scene that can rival Roy Cohn for sheer malignant chutzpah and theatrical malfeasance in the first degree. There are scumbags, to be sure, but they just don't have that aura about them, that built-in circus of paradoxical perversion and well-deserved notoriety. There's no one that makes you go, "Ooooooooooooh, he's scary." You've got bloviating bimbos such as Ann Coulter foaming at the apparently Botox-enhanced pout about the glorious Joe McCarthy, but she has only Bill O'Reilly and the limited power of her own invective to back her up. And no one will tell O'Reilly to stop dropping his pencil so he can look up her skirt—they need each other as a shark needs a remora, and freely switch roles as circumstances dictate. It's a disgusting spectacle, but spectacle is as far as it goes. Cohn had invective, intellect, a killer instinct, the power of subpoena, friendly judges, Mafioso, his mom and dad, and the weight of the blueblood establishment (up to a point) backing him up across the span of his entire lifetime. Cohn's position in the culture was such that he could scorn the establishment from one side of his faux-populist, pro–little guy mouth even as he suckled the power structure from the other, and get away with it again and again.

Cohn did not spin conspiracy theories out of Washington suicides, as the woefully inadequate heirs to his throne tried to do after the Vince Foster tragedy; he prompted suicides based on the Commie conspiracy, a much more insidious and craven abuse of power. He was able to strong-arm Judge Irving Kaufman, via wildly inappropriate ex parte communications, to sentence Ethel Rosenberg to the death penalty instead of life. That's power, my friends. Coulter, O'Reilly, David Brock, Matt Drudge, John Fund, Pill-poppin' Rush Limbaugh, John Ashcroft, David Brooks, William "Know When to Fold 'Em" Bennett, and the Gollum character from the *Lord of the Rings* trilogy—stick 'em all in a blender and you might come close to the lethal margarita that was Roy Cohn.

The other trope is one that figures Cohn as a victim, both of anti-Semitism and homophobia, and explains, if not explains-away, his reprehensible blackmail tactics of the 1950s. I've been exposed to a peculiar whiff of this argument coming from that portion of the left that is slowly driving itself into extinction with its relentless, true-believer fixation on identity politics as the be-all-end-all. Somehow Cohn is to be provisionally pitied for his reaction(ary)-formation in the face of potential persecution. The trouble with this positionality is that, even if you believe Cohn reacted out of a fear of being outed as a gay man—certain death in 1950s America, if not literal, then at least professional—by all indications, Roy Cohn never once considered himself to actually be a gay man. Despite the fact that he had sex with men. D'oh! If anything, one might argue Cohn was way ahead of the sexual-politics curve in this regard, unwittingly of course; his actions did not dictate or codify his identity, in fact, it was vice versa. Whatever you might think of that theory, hypocrisy in the service of self-protection was the least of Roy Cohn's sins. In the end, it really doesn't make a difference one way or the other if he and David Schine were, in fact, teabagging along the Thames during their infamous 1950s European book-burning tour. Whether he was gay or not, his actions on behalf of McCarthy and Hoover alone earned him the eternal crumbum sobriquet, for sure. And, besides, as far as I can tell, Roy Cohn never put himself forward as a champion of anything other than himself and his chosen cause célèbres. The fact is, Roy Cohn was gay! gay! gay! And increasingly flagrant about his "lifestyle" ("their" word) as the years went by, as indicated by his biographers.

All the insiders knew it, his pal Barbara Walters knew it, and as he made his way through the swinging seventies, putting his time in at Studio 54 like every other hip New Yorker of the era, anyone who saw him in action knew it, too. And yet he managed to keep this a "secret" from the masses for his whole life. That's how scary, and influential, and persuasive he was. The catechisms of the cult of personality protected him, and his main redeeming quality— a fetishistic obsession with loyalty—seemed to keep his pals on the gossip pages from ever wink-winking at his expense.

As his biographers have noted, he actively fought against attempts to "out" him, used his power to persecute those who dared push the envelope on this issue, and, as is well-reported, went so far as to actively campaign against gay-rights legislation in New York City in the last years of his life. What did he care—he didn't need the extra protection. Well . . . that's not exactly true: He could have used a Trojan. The point is, Cohn was hell-bent on keeping his private life private, as was his right—even if it meant he was hell-bound. Like it or not, that right was not abridged because he chose to persecute others based on their personal ideological convictions. The closet he occupied, besides being neon lit, as Sidney Zion writes in his Cohn biography, also had a back door through which he could escape if the "fags," as he reportedly liked to call "them," got wind of his double-life deceit. He was above all, a Master of Deceit, and a back-door man in all manner of the expression.

As for the notion that he was victimized as well by anti-Semitism, there is no denying that Hate-the-Jew is an old and vicious pastime in this country. But let's get real here: Roy Cohn enjoyed class privilege, cultural privilege, and political privilege for his entire life. He used this privilege, for example, to jump to the head of the line and help himself to ample quantities of the life-extending AZT treatment, even as he denied having AIDS in the first place. He truly thought his life was more valuable than mine or yours, and so, fuck him for all eternity. I find him to be a repulsive figure not because he was a bad Jew, or a hypocritical homosexual, but because of his bragging about his precocious, privileged, mama's-boy status. His father was a powerful judge, his mother came from old money, and Cohn at an early age was forming alliances with all of the major and minor power brokers of the time, from the gossip columnists to the Tammany politicos. His Uncle Bernie Marcus may well have been victimized by anti-Semitism, and railroaded into prison over trumped up charges, but in order to claim victim status, you yourself have to prove that there was some horrible outcome to your life because of the actions of others. And for Roy Cohn, there simply wasn't any consequence, at least not until the last few years of his life, when he faced disbarment and death. Both being inevitabilities in his case. America may well have been, and may well continue to be, a Jew Hating Nation at heart, but there's no possible way to excuse his behavior in convincing Kaufman to execute Ethel Rosenberg, as one might excuse the desperate decisions made by, say, Jewish collaborators in the Warsaw Ghetto, circa 1942. You can understand the latter act of self-preservation. Better them than me, right? But Roy Cohn felt no survivor's guilt after they fried Ethel; in fact, in his autobiography he actually brags about his influence over the judge. So, no, Roy Cohn was no victim, and to trumpet him as such, or to even hint at some reaction-formation explanation for his behavior over the years, is nothing less than a disgraceful insult to those gays and Jews who actually were humiliated, persecuted, and murdered based on their status.

Richard M. Nixon

✳

BY TODD GITLIN

THE FIRST PRESIDENT to grow up in Southern California, Richard Nixon was a rootless man, solitary, unanchored, and harsh, devoid of interests beyond politics and sports.

He made and remade himself repeatedly as he clambered to power, as cunning as he was insecure. He rose from Congress to the Senate to the vice presidency and eventually to the White House on the strength of fervent anti-Communism, along the way attacking President Truman as "a graduate of Dean Acheson's Cowardly College of Communist Containment." Later, during his presidency, he welcomed Acheson as a valued adviser—and heard the former secretary of state urge him not to negotiate with Communist Russia or China, both of which Nixon proceeded to negotiate with. He prolonged the Vietnam War for more than five years—longer than any of his predecessors—while proclaiming his commitment to achieving "peace with honor," meaning peace with bombardment. He accelerated the air war while withdrawing American troops, thus keeping the war off the TV screen. While responsible for the heaviest air assaults in history, all directed against Communist countries, he was the first American president to visit other Communist countries and bargain with their rulers, masterfully playing China against the USSR and the USSR against China. After he fell from power, he remained an admired statesman in the eyes of the ruling classes of these two great Communist powers.

Throughout almost forty years in politics, through many downfalls and the crises he cherished as tests of his own nerve, he lashed himself to the mast of his own ambition. Often tiptoeing at the edge of a precipice, he understood his life as a series of crises (*Six Crises* was his first book). As a writer and speaker he was graceless, but he was one of America's most intelligent presidents, writing draft after draft of his most important speeches, committing the final versions to memory. In law school, he was renowned for his "iron butt." He prided himself on his intellect, his mastery of big pictures and tiny details alike. He was physically awkward and puritanical, indifferent to style, though he learned to appreciate fine French wines. Austere, he permitted himself five minutes for breakfast, five for lunch (usually cottage cheese). In the middle of his first term as president, he recorded this memo to himself: "Stop recreation except purely for exercise."

In 1952, General Eisenhower chose him for his running mate, largely on the strength of Nixon's successful crusade to see the State Department official Alger Hiss tried as a Soviet spy. (Excoriated by liberals, Nixon was probably right that time.) When Eisenhower seemed ready to dump him because he was charged with availing himself of a businessmen's slush fund, Nixon surprised everyone by coming back from political death. He narrowly lost his first run for the presidency, against John F. Kennedy in 1960, possibly on the strength of stolen votes in Illinois. He lost his next race two years later, for the California governorship, and famously told reporters they wouldn't "have Nixon to kick around anymore." But he was indefatigable. In 1968, he won the presidency with less than 44 percent of the vote, thanks to the third-party candidacy of George Wallace, who won 13 percent. Nixon then won for the second time by the largest margin in American history, winning over 60 percent of the popular vote, and 49 states, against George McGovern in 1972.

Lose or win, he was obsessed by the Kennedys, spoke of them every day. He hated "the establishment." He told Garry Wills he despised "people just lying around at Palm Beach." (Once in the White House he said: "The elite have been showing signs of decadence and weakness; the more people who are educated the more likely we are to become brighter in the head but weaker in the spine.") He reviled "the Jews" and held blacks to be genetically inferior. "God," he said once, "I hate spending time with intellectuals. There's something feminine about them." He wore, Wills wrote, "a permanent air of violation." In private and sometimes in public, he was a man of fathomless bitterness and deviousness.

Nixon, the most secretive of presidents (until George W. Bush), left the most extensive records yet of the White House's inner workings: the tape recordings that brought his administration crashing down; extensive notes by Nixon and others; documents proving that, among other things, he authorized thirteen months of secret bombing missions over Cambodia in 1969 and 1970, keeping phony records to disguise them as missions confined to Vietnam. Nixon, with a clear sense of his historic importance, ended up leaving a voluminous record of his own pathology: his spitefulness, pettiness, corruption, drunkenness, explosive rage, and compounded lies. "I gave them a sword," he ended up saying of his enemies. Yet he seems never to have hesitated in his ruthlessness—the very ruthlessness that undermined him and made his name to this day synonymous with both destructive deceit and self-destruction.

Purporting to celebrate the common people, he left ample evidence of his contempt for most of their political concerns —"building outhouses in Peoria" was a term he used for domestic questions. He turned much of domestic policy over to his staff. Yet in office, he accommodated the concerns of liberals, supporting guaranteed income, affirmative action, environmental reform, price controls, and other such policies, in order to woo Democrats away from their party, isolate the far left, and piece together an enduring Republican majority.

Early in his political career, his deviousness earned him the epithet "Tricky Dick," but he turned his flexibility to his advantage, reconstituting himself after repeated early downfalls and devising reincarnations as a "new Nixon." When, in 1952, as General Eisenhower's running-mate, he came under fire for corruption, he saved his political career by appealing on television for sympathy as a lover of dogs, family, and good Republican cloth coats, making the first significant political use of the small screen for impression management. Out-debated and out-impressioned by John F. Kennedy in the presidential campaign debates of 1960, he came back eight years later with the first successful use of pseudo-documentary techniques in political commercials.

His deviousness extended to global maneuvers on a potentially catastrophic scale. He manipulated the South Vietnamese leadership to help him win election in 1968, and manipulated them again in order to betray them when making deferred peace in 1972 and 1973. He relished the idea of acting erratically in order to convince enemies—like North Vietnam—that he was a madman whom it would be wiser to obey than to resist. In 1969, he ordered American nuclear bombers onto full alert so that Soviet spies would notify the North Vietnamese and they would feel a full measure of fear. He pulverized Hanoi with the Christmas bombing of 1972 in order to win points at the bargaining table. During his presidency, as he proclaimed that the United States was on its way out of Vietnam, his armed forces were responsible for the deaths of more than a million, possibly two million, Vietnamese. As he planned the invasion of Cambodia in 1970, he said privately: "Troop withdrawal was a boy's job. Cambodia is a man's job."

Insecurity ruled him. At the height of his political success, he was constantly scheming for future advantage. Thus, for example, he devoted much political energy in his second term to ensuring that George Wallace would not again run as an independent and deprive him of an electoral majority. He kept enemies lists. No sooner did he take up residence in the White House than he set up an independent reelection campaign apparatus outside the Republican National Committee and proceeded to collect funds for use in his second presidential election. Here was one starting point for the concatenation of crimes and corruptions that became known collectively as Watergate.

His paranoia made him a great overreacher. His impeachment might not have been feasible but for the elaborate taping system he himself installed in the White House. Obsessed by the antiwar movement, he approved many crimes, some of which were carried out (burglaries, assaults, fund diversions, tax investigations) and others of which were not (firebombing). Toward this end, he housed a clandestine mayhem squad (the "Plumbers") in the White House itself. He inspired both great loyalty and great scheming from his staff, and proved willing to fire those closest to him.

He was the first president to see his vice president, Spiro Agnew, resign because of corruption. Facing impeachment, he became the first president to resign. Succeeding in being pardoned by his successor, Gerald Ford, he lived twenty more years, writing books, nursing resentments, striving to rise above them, and cultivating a reputation as elder statesman.

✳   ✳   ✳

Henry Kissinger

※

BY CHRISTOPHER HITCHENS

ERROL MORRIS'S PRAISEWORTHY if lenient documentary *The Fog of War* occupied a good deal of attention during the fall of 2003 and spring of 2004, not so much for what it disclosed about the hidden history of the Vietnam War but for what it suggested about the personality of Robert McNamara. Here was a former senior statesman, prickly no doubt and still vain to a certain degree, who nonetheless felt that he owed his fellow citizens something by way of an explanation. He had prolonged a hideous war in which he had privately ceased to believe, and had suffered some agonies of conscience and reflection as a consequence. I don't wish to exaggerate this—I was at one point scheduled to introduce the former secretary of defense at a public forum following the film's Telluride premiere, and found him hearty and canny enough when we chatted by phone—but McNamara has also added to our store of knowledge about the near-catastrophe of the 1962 Cuban missile crisis, and together with co-veterans William Colby and McGeorge Bundy took an active interest in detente and disarmament, along with the requisite moral self-scrutiny, in the 1980s.

Contrast this relative frankness and disclosure with the figure of Henry Kissinger. Twice in the recent past, when asked by interviewers about his role in the events in Cambodia and Chile, he has either walked off the set or exploded in pique (and this is only at the British Broadcasting Corporation). In the United States, he almost never "grants" an interview except with pre-selected questioners and pre-determined questions. He has published volumes of memoirs, based on state papers appropriated and monopolized by himself, which the passage of time has shown to be riddled with self-serving falsifications. He has bristled at the suggestion that his syndicated column should identify him as the representative of corporations that have an interest in the questions he "discusses." (The *Washington Post* finally agreed to do this, after several of his articles defended the trade relationship with China, but only after complaints from congressmen.) And, when offered the high honor of chairmanship of the commission to investigate the atrocities of September 11, 2001, he first accepted and then—when it became evident that he would have to publish the client list of Kissinger Associates— abruptly withdrew his name.

Of those who were involved in the coup against the United States Constitution that bears the generic name of "Watergate," he is the only one to have escaped prosecution. He helped to prosecute the illegal and secret war that led to the bugging and harassment of dissenters within the government, and he also helped to initiate and forward the illegal bugging itself. Nixon had to accept a "pardon" to avoid impeachment, Agnew had to resign and face prosecution for corruption, and Attorney General Mitchell actually went to jail. But Kissinger survived, and continues to peddle a mendacious version of those events. Of the dictators he helped to install, or whose vicious rule he helped prolong, almost all are in jail or are avoiding indictment on the grounds of mental or physical incapacity. Just look at the list of his "partners." Brigadier Ioannides and Colonel Papadopoulos of Greece were imprisoned for life, convicted of torture and murder and subversion of democracy.

General Jorge Videla of Argentina is in prison for similar crimes, but also for the fairly distinctive one of selling the babies of the rape victims in his secret jails. General Pinochet of Chile was indicted in his own country as well as in Europe, for kidnap and torture and murder, and escaped trial because his democratic successors were more merciful than he had ever been when he pled old age and infirmity. General Suharto of Indonesia avoided prosecution on charges of massive corruption and brutality because he, too, went from supreme power to an opportunistic claim of mental and physical incompetence. What a crew! And of this second gallery of thugs, Henry Kissinger is once again the last man standing. (In the case of General Suharto, a full inquiry would also have shown a vast Kissinger presence on the boards of Indonesia's army-run "crony capitalism.")

There are those who still say that Kissinger may have been ruthless in his time but that the Cold War was not for the faint-hearted. What merit does this claim possess? In the first place, it was noticeable that Kissinger in office was always flattering to Leonid Brezhnev and Mao Zedong, and always ready to bargain with them. He sternly opposed any attempt by the Senate to link the plight of Soviet Jewry to his top-table dealings. He successfully prevented President Ford from receiving Aleksandr Solzhenitsyn at the White House, for the same reason. And he was the only American of any stature to defend the Chinese Communist Party's decision to massacre the students of Tiananmen Square in the spring of 1989. (Given the number of senior Party members who have since called for a renunciation of this atrocity, this makes Kissinger an ultra-reactionary even in Stalinist terms.) He was also the leading advocate of non-intervention against Slobodan Milosevic during the bloody campaign for an ethnically-cleansed "Greater Serbia." In the latter two cases, interests represented by Kissinger Associates helped to dictate his public line, because he does now have a second career as "facilitator" between dictatorships and the corporations who love them. This consideration should not obscure the main point that in Henry Kissinger we have a man who managed to be soft on fascism *and* soft on Communism, often both at the same time.

A slightly less confident defense argues that realpolitik is not for the squeamish, and that eggs must be broken if omelettes are to be made. One can see the smashed eggs but where, please, is the omelette? How were Cambodia and Laos and Vietnam ameliorated by Kissinger's attentions? What improvement was made to Chile by the twenty-year interruption of its (now-restored) tradition of democratic elections? The Cyprus imbroglio of 1974 led to mass death and dispossession on the island itself, to a near-war between two NATO countries, and to an unworkable partition which has wasted more than a quarter-century of everybody's time before being partially undone. Where is the success here, pray tell? And perhaps it can be explained to the simple-minded how the near-extirpation of the people of East Timor helped advance the development of Indonesia, or indeed to arrest the spread of Communism. Sometimes one can trace a definite result from Kissinger's panicky and high-handed interventions: his helping to start a tribal war in Angola, for example, probably accelerated the collapse of the South African apartheid regime that he was trying to protect. However, it undoubtedly retarded the post-colonial life of Angola by a mutilated generation or two. This is not statesmanship, of the old-school Bismarckian or Metternichian type. It doesn't pragmatically stabilize the "balance of power." It fiddles angrily with it for a brief moment and then walks away as "deniably" as possible from the carnage and disaster.

And then the lies . . . Kissinger told the readers of his memoirs that he had not known, even though he was in the same room, that General Suharto planned to send Indonesian forces across the Timorese border the next day. But declassified documents have caught up with his perjured account, obviated the authority of his purloined state papers, and shown that he was an intimate partner in the planning of the illegal aggression. Kissinger assured the Congress of the United States that he had made available all the relevant papers in the matter of the military coup in Chile, but an initiative by Congressman Maurice Hinchey of New York, decades later, was required to bring the actual documents to the light of day—and they tell a very different story. If the Kissinger memoirs had been written by a working professor instead of a pseudo-academic and full-time lobbyist, he would have been fired.

To pseudo-academic and lobbyist and apologist, and re-writer of history, one could add the role of socialite. The lure of the gala and the black tie and the flashbulb still seems as magnetic as ever it did, when he was a celebrity "walker" for starlets and media babes. (The "action" in these cases, according to all informed reports, ceased when the cameras were turned off.) Kissinger even managed to contrive a relationship as some kind of foreign policy "advisor" to Princess Diana, the uncrowned queen of the celeb universe, and made an ostentatious appearance at her funeral. Perhaps one should not object to the rubbing of shoulders, the pressing of flesh and the rest of it: he is as entitled as anyone else to seek amusement and distraction in this way. However, one did not see Robert McNamara or William Colby ceaselessly courting the glare of fashion in such a manner. Perhaps they even thought, with so many deaths to explain or justify, that there would be something a little inappropriate, even macabre, in constant resort to high society and Park Avenue glitz. What is made apparent, by his vulgar pursuit of renown in this department, is that Kissinger has no conscience, no sense of embarrassment, no feeling of remorse let alone of shame.

And this is horrifyingly impressive from any point of view. Even if Kissinger can persuade himself that the secret war in Cambodia was justified, he must still "know" at some level that he ordered the killing of many thousands of people. He must be aware of the gigantic loss of life in East Timor. And on a micro-scale, he must remember that he ordered the elimination of named individuals—General Rene Schneider of Chile, for example, or Archbishop Makarios of Cyprus—who stood in his way. It's one thing to soberly accept responsibility for such things, and another to be seen making jokes about "power as an aphrodisiac" (not his original formulation, though he likes to take credit for it) while surrounded by empty-headed and sycophantic hostesses.

Of course, where he can, Kissinger tries to avoid the "credit." He attempted with some success to prevent subordinates from testifying about Cyprus and Chile, and has personally refused to answer questions from magistrates in three democratic countries (Argentina, Chile and France) who have sought his testimony in cases of torture, murder and "disappearance." Suddenly, his love for the limelight

deserts him and he shrinks away, cowering behind a bat-
tery of lawyers. Let us just remember, though, that these
inquiries came from people who are seeking to know the
whereabouts of their loved ones; people who have been
living in a hell of uncertainty and fear for many decades.
Our hero could help them to clarify much that is unknown,
but he hoards the documents or tries to put them under
seal (having extracted his ration of profit from their selective publication) and knowingly prolongs the misery.

It is altogether right that, in the presidential campaign
of 2004, American society should still be preoccupied
with what happened in Vietnam, and with the abuses of
power at home that allowed the continuation of an
already evil war overseas. Now would be the perfect
moment to reopen the hearings that Congress once held
on this grave issue. We now know, from the memoirs and
confessions of many participants, what Congress then
could not. We know that in 1968, envoys of the Nixon
presidential campaign went behind the back of the
Johnson-Humphrey administration, and deliberately,
covertly, sabotaged the peace negotiations then in
progress in Paris. They offered the South Vietnamese
junta a better deal if it would withdraw from the talks
on election eve, which it did. For his part in this treach-
erous undertaking (he had been Nixon's "mole" in the
American delegation in Paris) Kissinger was rewarded
with high office in a cabinet that imploded in corruption
after protracting and widening the war, and then settling
it on the same terms that had been available in 1968. It
was in those years of shame that John Kerry was
deployed to commit the atrocities at which he later
protested. Those whose names appear on the Vietnam

memorial after January 1969, and those Vietnamese, Cambodians, and Laotians whose names would fill more walls than we can bear to think about, were immolated for the vanity and greed and reputation of Richard Nixon and Henry Kissinger, and at least we can claim that their blood still troubles us a little.

There will be no "healing" of that appalling wound if Henry Kissinger is allowed to end his career unindicted. He has disfigured and befouled the planet with his war crimes, and has done serious damage to the United States Constitution into the bargain. He is a liar, a coward and a murderer, and a falsifier of history. Is there, then, no decency at last? It is purely indecent to have to think of him alive—and prosperous, and smug, and feted—with all those good people dead.

George W. Bush

BY TODD GITLIN

THE ASCENDANCY OF George W. Bush was an earthquake of historic proportions. A rupture of such consequence may have the look of a freak of nature—a product of Florida shenanigans, Al Gore's campaign feebleness, Ralph Nader's megalomania, and other oddities. But as in nature, a political earthquake is a convulsion with a history. It's a surprise that, on further inspection, isn't wholly surprising.

The 2000 victory of George W. Bush in the Electoral College and the Supreme Court of the United States was at once the triumph of a political dynamo and the ascendancy of an idea about America. The dynamo was impressive by itself. It was a long-term strategic merger of fundamentalist Christians and business interests, a merger secured in the late 1970s and consolidated during the Reagan presidency, generating a stupendous fundraising machine and a supply of passionate activists. Both moralist restoration and corporate priorities represented rollbacks against progressive achievements. The latter, exemplified by Bush's emphasis on tort reform starting during his successful campaign for the governorship of Texas against the Democrat Ann Richards in 1994, generated vast campaign funds—a total of $4.1 million from corporations and individuals connected with corporate tort reform efforts for his two gubernatorial campaigns. Bush rewarded these interests with seven tort reform laws passed during his first legislative session.

The Bush-Cheney team in 2000 was an unusually pure distillation of corporate privilege. As Rob Reiner said during the 2000 campaign, "Who said the Republican ticket doesn't respect diversity? They represent *two different* oil companies!" Bush and Cheney were exemplars of crony capitalism at its crudest, and their policies in office, not surprisingly, systematically siphoned money out of the hands of the majority and into corporate treasuries. For its profits, oil is strikingly dependent on government subsidies, of which the oil depletion allowance is a conspicuous example. For Bush, trickle-down economics is more than an ideology; it is a way of life. His oil experience, even more than his father's, consists of failing upward—investing other people's (cronies' and relatives') money, parlaying old school and family networks into a reputation for connections, which in turn bought him access to still more funds even as his oil ventures didn't pan out. He likewise parlayed connections into a bargain-basement, vastly profitable purchase of the Texas Rangers, his principal administrative achievement before reaching the Texas governor's mansion.

Meanwhile, the Republicans' moral restoration crusade, exemplified by Bush's February 2004 endorsement of a constitutional amendment to ban gay marriage, generated a different sort of payoff: generating vast resentment on the part of millenarian cadres. That they would have trouble actually rolling back decades of cultural liberalization would not deprive them of political usefulness. To the contrary: Their frustration (failure to reverse Supreme Court decisions restricting school prayer and Bible readings, failure to repeal the crudities of popular culture, failure to drive Bill Clinton from office) would only fuel their passion to drive the infidels from Washington.

The right's business-moralist merger, linked with a disingenuous appeal to "compassionate conservatism" and "changing the tone in Washington," achieved the Republican nomination for the young Bush after a decidedly flimsy political career; and continued with victory in the Florida debacle; and subsequent triumphs in the 2002 midterm elections, in redistricting battles, in fights over Medicare and other issues. Once in power, Bush's machine corralled Republicans in Congress and won victories in foreign policy, tax policy, environmental policy, and virtually every other sphere of governance.

But an organizational dynamo could not have managed this immense transformation all by itself. To win an election— even, in the last resort, thanks to the Supreme Court's unprecedented intervention—was a managerial achievement of impressive proportions. But the rules of politics require more than adroit strategizing and organizational discipline. Politics is personal. George W. Bush could not have been elected president, or retained such popularity as he has retained, if he had not—at least in appearance—embodied images, moods, and ideas that many Americans harbor about themselves and their country. He was not only American, he was *America's*. These are not the only images, moods, and ideas about America, and they are not necessarily the most popular ones—Bush fell 550,000 votes short of that mark—but they are colossal.

1. The populist

This son of dynastic privilege is not completely a fraud—though he embellishes the down-home side of his résumé, as in his repeated insistence that (in contrast to Al Gore, who attended Washington's exclusive, private St. Albans School) he attended San Jacinto Junior High School, when he did so for all of one year before heading off to board at Andover. As a child of privilege, he identifies with "the little guy" in the strained, self-protective way that only an anxious dynast can do. It is not incidental to his sense of himself that he understands himself that way. The worshipful son of a hypersuccessful father, who was in turn the son of a United States Senator and the grandson of industrial and financial tycoons, young Bush grew up *feeling* like "the little guy." At Yale, Class of 1968, he belonged to a social upper crust that was in the process of being displaced by smarter, more accomplished public school graduates and '68ers—a big guy brought low, as if he were nothing more than a little guy after all. (His Yale fraternity rushed four hundred boys during his sophomore year but barely

half that number the next year.) His sincerity about being
one of the little guys is mixed with resentment against "elitists" and "snobs" who wouldn't know how to appreciate an
erstwhile head cheerleader or fraternity schmoozer.

2. The down-to-earth man of action

Bush frequently expressed his disdain for complexity: "I
haven't thought about the nuance of it." "Look, my job
isn't to try to nuance. My job is to tell people what I think."
During the 2000 campaign, Bush's ignorance of the names
of foreign leaders became journalists' prime story line on
him. This placed the bar so low that all Bush had to do was
rattle off a few facts, or factesque claims, to perform
"above expectations." There was no political problem in
his lacking facts. To the contrary: His ignorance ingratiated him with uneducated voters, especially white men. To
his supporters, Bush's simple-mindedness was not an
impediment. His impatience with complexity signified
that he knew—viscerally—what really counted. The
enemy consisted of fancy-ass cloud-sitting nuance-prone
elitists, but he knew how things really were, which is what
kept him down to earth and gave him the assurance of
moral clarity. His native hue of resolution was never sick-
lied o'er with the pale cast of thought. Bush the plain-
talking man of action was perfectly tailored to morph into
Bush the war president.

The press's line on Bush in 2000—genial if factually
challenged—missed the point about both his incapacities.
He was unreasonable but shrewd, self-deluding and mendacious as required. As in the case of Iraq's purported
weapons of mass destruction, his intuition was a substitute
for both evidence and logic. In presidential campaign

debates, in press conferences and in rare interviews, he never displayed reason, never sorted through alternative hypotheses to form a conclusion. Former treasury secretary Paul O'Neill told reporter Ron Suskind that Bush seemed utterly uninterested in debate among his advisers. Things were so, in other words, because he knew they were so. "With his level of experience," the pragmatist O'Neill told Suskind (as quoted in *The Price of Loyalty*), "I would not be able to support his level of conviction." Bush did not ask questions, even of his senior staff. He did not read reports— or even O'Neill's short memos. According to Christine Todd Whitman, his EPA chief, he did not explain himself, did not (according to Suskind) "analyze a complex issue, parse opposing positions, and settle on a judicious path. In fact, no one—inside or outside the government, here or across the globe—had heard him do that to any significant degree."

Was this because Bush knew how to remain "on message?" More likely, it was the other way around: Bush stayed "on message" because he dared not deviate. He stayed on course because a single swerve would threaten to wipe out the course altogether.

3. The good old boy

In Bush's world, to be manly and moral is to be visceral. You know what to do by surrounding yourself with people who appear to follow your lead even when you are following theirs. As a crony capitalist, Bush was like a gambler with a free draw. Intuition was his forte in the oil business, even if it struck no gushers.

Since at least his time cheerleading at Andover, George W. Bush made friends—buddies, at any rate. He was skilled, like his father, at remembering names and faces.

From prep school head cheerleader and Yale fraternity chief onward, he was in the habit of affixing nicknames on everyone he has ever met, apparently—a habit that diminished everyone he knew and established his power and superiority. He enjoyed teasing, evidently more than being teased. Until he gave up drinking at age forty (or so he claimed), he had a well-known heroic capacity for partying. These skills suited him well for a career in crony capitalism, where success is a confidence game in which the players are willing to pay for the rewards they expect to accrue to the right company. They also suited him well for political ascendancy in a state whose governors are deprived of great powers and whose social functions are therefore especially significant.

4. The sinner saved

Bush's official personal story is one of redemption earned, salvation achieved by force of will, thus a proof of his character. Whatever advantages he began with, he dissipated through youthful recklessness, so he was no longer burdened by privilege—after all, he squandered its advantages. Having recovered, however, he emerged as a man like all men: a sinner humbled, reclaimed, reborn, reinvented—truly self-made.

Christianity without suffering, regeneration without sacrifice—this is not Christianity in the spirit of the New Testament, but rather, a clarion call to "fundamental" (a word he likes to repeat) values. His gospel validates the authority of the father, the minister, and the commander-in-chief. It is a gospel at peace with a social Darwinist vision of social rewards. It affirms that, by and large, people achieve their just desserts.

5. The lucky man.

Bush is no fool. He knows he is a dynast, not even close to a self-made man. Yet this doesn't undermine his popularity. People admire the lucky and feel cared for by the grace of dynastic succession. Luck is a testament to the value of optimism, and optimism has the texture of an American religion. When people acknowledge that the world is run by "lucky devils," they defend against the sinking knowledge of their own failure. They recognize that the world is unfair and at the same time protect themselves from caustic resentment.

It isn't hard to establish that Bush has done yeoman service for the wealthy. But his plutocratic policies are reasonably popular—until they fail the pragmatic test and do not produce jobs—because a considerable number of voters identify with the overprivileged. They are in thrall to their optimism.

6. The sportsman

Whether Bush became chief managing partner of the Texas Rangers in order to position himself for a political career, or vice versa, he surely ingratiated himself with a Texas Republican base when he led a consortium to buy the Rangers in 1988. It was this well-lubricated investment that positioned him as a popular figure. He was then in a position to persuade the voters of Arlington, Texas, to bear the burden of a bond issue that would pay for the Rangers' new stadium while expropriating local properties, thus permitting his $606,302 investment to grow almost twenty-five-fold, to $14.9 million, within ten years.

In modern societies, the sports entrepreneur, whatever

his property deals, has an opportunity for grace. Part master builder, part pioneer, part celebrity, a mover and shaker who serves the larger interests of leisure, a virtual public servant, he appears as the most generous of donors, a paterfamilias who endows the populace with its due—glory and vigor, and the chance for participation, however vicarious, in spectacular, transcendent experience.

7. The guardian against the government

Bush could not have mobilized Republicans just because he was a dynastic scion, or matched their idea of presidential demeanor. A decisive element of what made them rally to him, and conclude that he was electable, was that he shared their suspicion of government—at least rhetorically. As governor, he tilted toward oil and gas interests— interests in which he was deeply interested by experience as well as belief—sharing their view that many of their troubles stem from federal policies. The principle that "It's not the government's money, it's your money" is, however, more than a front for corporate prerogatives. It expresses a "vision thing"— an idea about freedom intertwined with a hatred of federal power that has deep roots in America. This idea runs especially deep in the West and the former slave-owning Confederate South—the "red states" that constitute Bush's base. It is the voice of land against regulation, property against equity. It is plutocracy with a populist face.

In short, Bush's born-again redemption and gliding career consolidated a merger of the Bible Belt and the Oil Belt. He invested and reinvested in popular themes to win support for his two main commitments: open-ended unilateralist war and plutocratic economics. Artfully, he exploited his weaknesses and magnified his strengths to leave an indelible mark on the American government and people.

PURGATORY—EITHER SIDE OF THE FLIPPED COIN

Thomas Alva Edison, John Reed, Walt Disney, Huey Long, Pete Rose

As noted in the introduction, there are few Americans with the complex legacy of Lyndon Johnson. He was a great president for eighteen months, when he pushed through the Voting Rights Act and pressed the Great Society/War on Poverty agenda. Then almost overnight, he went from FDR to King Lear, escalating the Vietnam War to hideous proportion, destroying himself in the bargain. The Americans noted here are in the same tradition of mixed properties: they did good, but they also did bad. These are the poetic, tragic people of this book, the ones with the flaw that, whatever their intentions, has sullied their memory. Thomas Edison might have been a cad and a bully, but try reading a book in a dark room without his contribution to home convenience. Huey Long could have been a great president if he weren't such a corrupt governor. Pete Rose, aka Charlie Hustle, appears here by virtue of having one of the best offenses (all those hits) combined with the worst defense (to explain away his crimes against the national pastime). These are the divided souls of the nation, half in heaven, half in hell.

Thomas Alva Edison

BY STEPHEN S. HALL

The Cur of Menlo Park

In the summer of 1888, Thomas Edison invited a newspaper reporter and several other observers to his laboratory complex in Orange, New Jersey, to witness one of the most abominable experiments in the history of electricity. A mongrel dog had been obtained for the occasion, and was forced to stand on a metal plate while being urged to drink from a metal pan of water. Separate electrodes, conducting 1,500 volts of alternating current, were attached to the plate and pan; with the first sip, the dog would complete a lethal circuit. The dog, however, was not thirsty; indeed, as described in Mark Essig's *Edison & The Electric Chair*, it seemed to know exactly what was going on, struggling desperately to escape the trap. Nonetheless, it accidentally grazed the water pan with one paw and was instantly electrocuted. "There was a quick contortion," the *New York World* reported, "a smothered yelp, and the little cur dog fell dead."

What makes the "experiment" especially cruel is not that the unwilling dog died; scientists have been killing animals in the name of science for hundreds of years, with the arguable justification that some measure of human knowledge has been gained in the admittedly lopsided bargain. But Edison's demonstration was essentially a publicity stunt, and in fact one might even accord it the historical distinction of marking one of the earliest alliances of corporate propaganda and junk science. The experiment was part of a disingenuous campaign (during which many more animals perished) designed to convince the public that alternating current, an electricity distribution system that was a brainchild of the famously mysterious Nikola Tesla and was commercialized by rivals of the Edison Electric Light Company, was especially suitable for prison executions, precisely because it was so dangerous and unsuitable for public use. The little cur dog's demise represents an early casualty in a fascinating nineteenth-century technological contretemps known as the "battle of the currents," during which America's most famous inventor shed decades of scientific rigor in the interests of a corporate agenda. If science is the dispassionate search for truth, then the battle of the currents marked Edison's acquiescence to the notion that truth as a social good might, under certain circumstances, be trumped, those circumstances being both corporate economic advantage and personal ego gratification.

Given his status as an American icon, it may seem odd to place Thomas Alva Edison in the company of miscreants. By any measure, he was a prodigious inventor who combined unusual persistence with a breathtaking ability to think outside the box. If anyone doubts the long reach of truly visionary technological innovation, consider the fact that virtually every dominant cultural entertainment of twenty-first-century life—popular music, moving pictures (in every sense), and even personal telecommunications—were invented by a man born in 1847. If one cares to trace the genealogy of industrial wealth in today's global economy back to its initial proof of principle, it is fair to say that every movie and media conglomerate (Fox, Sony, Warner's, Universal, to name but a few), every music-making company (from Deutsche Grammophon and EMI to Pioneer and Bose and Panasonic), every telecommunications company (Verizon, Nokia, Sprint), every company devoted to the generation and dissemination of electrical power (General Electric, Westinghouse) can trace the origin of its mission, and the feed stock of its capital worth, to ideas either generated or improved upon by the man known as "the wizard of Menlo Park."

Edison's life story uniquely complemented the mythologies demanded by both emergent capitalism and American democracy, i.e., that an eccentric Ohio-born loner, by dint of toil and intellect, could become a titan of industry and revolutionize civilized life. It was not simply a rags-to-riches myth, but also an argument about the meritocracy of ideas in a Jeffersonian context of enlightened self-interest, progress wedded to technological innovation. And yet mythology is built in part by selective omission, and Edison's "genius" was purchased at considerable psychological cost.

His sympathetic biographer Mathew Josephson describes how as a young boy growing up in Milan, Ohio, Edison suffered a public whipping by his father; indeed, Edison's father announced the event in advance and invited townspeople to witness the humiliation. Little wonder that Edison was always considered emotionally remote, if not affectively inert, by family, friends, and colleagues. Josephson also recounts the famous childhood episode when Edison and a playmate went swimming. The playmate disappeared and was later found drowned; Edison neither attempted to rescue his friend nor sought adult help, and didn't even mention the disappearance to anyone. For his reticence, he was beaten again.

It is the mythology of the lone-wolf inventor that plays so well against one of Edison's least-appealing, and perhaps most enduring, legacies: the corporate mogul. Every biographer recalls the energy and pluck of twelve-year-old Edison selling newspapers on trains to make money; fewer make the contrapuntal connection that barely a decade later he was collaborating with Jay Gould, the ultimate railroad robber baron of the nineteenth century, to undermine the patents of a rival telegraph company. Very early on, he had learned that the meritocracy of ideas was often at odds with good business and financial reward. It was capital from Gould, in fact, that allowed Edison to establish his first research facility in New Jersey.

The most revealing window on Edison's industrial soul, however, emerged from the seemingly obscure "battle of the currents." In the early 1880s, the Edison Electric Light Company and its subsidiaries began to wire American cities to deliver electricity to homes and businesses. Edison opted for direct current, a form of power that was difficult to distribute and not particularly efficient. The rival industrialist George Westinghouse developed a system using alternating current, which was much easier to conduct over long distances and thus could be distributed to many smaller communities in the country, in effect democratizing the benefits of the new technology. As historian Thomas P. Hughes noted in his landmark study *Networks of Power*, Edison and his supporters resorted to "unorthodox political tactics" during a campaign he characterized as "one private enterprise's endeavor, through political power and legislation, to outlaw the technological advantage of another."

Edison, the outsider/loner become ultimate corporate

monopolist, sought to discredit alternating current in every way possible. When the state of New York began to consider electrocution as an alternative to hanging in capital punishment cases, Edison and his cronies conducted dubious animal experiments to show that alternating current was much more dangerous—thus, perfect for execution. But in fighting Westinghouse and alternating current, Edison invented something for which he has received no patents and no credit: the insidious strategy of corrupting science to advance corporate ends, a strategy that depends in no small part on the deliberate, cynical attempt to confuse the public.

The tactics for this campaign of corporate disinformation will sound very familiar to modern ears. In an orchestrated campaign to discredit alternating current, Edison manipulated the press (as in his little dog execution), lobbied government officials (wining and dining them and, if failing there, bribing them), and surreptitiously funded supposedly independent experts who offered "scientific" evidence proving the dangers of alternating current. In every instance, the aim was to undermine public confidence in widely accepted scientific fact. Since its invention by Edison Electric, forerunner of General Electric, such junk science has served the purposes of the tobacco industry, the power industry, all manner of corporate polluters, and has now contaminated the public discourse involving crucial ecological issues like global warming and environmental toxins—disputes whose resolution depends on whether science is used to clarify or obfuscate the problem. (In the "battle of the currents," the technical superiority of alternating current ultimately prevailed—it is still the current that feeds our refrigerators, our stereos, our televisions.)

With that environmental legacy in mind, it is worth recalling a brief conversation between Edison and his secretary as they took in the picturesque view from Glenmount, his twenty-three-room mansion in New Jersey overlooking the Orange River Valley.

"See that valley?" Edison remarked.

"Yes, it's a beautiful valley," the secretary replied.

"Well, I'm going to make it more beautiful," Edison continued. "I'm going to dot it with factories." And indeed, the popular culture, the corporate landscape, and the environmental state of the planet we have all inherited is still dominated by the aesthetic of Thomas Edison, a man so culturally tone-deaf that he thought it perfectly logical to solicit the dogs for his canine executions from, of all places, the Society for the Prevention of Cruelty to Animals.

John Reed

BY WILL BLYTHE

"We had tickets to the ballet at the Marinsky Theater— all the theaters were open—but it was too exciting out of doors." So the American journalist John Reed wrote without a speck of irony about the night of November 7, 1917, in his peculiarly famous book *Ten Days That Shook the World*. With his gal pal, Louise Bryant, he was in Petrograd, and the Bolshevik coup against the Provisional Government led by Alexander Kerensky was in full swing. Thus Reed was faced with a choice in entertainments that suggests an odd equivalence between the two: ballet or revolution? What does the Fodor's have to say, darling? Reed chose revolution, that supremely aesthetic spectacle to the hungry twentieth-century eye with its omnivorous desire to see everything that can be seen. It would have had to have been a very good ballet to compete.

So, John Reed, the romantic, out in the streets, taking in the Revolution. He was thirty years old. He wanted to see the dawn of a new world.

At his least harmful, Reed was an enthusiast. One of his enthusiasms was the working man. Reed's journalistic career began in April 1912 when he served four days in the Passaic County, New Jersey, jail alongside striking silk workers led by Big Bill Haywood. When asked his profession by the sentencing magistrate, Reed answered with a smile, "Poet." He wrote a story about his prison sojourn that gave him something of a reputation in left-leaning circles, and then put his poetical skills to the task by creating a musical revue featuring striking workers and their families.

He felt, it seems, that the silk workers—gritty, obdurate, and usually ethnic—were more real than he was. After all, he started out life as a cosseted rich boy from out West. Like Teddy Roosevelt, who would eventually detest him, Reed had been a sickly child. But reality required toughness. It was the era of tramp steamers, Jack London, Ivy League football, manliness. He wanted a larger life, immersion in the authentic. He had been a cheerleader at Harvard, spookily intense, and now he wanted a new team to cheer for. Reed first went to Russia in 1915 on assignment for *Metropolitan Magazine*. He was five years out of college, a year or so from having ridden with Pancho Villa

in Mexico. He and his friend, the newspaper artist
Boardman Robinson, crossed the border into Russia
wearing jodhpurs, boots, and cowboy hats, and before they
could whoop yippee-ai-o-ki-ay, they had blundered right
into the Tsarist police, who imprisoned them briefly and
then threw them out of the country.

He went back to Russia in September, 1917, on assignment for *The Masses*, the socialist magazine edited by Max
Eastman. He spoke barely a word of Russian, just enough
to proclaim. *"Da, amerikanski sotsialist!"* He knew little of
the country's history. But qualifications were hardly necessary for a junior year abroad flirtation with the originators
of Soviet totalitarianism. In fact, they might have impeded
a love affair. Reed owned an American charm and open-
ness, and walked about unweathered, as if the worst storms
of history had missed his shores. These qualities must have
been a tad amusing to the Bolsheviks. In his book *Heroes I
Have Known*, Eastman had this to say about his friend John
Reed at the time of his second Russian expedition. "He
walked in there," wrote Eastman, "bursting with exuber-
ance and faith in revolution, zeal to understand it too,
found Lenin a laughing man, a man you could make friends
with, and trust and understand, felt himself perfectly at
home in the new proletarian state, and settled down to live
there awhile."

Found Lenin a laughing man. You wonder whom Lenin
was laughing at, but nonetheless, Reed's timing was impec-
cable. Based in Petrograd, he watched at close range the fall
of the provisional government and the seizure of power by
the Bolsheviks. "For color and terror and grandeur," he
wrote, "this makes Mexico look pale." That democracy was
undercut by Bolshevik subterfuge, he did not note.

Ten Days That Shook the World, the book that issued two years later from his five-month tour, possesses a giddy, careering quality—like a thrill-ride over the barricades, bullets whizzing overhead. It lacks analysis, purveying instead pure revolutionary sensation. It's the closest thing to the buzz of twenty-four-hour cable news that 1919 had to offer, a welter of headlines and proclamations, spot interviews and glamorous backdrops. The Constituent Assembly is dissolved! The Winter Palace is stormed! Trotsky sneers! Lenin thunders! The Supreme Soviet Leader turns a chamber of adversaries into a cheering throng! (Now *there's* a successful Soviet Electrification Program.)

The book presents Reed as an embedded journalist with Bolshevik credentials, racing to the front in some Red Guard's little deuce coup d'etat (a special model, vintage 1917). At one point, the reporter finds himself quite literally up against the wall, on the verge of being shot by two Bolshevik dolts who can't understand his documents, only to be rescued by an old babushka who can read. You sense Reed's delight not only in survival but in bringing the anecdote home. *Ten Days That Shook the World* is an early-twentieth-century example of the amoral pleasures to be had at the Apocalypse—for the observer, the journalist, anyway. The one who gets to go home.

For all of its speedy reportage, the prose sometimes takes a theological turn. "Slowly from the Red Square ebbed the proletarian tide," Reed writes about a visit to Moscow in November 1917. "I suddenly realized that the devout Russian people no longer needed priests to pray them into heaven. On earth they were building a kingdom more bright than any heaven had to offer, and for which it was a glory to die."

If history is any indication, it is unlikely that the devout Russian people realized what a glory it was to die for the Revolution, though a great many would continue to have the opportunity for just such a shining realization.

Reed's portrayal of Lenin, the architect of all that glory, borders on the hagiographic, as if the self-appointed Soviet leader were the St. Francis Assisi of Bolshevism, birds alighting on his homely, secular head as he shambles into the teeming hall: "A thundering wave of cheers announced the entrance of the presidium, with Lenin—great Lenin—among them. A short, stocky figure, with a big head set down on his shoulders, bald and bulging. Dressed in shabby clothes, his trousers much too long for him. Unimpressive, to be the idol of the mob, loved and revered as perhaps few leaders in history have been."

Lenin reciprocated the encomium, writing the foreword to his acolyte's book: "Unreservedly do I recommend it to the workers of the world. It gives a truthful and most vivid exposition of the events so significant to the comprehension of what really is the Proletarian Revolution and the Dictatorship of the Proletariat."

The book was published on March 19, 1919, and sold nine thousand copies within three months—a reputable figure—and millions in the years thereafter. It strongly influenced the way the West viewed the Soviet project, romanticizing its leaders, turning the entire endeavor into a quick-cutting Pathe newsreel glamorizing the birth of a totalitarian state.

In fact, with *Ten Days*, Reed has written advertisements for a tyrant, sent home bedazzled dispatches from a putsch. Here is a not unfamiliar example of the journalist as power-tropic, his sympathies tilting toward the strongman who grants him access, who breaks bread—or, is it eggs?—with him. For it was Lenin who famously said in regard to revolution, that you had to crack a few eggs to make an omelette. Delighting in the spectacle of cataclysm as much as the promise of utopia, Reed measured the Russian Revolution by its largest aims, not its smallest targets—the benighted citizens who threatened Lenin's grasp on power. And from early on, that meant nearly everyone—including former colleagues. Mensheviks, Left Socialist revolutionaries, and even Bolsheviks themselves—the gravepits began filling with such righteous comrades early in Lenin's tenure. Lenin and his colleagues destroyed the possibility for a liberal democracy in post-Czarist Russia, and Reed was there to commemorate their every manifesto. In the introduction to the Modern Library edition of *Ten Days That Shook the World*, Bertram Wolfe cites one of the subjects of the book, saying that it was "the work of an innocent who did not know whether he was attending a wedding or a funeral."

It was a funeral. Lenin, the dictator of the proletariat who had never once set foot in a factory or on a farm, liked to quote Robespierre: "The attribute of popular government in revolution is at one and the same time, virtue and terror, virtue without terror is fatal, terror without virtue is impotent. The terror is nothing but justice; prompt, severe, inflexible: it is thus an emanation of virtue." Lenin ruthlessly suppressed any political opposition, vested all power in the Communist Party, and established the Cheka, a secret police force. M. Y. Latsis, a Cheka official, proposed that guilt was not a matter of act but of class. "We are not carrying out war against individuals," he proclaimed. "We are exterminating the bourgeoisie as a class. We are not looking for evidence or witnesses to reveal deeds or words against the Soviet power. The first question we ask is—to what class does he belong, what are his origins, upbringing, education or profession? These questions define the fate of the accused. This is the essence of the Red Terror."

In June 1918, Reed admitted that in Russia there had been violations of the right to freedom of speech, that there had been illegal searches and requisitions, and that people had been arrested. None of this, he asserted, made for a tyrannical regime.

Somewhere in the last three years of Reed's life—he died in Russia of typhus in 1920 and was buried at the Kremlin—his appetite for sensation and his youthful large-heartedness were replaced by a desire for absolute faith. Naïveté is bad enough for a journalist, but an innocent abroad is less dangerous than a true believer. Reed was looking for something to turn his life serious, to give it gravity, weight, solidity. He desired a conversion experience. He was a journalist now hunting not a story but a cause. A religion, in fact. When he returned to Russia for the third time in 1918 after a stay in New York where he had finished *Ten Days*, Reed ridiculed those "playing at art, playing at love, playing at rebellion."

Truly, he knew of what he spoke. He would make up for youthful naïveté with the certainty of newfound conviction. He would no longer play at revolution. He became programmatic, quoting Marxist boilerplate with the same unforgiving implacability of a Bible-toting Jerry Falwell. At one time, he worked in the Bureau of the International Revolutionary Propaganda, a section of the Bureau of Foreign Affairs. God may have been replaced by History for the Marxist faithful, but *It* was as demanding as *He*. Marxism was a librarian's religion, an intellectual's faith. Lenin's interpretations of Marxist theory were conveniently elastic, but he and Trotsky proved themselves capable of a ferocity for which the study would have seemed lax preparation. This violence was the last test in proving themselves worthy of wielding power—as if intellectuals, theoreticians, those pale creatures of the study must convince themselves that they can kill as easily as a farmer slaughters a pig. Utopia awaits once the place has been sanitized by killing and cowing everyone that would actually be in it.

By the time Reed had resettled in Russia from 1918 to 1920, he knew the oppressive, violent nature of the Revolution but his idealism had coarsened. He had become a practical man. Hardheaded in the Bolshevik way. He knew, for instance, of the Bolsheviks's rushed execution of five hundred "counter-revolutionaries" the night before the long-promised (and temporary) abolition of the death penalty. The incident distressed Emma Goldman, the anarchist who had arrived in Russia after having been deported from the United States. In Goldman's account, Reed reassured her that she would get past her consternation: "You're a little confused because you've only dealt with the Revolution in theory. Cheer up and make me a cup of that good old American coffee you have brought with you."

When Goldman spoke sympathetically of their former allies, Russian socialists who had now aligned themselves with the Whites in their war against the Bolsheviks, Reed expressed exasperation. "I don't give a damn for their past. To the wall with them! I say. I have learned one mighty expressive Russian word, *'rasstrelyat!'* The word means to execute by shooting. Once Reed had cheered for the *Harvard Crimson*, now he cheered for the Red

Army. Like many Western intellectuals of the twentieth century, his ethical standards were limber: he accepted atrocities abroad that would have driven him to rebellion in his own country.

Reed was not without quicksilver perceptions, which makes his accommodation to Lenin's "exterminations" (One of the leader's favorite words: In his 1918 essay "How to Organize the Competition," Lenin announced the goal of "purging the Russian land of all kinds of harmful insects.") all the more distressing. He was watchful of Stalin, for instance, noting just before his death, "He's not an intellectual like the other people you will meet. He's not even particularly well informed, but he knows what he wants. He's got will power, and he's going to be on top of the pile one day."

Of course, Reed may have observed this with some admiration. In Russia, he suffered from an admiration for power, perhaps viewing Bolshevism as the antithesis of capitalism, whose rough-riding force he understandably decried. But Lenin and his gang loved power more than reformation, power more than citizenry, power more than freedom. They were tyrants. Some historians think Reed came to understand this and died disillusioned with the Revolution. Other observers believed "he died still a Bolshevik, and proud of it."

In any event, John Reed besmirched a reasonable (if overly inflated with the effluvia of self) opposition to the cruelties of capital by lavishing praise on a murderous and undeserving representative of capitalism's alternative. He was one of the first intellectuals and journalists of the twentieth century to do so, but he was hardly the last.

✳   ✳   ✳

Judith Coburn

Walt Disney
✹

BY JUDITH COBURN

Snow White Takes the Big Gulp

Once upon a time there was a little girl who, like all the little children in the world and even their parents, grew up in the house Uncle Walt built, with Mickey Mouse and Donald Duck. Like Dumbo, she thought she couldn't fly. But she became a writer anyway and even once got to visit the studio built by Uncle Walt and got a chance to write a Disney movie.

Flying down to L.A. to meet with Uncle Walt's people, the little girl couldn't make up her mind whether she felt like Cinderella or Snow White. She knew she wasn't the fairest in the land like Snow White. Maybe she would be if the movie turned out to be a glass slipper. But that was Cinderella. Actually, the little girl wasn't worried because Uncle Walt always made sure the handsome Prince rescued the little heroine no matter what.

And anyway, Uncle Walt was a midwesterner, just like the little girl, only he was from Chicago and born a long time ago, in 1901. The little girl had once read a book about Uncle Walt by Richard Schickel, which said Uncle Walt was a go-getter, not really an artist, but an inventor-entrepreneur like Henry Ford, who wanted to get rich. That he grew up poor and had to invent a lot of the ways to make cartoons himself and gambled all his own savings to build his studio, which he opened in 1928. But Schickel also wrote a lot of snobby stuff about the Midwest in his book, like how practical everyone there is and how midwesterners like Uncle Walt had "the habit to ask 'how much,' 'how far,' and sometimes simply 'how.' But rarely asked 'why.' " The little girl didn't know why he wrote that but she thought he was right about Uncle Walt.

Actually, the little girl didn't want to write a movie for kids but one for grown-ups. She and her writing partner Pooh wanted to make a picture about a crazy anthropologist who went down to the coast of Nicaragua to study some turtle fishermen but who got studied by them instead. Since it didn't have any sex or drugs in it, only turtles, Pooh's and the little girl's agent thought one of Uncle Walt's new guys, who turned out to have gone to Harvard with Pooh, might greenlight it, as the little girl, who was already learning to talk Hollywood, told Pooh on the phone.

Pooh and the little girl rented a subcompact which was almost too small for Pooh to fit in and drove out to Uncle Walt's studio in Burbank. It was just like Disneyland! The little girl had heard Uncle Walt was a loner and a control freak and had a thing about cleanliness. But this was awesome! All the walkways were clean enough to eat off and the grass was so perfect it looked like Astroturf. Each office had a mailbox outside it in the shape of Mickey or Donald. Inside, all the people chirped at them cheerfully just like the characters in Uncle Walt's movies and the little girl wondered if they all had to whistle while they worked. But Pooh pointed out how many AA meetings were advertised on the company bulletin boards.

The little girl had been to Disneyland only once, when she got in for free, posing as a nurse escorting two Vietnam veterans on furlough from the local loony bin for the day. High on acid and nitrous oxide siphoned off a whipped

cream canister from a nearby ice cream parlor, they wanted
to see if they could crack Disneyland's infamous no drugs
and alcohol rule. But that was part of an X-rated movie the
little girl hoped to get John Waters to direct. OK, also a little
like the cartoon Uncle Walt actually made with his friend
Salvador Dali in 1946, the one thing he made that
expanded consciousness like real art instead of reducing it
to kitsch. Which is funny, because the little girl remembered that Uncle Walt had once told a journalist right
before he died, "I always had a nightmare. I dream one of
my pictures has ended up in an art theater."

At the studio, Uncle Walt's guy was a small fellow but
he sat behind a desktop big enough to ice skate on and fingered a big set of brass knuckles during their pitch, which
confused the little girl. She knew all Disney pictures had a
good guy and a bad guy, so was this the bad guy? After
Pooh and the little girl told about the anthropologist and
the turtle fishermen, Uncle Walt's guy swung around in
his big chair, like the Wizard of Oz, the little girl thought,
but didn't want to mention it since that wasn't a Disney
picture.

Uncle Walt's guy said he didn't think most people knew
where Nicaragua was, which the little girl thought was
funny, since there was a war on there at the time, but
maybe they didn't know about it in Disney World. Uncle
Walt's guy said he had just the picture for them, though,
even the same plot. It was about Humphrey the whale,
who had split from the ocean and tried to swim to Sacramento. The little girl had read about Humphrey on the
front page of the *San Francisco Chronicle* but she didn't
really see what that had to do with turtle fishermen except
maybe both pictures might star water. She could tell Pooh

didn't get it either, because he scrunched down in his chair and wouldn't look at her, which always meant he would burst out laughing if he did.

But she understood when she looked over at Uncle Walt's guy and his nose seemed to be getting longer and longer. Then she knew Humphrey was a story Uncle Walt would like.

The little girl and Pooh ran out to their subcompact, raced off the lot, pulled off the freeway and hooted with laughter like the hipster crows in *Dumbo. Dumbo!* The little girl really felt like Snow White—the glass slipper might even turn into an Oscar—when she thought about writing a major motion picture like *Dumbo.* No matter how many rants the little girl got off about the monoculture and American cultural imperialism and appropriation of the world's greatest fairy tales and dumbing down and little kids in Cambodian refugee camps with faded Mickey Mouse T-shirts recycled from rich kids' trips to Anaheim and all-white silly girls waiting for their all-white dumber princes to come while dwarves and pigs had all the fun, the little girl had a weakness for Dumbo.

So Pooh and the little girl flew back up North and started walking around under the big redwoods trying to talk like Humphrey. He not she because that was what Uncle Walt would want. And no one had to tell the little girl and Pooh what Uncle Walt would want. They were Disney kids like everyone else. Humphrey couldn't be a girl because he was an adventurer and he couldn't be black or Jewish or gay either because those people didn't exist in Uncle Walt's world except when he didn't like someone, Richard Schickel wrote, and called that person "fag." There couldn't be a nice Mom and there had to be a mean stepmother, just like in most of Uncle Walt's cartoons. And there had to be a happy ending just like all the remakes Uncle Walt had done of the world's greatest fairy tales, no matter how scary and dark the originals were.

The little girl had just been to the library and discovered a whole postmodern industry critiquing Uncle Walt's characters and how they demeaned people, books with titles like *From Mouse to Mermaid: the Politics of Film, Gender and Culture.* What they said was probably true but every time the little girl saw words like gender or deconstruction, she got a headache and had to lie down until it went away. And those books with their klutzy formulas just made her want to rent *Fantasia* again, which, no matter what anyone says, is one of the top ten movies *ever.*

Then Pooh and the little girl found out from Uncle Walt's guy that *Humphrey* wouldn't even be a cartoon like *Dumbo* but a realistic movie like Uncle Walt's dorky *Wonderful World of Disney* on TV. Uncle Walt's guys said the cartoon was dead, which was only three months before *Who Framed Roger Rabbit* came out but long before Pixar even existed. But they were Disney, so they knew. Oh no! said the little girl—big gray blobs floating around on screen. Maybe we should make it a French film and have actual sounds of whales canoodling, with our dialogue in subtitles.

All these rules began to make Pooh feel like Eeyore but the little girl told him not to go there since Disney's Pooh pictures were really bad. The little girl thought that maybe if they ate a lot of Big Macs and drank a lot of Big Gulps that might help to raise their blood sugar and lower their IQs. And to think about synergy, which Uncle Walt had invented, for God's sake, like what would the Humphrey doll look like and who could do the lyrics for *Humphrey!*

The Musical! And whether they could get any Hamlet in somewhere like in *The Lion King.* ("To swim, or not to swim?") The little girl had read that Edmund Wilson said that Uncle Walt had invented "an infallible formula to provoke an audience's automatic reaction," and she told Pooh that's what they had to do. And pretty soon they were amusing themselves to death while mindlessly simplifying, just like the little girl had read about in Professor Postman's awesome tome.

Back down to Burbank Pooh and the little girl flew to meet with a whole posse of Uncle Walt's guys, all dressed in their required Disney uniform of dark suits and ties and all chewing gum like Clarabelle the Cow. The little girl and Pooh told how the movie would go and the big boss, only one down from Jeffrey Katzenberg, said he really loved how they had "anthro- . . . anthropo- . . . , uh, you know . . . the whale." And Pooh and the little girl worried that they hadn't dumbed down enough since they still remembered how to pronounce "anthropomorphize" and what it meant and that that might put them off the picture. But everyone stood up and shook hands and said they had a deal.

But it all turned out not to have a happy ending, even if that's the way it's supposed to end in Disneyland. The next morning, the little girl and Pooh were summoned, before breakfast, to a conference call and told the picture was off. Well, this was nothing new, the little girl knew, since Uncle Walt had once busted a cartoonists' union at his studio. Not to mention that he named names before all those rabid anti-Communist committees that led to the Hollywood blacklist.

Little did Pooh and the little girl know that Jeffrey Katzenberg would also soon be purged and that eventually

Uncle Walt's company would be known more for amusement parks and corporate despotism than cartoons and that the world's greatest cartooning would fall into the hands of Frenchmen, Japanese, and Jews. And even computers.

Pooh and the little girl came out OK though because their agent got them hush money for promising not to tell anyone Disney had welshed on a deal. The little girl crossed her fingers behind her back when she promised. Just like Truman, in her favorite Peter Weir movie, *The Truman Show*, the little girl was happy to grow up and escape from a land like "Celebration," the cleanest little town you could imagine, that Uncle Walt had actually built in Florida near Disney World. The movie was made there but it wasn't a Disney picture.

Huey Long

BY ARTHUR KEMPTON

FROM RAILROAD COMMISSION to grave, Huey P. Long's political life lasted sixteen years, long enough in his case to have been called a Communist and a Fascist out of different sides of the same mouths. No holder of high office in America ever took positions on social and economic issues as hostile to the class interests of official America as Long's were. And no American politician ever concentrated in himself as much control over so large an apparatus of government as this dogmatic enemy of concentrated wealth did in Louisiana.

A ruthless pursuer of the common good, Long felt beset by implacable enmities, and blamed those who bore them for making him behave badly in the service of his high ideals. "Every thing I did, I've had to do with one hand," he sniffed, "because I've had to fight with the other." During the last decade of the century before last, Huey Long sprang into life bristling with nervous energy, third son of a northeast Louisiana man of minor small-town property and his higher-born wife. He was the seventh child of ten in a household that fostered in its best-known adult an absence of normal family feelings.

Long's career in politics purely expressed his lifelong predisposition against established order. He was tossed out of high school midway through his senior year for trying to unseat the principal. As he later would put it, "I have always fought the regime." At seventeen, the displaced schoolboy was discovering his aptitude for selling cooking grease made from cottonseed oil. A year later, he was working in Memphis, handling the regional sales of a Texas meat packer's canned goods. His older brothers tried to steer him toward respectability; one's intercession brought him to Oklahoma, where he was meant to enroll in college. Within a year, Huey was back in Memphis, mildly prosperous from selling starch.

In the making of Huey Long, nature had marred a face fit for a shirt-collar model with the red-clubbed nose of a baggy-pants clown. This would work to his vocational advantage. It kept him from being too much better-looking than his customers, and seeming regular was a prerequisite of putting a buyer at ease. Before long, he was selling patent medicine across northeast Louisiana, Arkansas, and Mississippi. On the road, he entertained himself at campaign rallies. For Huey, a political season spent watching old-school redneck stemwinders like Jeff Davis, James T. Vardaman, and Theodore Bilbo rail against the plutocracy was a semester at demagogue school.

In 1914, his brother Julius arranged for him to study law at Tulane University. The next year, at twenty-one, Long was admitted to the Louisiana bar, and opened a sparse practice in Negro divorces and workman's compensation cases around Shreveport. To make ends meet, he was obliged to go back on the road selling cans for kerosene heating oil. Ten years into his law practice, Long was a busy litigator of disputes over land titles, oil patch holdings, personal damages, and the claims of two small local petroleum interests against Standard Oil Company of Louisiana. By then he was well into his service on the state's Railroad Commission, having won election when he was twenty-five.

In this underlit agency's authority to regulate railroads, telephone and telegraph companies, and pipelines, Huey saw a stage full of bit players awaiting the entrance of a swashbuckling star. He'd told an associate that he would run for railroad commissioner, win, and then go on to become governor. However lively its politics, Louisiana was in a deep southern state of socio-economic languor during the first quarter of the twentieth century. Its wealth came from what could be grown in or taken out of the ground: crops, trees, oil, and gas. Most of the money made on Louisiana soil migrated north. Most of what remained subsidized an oligarchy of planters, merchants, and politicos—the permanent government of a "feudal democracy." Unchallenged for forty years, Louisiana's establishment presided smugly over a citizenry whose average yearly income was among the lowest in the nation. The times were crackling with social resentments and fervid popular yearnings; the benighted South was a hotbed then of jack-leg prophets and millenarian cultists.

The electorate was susceptible to the advent of some fresh tribune of the people with a gift for making himself conspicuous. Born restless, Huey Long had been in a hurry ever since. And because Louisiana's ruling elite had never bothered to impose organizational disciplines on its political class, there were no sergeants-at-arms among state Democrats who could make a pushy young outsider wait his turn. Long spent his several years on the rechristened Public Services Commission arranging to run for governor: striking political bargains to forge necessary alliances, making himself better known by fighting phone company rate hikes, vilifying the state's leadership as paid corporate stooges, and jousting with Standard Oil, the octopus that had become as much an object of his obsession as the white whale was to Ahab. In 1924, he ran and lost, but made a strong showing. Since no governor of Louisiana could succeed himself, Long never had to break stride in the pursuit of his next chance.

In 1928, thirty-four-year-old Huey Long ran for governor on a platform of free textbooks, financial assistance to local school districts, toll-free bridges, paved roads, and improved hospitals. "Longism" was hotly denounced by newspaper editorialists and most other holders of the state's important property. To counter, Huey launched his pioneering career as a political mass marketer by blanketing the state with about a million campaign circulars. A full-fledged player now at what he called the "sport of kings," he adopted as his uniform

double-breasted pinstripes and white linen suits—a
country lawyer's simulation of well-bred style. Long made
his way with a salesman's knack for appearing cut from
a slightly better grade of the same cloth as his customers
were. In his case, these comprised a class known to polite
society as peckerwoods and rubes.

On the stump, the ferocity of his invective so outraged
opposition supporters that some in his audiences came
after him with flying fists. A physical coward unafraid to
be a reckless provocateur, his vituperations once caused a
former governor he'd tongue-whipped from a speaker's
platform to chase Long out of a hotel lobby and pummel
him in an elevator. Unbeholdened to such powers-that-
were, Huey Long was swept into office with half again as
many votes as were cast for his nearest rival.

Once elected, he set about bending state government
to his will. Recognizing jobs and contracts as government's
true currency, Long reached for as much control over as
many of these as he could grasp. He wrested state agencies and commissions out of unfriendly hands, then used
his grip on patronage to squeeze legislators who opposed
him. "A deck has fifty-two cards," he advised the parties
to one negotiation, "and in Baton Rouge I hold all fifty-
two . . . and can shuffle and deal as I please."

Heady with having his way, he dubbed himself the
"Kingfish," after the comic character on the radio show
Amos 'n' Andy. He stashed his family in Baton Rouge while
he lodged in a New Orleans hotel suite with his own
Mystic Knights of the Sea. There, nestled among body-
guards, bag men, and political cronies, he did the people's
business: strong-arming natural gas service into New
Orleans, ramrodding a bond issue through to pay for road

construction, trying to steamroll the legislature into taxing oil companies to buy books for schoolchildren.

The oil tax proved one affront too many for the oligarchs to bear. After a year of wriggling under Long's thumb, the hard-pressed bloc of statehouse conservatives rose against him, serving up a bill of impeachment with nineteen charges ranging from bribery and misusing public money to fondling a stripper in a French Quarter nightspot. Long's ways and means were no doubt uncouth, but his true impeachable offense was opposing the interests of Standard Oil. In his own defense, Huey ran an all-out political campaign in public, and bared his knuckles in back-room caucuses. He churned out waves of leaflets, and had them delivered in state custody to most Louisiana doorsteps on the day after they were printed. He criss-crossed the state, speaking at rallies and on radio, keeping up a steady rat-a-tat-tat of diatribe against Standard Oil and its "paid agents" in Baton Rouge.

At every stop, he would abuse the most prominent of his local opposition in nasty, personal terms. Upon hearing Long impugn his honesty and mock his deafness, a judge in Opelousas spat back that his tormenter was bound to "end either in the insane asylum or the penitentiary." In retorting, the scalded patrician had expressed a shared conviction of his class that was hardening into its common purpose.

In the end, Long bought and extorted one more vote than he needed to survive. The battle left him scarred, and shadowed the rest of his political life. Some who were close to him said that impeachment changed Huey Long from heartfelt reformer to a manic conglomerator of power and remorseless settler of scores. He started building things apace: paved roads, bridges, a new capitol, and other public buildings. Long poured money into the state university, which he adopted as his own. He obsessed over the football team, led cheers at pep rallies, wrote fight songs, hired and fired coaches and deans, elected class presidents, and pulled the strings of student government when it suited him. Huey seemed to relish the life as big man on campus he'd missed while he was getting his practical education on the road.

The refinement of his political organization in the crucible of impeachment spurred Long to keep on running: by then, he was conducting a perpetual campaign. He started his own newspaper—devoted to sports, gossip, movies, fashions, advice to the lovelorn, and the latest news and opinions of Huey Long—which claimed a weekly circulation of one hundred twenty-five thousand. The most effective of the governor's social programs—an adult literacy offensive—created a hundred thousand more potential readers of the *Louisiana Progress.* In 1930, halfway through his term as governor, he ran for the United States Senate. His election brought Long onto the national stage he thought befitting a political actor of his stature, without disturbing his focus on Louisiana's everyday affairs of state. He gave the Senate no more respect than he had the legislature back home: disdaining its leaders, traditions, and protocols; assuming as his due, all privileges of club membership without waiting for them to be conferred. He slighted his committee assignments, rarely bothering to show up for meetings. Indeed, three weeks after his arrival, he repaired to New Orleans for a month, snorting that Democrats in Washington were cowering before Herbert Hoover like "a whipped rooster."

When Long returned, he began taking the floor without regard to the topic of debate to decry the "handful of men" who "own all the money in the country," and were the cause of America's economic collapse.

Huey knew that show was the business on any stage, however decorous its trappings. When in full cry, he would run his fingers through his hair, and swing his fists for emphasis, bobbing and weaving like Jack Dempsey in the ring. Newspapermen appreciated Long's color and flair, and started the publicity mill grinding. The Kingfish was ready to spread.

But if Long was showy, he was also a sharp rhetorician with a photographic memory and gift for extemporizing. He came to politics as a lawyer from Shreveport with a salesman's mental file of quotations from the Bible and *Saturday Evening Post* that he'd relied on to bolster an argument or close a deal. In the Senate, he would rise from a desk stacked with books, pamphlets, and documents, from which to pull citations to hammer home the points that scaffolded a case he could stand on his feet and make for hours. A colleague from Idaho once observed that Long was the only man he ever knew who could "argue from a wrong premise to a right conclusion."

In 1931, he launched himself into the national fray; first, in Arkansas, where his hard stumping carried back to the Senate a woman who'd inherited her office from a dead husband, and was considered unelectable by party regulars. This demonstration of Long's star power made shiny the eyes of men who were trying to get Franklin Roosevelt elected to the presidency. They enlisted him into their campaign. Long was invited to lunch at Hyde Park to discuss arrangements for his cross-country speaking tour. He dressed for this occasion in a "loud suit, an orchid shirt and a pink necktie." Far as he'd come, Huey made no better impression at the stately Hudson Valley retreat of one of New York's oldest families than he had in Shreveport's better drawing rooms; in neither setting could Long overcome the social deficit of not being a gentleman. His alliance with Roosevelt would barely outlast the electoral triumph it helped secure. Within months, Long was disparaging the new administration. Roosevelt retaliated by cutting Long out of federal patronage in Louisiana, thus giving direct aid and comfort to his enemies there, who lay coiled and seething. Bitter and desperate enough by then to start raising secret militias, Long's haters were preparing to strike.

With his political star hitched to the hoi polloi, Huey freely made public mockery of its class enemies. He wrote a letter to have his name removed from the Washington *Social Register*, declining an association with a local "elite" he wryly characterized as "insufficiently cultured" to learn how to eat potlikker properly. His conscience, he noted, was disturbed at having supplanted someone worthier of this distinction, his sleep unsettled by dreaming of "phantoms of the deserving excluded, who seem as though they were trying to lisp, 'How could you.' "

But privately, he lived as a man would who believed himself in constant peril. Even in Washington, well removed from Louisiana's hot-blooded rancors, he encamped at the Mayflower Hotel with a live-in detachment of three state police officers. He wouldn't venture onto a golf course without a bodyguard along toting a sawed-off shotgun. His sense of besiegement heightened in 1933, after the Long "machine" conveyed its boss's chosen candidate into Louisiana's other senate seat. With Roosevelt's complicity, the state's dogged faction of howling "anti-Longites" prevailed on the Senate's leadership to hold hearings on their claims of electoral improprieties, and on Long's fitness to serve. The ringleader of Long's homegrown opposition branded him "a dangerous paranoiac." For his part, Huey—who saw himself as a knight templar of the commonweal—blamed his enemies' militant zealotry for forcing him to act ruthlessly in a righteous cause. He was resigned to being forever embattled. "I've never held a public office," he sighed, "when I was not under some threat of removal. . . ."

Having weathered this latest big wind from down home, Long blew hard in Washington. In 1934, he turned his rhetorical flame-thrower on Roosevelt, comparing the administration's efforts at Depression relief to a "farmer feeding corn to hogs, calling them up from here, there, and yonder, throwing them a handful of corn." According to Long, nothing less than "a fundamental change in the economic system" would fix America. He introduced a bill in the Senate to limit fortunes, inheritances, and yearly incomes, and to provide pensions for needy citizens over sixty. He bought a half-hour of air time on network radio to exhort the nation to join his "fight to decentralize wealth." In it he proposed to tax the rich to provide every American family with a five thousand dollar-"homestead" grant, "enough for a home, an automobile, a radio, and the ordinary conveniences," and a guaranteed annual income of two to three thousand dollars. Moreover, the federal government would pay the college costs of worthy students, share the financing of public education with states, pay bonuses to veterans, limit the work week to thirty hours, and buy and store agricultural surpluses to protect farmers from the vicissitudes of the marketplace.

Long never tried to introduce into Louisiana any of the social welfare programs he talked about in Washington. He was casting himself as the leader of a national movement, laying groundwork for a presidential campaign. He started the Share Our Wealth society, which served as the home office of a coast-to-coast chain of local franchises. In Louisiana, these Share Our Wealth clubs were cogs in Long's "machine."

By 1934, the Long package was being hawked by Gerald L. K. Smith, an evangelical cleric Huey hired as an organizer. Under his mentor's wing, this demagogue-in-training honed the radio-preaching chops that soon would make him, along with Father Charles Coughlin—another Long ally—one of the two most scurrilous white rabble-rousers of the first half of the twentieth century. The Share Our Wealth "movement" caught on like wild-fire; by the end of the year, there were clubs in every state—27,431 of them—with a claimed membership of nearly five million people.

As he hurtled on toward his "destiny's" gleaming, Long had to keep swatting away attackers on his rear flanks. He micromanaged the suppression of another attempted leg-islative coup, then sent national guardsmen to occupy the offices of the registrar of voters to assure the favorable out-come of a New Orleans mayoralty race. His enemies in Louisiana were growing increasingly agitated. Drive-by shooters fired five times into his house in New Orleans.

Now convinced that his bedevilers never meant to abate, he resolved to make his position impregnable, by crushing the opposition's die-hard remnant, and expanding his control over the public jobs that fed his organization. He pushed through bills that extended the state's authority over jobs, contracts, and other municipal functions. He "struck down" the city government of Alexandria, long a stronghold of defiance. He purged the state payroll of opposition sympathizers. He kept—and wielded—files thick with documentary evidence of the private indiscretions of his political foes.

By then, Huey had reduced his approach to governing to barest essentials. "I can frighten or buy ninety-nine out of every hundred men," he chortled. And, by deftly outmaneuvering his nemesis in the legislature, he finally got his oil tax. "I said I would tax Standard Oil if it was the last thing I ever did," Long crowed. "This time I'll pay off Standard Oil for the impeachment."

During the worst of the Depression, Huey Long directly controlled about twenty thousand jobs in Louisiana. Whenever called upon, these hirelings kicked back to his organization, by means of a "payroll tax" Long imposed. The cash in this pipeline flowed into the "deduct box" secreted in his New Orleans hotel suite, and back out to grease electoral processes across the state. He also "taxed" companies and individuals doing government business. He kept a hand in the pockets of about a thousand rich citizens, who anted up thousands of dollars on demand. As an unabashed co-mingler of personal and political incomes, the Kingfish prided himself on taking his under-the-table money out in the open.

Like some movie crime boss, he lived lavishly in hotels in three cities. Long took fat fees from acting as the state's lawyer in tort cases. He had interests in companies holding choice land for oil and gas leases. His enemies whispered of cash rake-offs from gambling operations, but if Long had any sources of corrupt income other than himself none were ever proven.

By the spring of 1935, he had driven his Louisiana hounders to ground. As he renewed his Senate attacks on the administration, sixty-five thousand letters a week were pouring into his Washington office. The national press was building him up as a presidential contender. He'd begun speaking in public about taking on Roosevelt, plotting a run in 1936 at the head of a break-away third party. Franklin Roosevelt now regarded Huey Long as a present danger. Federal law enforcement opened an investigation into political graft in Louisiana. Tax prosecutions were mounted against prominent Long associates. The United States Treasury sabotaged a Louisiana bond issue. Jobs in federal programs were used to prop up Long's bedraggled opposition, to create pockets of foreign influence in his sphere of control. In their secret counsels, the anti-Long die-hards spoke assuredly of having "all the resources of the United States government at [their] disposal." For his part, Long was willing to block the flow of sixty million New Deal dollars into Louisiana to keep them out of the wrong hands.

On the political front, Roosevelt sent a "special tax message" to Congress in May of 1935. In language redolent of Long's, he announced his intention to use taxation as an instrument of social reform. A "wider distribution of wealth," the president suggested, would quiet social unrest. With Roosevelt uneasily eyeing the next election, Long could rightly claim to have pushed him into closer company with America's wooly band of proletarian causists than any member of the Groton class of 1900 would've expected to have to endure.

Early in the next September, Senator Kingfish passed his forty-second birthday directing legislative traffic in Baton Rouge. One evening, as he strode through the capitol building ahead of his retinue, an addled young ear, nose, and throat specialist named Carl Weiss stepped from behind a pillar outside the governor's office and fired one shot from a small pistol into Long's midsection. Huey died a couple of days later, after surgery performed amidst a roomful of his hangers-on milling around the operating table, from the effects of bullet holes in kidney and colon compounded by inept doctoring. No motive has ever been definitively ascribed to Long's slayer. He couldn't say, because in subduing him Long's bodyguards riddled his body with more than thirty rounds, the blasts from their shotguns blowing half his face away. His family surmised that Dr. Weiss—a sensitive "idealist" and a believer in "right above everything"—after years of watching this swaggering wrongdoer's unchecked rise, had finally gone haywire and that night taken it upon himself to rid the world of a tyrant.

Huey's people were sure Weiss had been sent by the cabal of Long-haters who were known to have met two months before and contemplated murder. But then, stories abounded of conspirators in shuttered rooms drawing straws to decide which one would gut the Kingfish. It turned out there were three ongoing plots against Huey's life at the time of his death, but evidently Dr. Weiss wasn't involved in any of them.

Long spent his last hours of fitful consciousness trying to understand what had happened. For a man who insisted on round-the-clock armed guarding, he seemed oddly taken aback at the turn of events. "Who was that that shot me?"

he kept asking. When told, Huey, still uncomprehending, replied, "I don't know him . . . I wonder why he shot me." Even after he learned that his assailant was the son-in-law of a judge he was gerrymandering out of office, Long remained incredulous: "I don't know him," he repeated. "What did he want to shoot me for?" Having been a promiscuous giver of offense to men he thought important, perhaps the idea of being done in by some faceless spear-carrier in his life's grand pageant was beyond his reckoning.

With an attending crowd of doctors, family, cronies, and trough-feeders gathered around his bedside, Long slipped in and out of a coma, alternating in wakeful moments between hallucination and lucidity. As he lay dying, Long's most trusted lieutenant—his bag man—sensed that the time had come to honor the great man's spirit by sacrificing delicacy to high purpose. Near the end, Seymour Weiss twice leaned over the prostrate form of his principal and gently shook him awake. "Huey," he twice implored, "you've got to tell me. Where did you put the deduct box?" Both times, Long stirred, raised himself long enough to whisper, "Later, Seymour, later . . ." and fell back into unconsciousness. Overtaken by death as he never was in life, at the last he reportedly muttered, "God, don't let me die. I have so much to do." But other death-watchers thought they heard him say, "What will my poor boys at LSU do without me?" How like Huey Long, within whose prophetic career were contained so many elements of modern American political life, to die with one eye on the sublime and the other on a football team.

✳   ✳   ✳

Pete Rose

✳

BY VIC ZIEGEL

THE PETE ROSE who put his name on the cover of a book subtitled *My Prison Without Bars* is a Pete Rose who has to try a lot harder. That was never the case when Rose was a younger man, playing the game the way it should be played—running to first after earning a walk, punishing his body to break up a double play, diving head-first into shin guards to score a run. That kind of pain didn't matter. Pain, for him, was going oh-for-five, or leaving the winning run on base.

My Prison . . . is Rose's latest dive, the one meant to get him around a tag and into baseball's Hall of Fame. "Oh, yeah, I remember now, I did bet on baseball when I was managing the Reds." But never from the clubhouse, he wants us to understand. As if baseball's only concern was real estate's eleventh commandment: location, location, location.

The admission appears after fourteen years of head-first lying, fourteen years of telling assorted baseball commissioners they had the wrong guy. (What, me bet on baseball? Never, ever.)

The first rule of baseball is no betting allowed. Bet, and you're busted. The posters are hung in every clubhouse, in English and Spanish. (No betting, *no apostando*, no, no, no.) OK, Rose probably can't read Spanish, so that lets him off half-a-hook. But calling bookies to plunk down nickels and dimes has been frowned on since at least 1919, when the Chicago White Sox tanked the World Series. And got the great Shoeless Joe Jackson thrown out forever.

So why did Rose, who played the game hardest of all, treat the sport that meant so much to him, when he became a manager, like just another line on an income tax form? Well, if you listen to Fay Vincent, the former commissioner, Rose's rap sheet goes back to his time as a player. "Pete Rose is still lying," Vincent insists. "I don't think he knows how to tell the truth. I'm morally certain that Rose bet as a player. I'm virtually certain that he bet in Philadelphia in 1980 and '81."

Vincent's evidence? A baseball writer, whom he described as a close friend of Rose's, told him. I talked to the writer and, even over the telephone, you could see his eyes rolling. ("I never uttered those words. I never said that. I never said any of those things. It's untrue.")

One truth is that almost every baseball writer who stared down at Rose from a press box might have thought of him as a friend. There was no better interview in the game. He wouldn't duck a writer's question, would volunteer anecdotes and, like Donald O'Connor, he'd make 'em laugh.

Here are two examples that are mine alone. After a rookie pitcher for the god-awful Mets of the mid-sixties shut out his Reds, I had the bright idea of stepping into the loser's clubhouse and asking Rose what he thought of the rookie. Rose didn't hesitate. "He's better than Candy Soufax," he told me.

My job, I understood, was to play straight man. "Uh, Pete, don't you mean Sandy Koufax?"

Now Rose was shaking his head. "Come on, Vic, you know there's only one Sandy Koufax."

When I was in Cincinnati, I'd sometimes run into Rose at the local racetrack. He loves betting on the ponies. No baseball poster said he couldn't. So we'd talk horses, and exchange harmless lies. After I was off the baseball beat for a few years, we ran into each other, and I asked, naturally, how the horses were treating him. "Great," he shot back. "Never better. I'm in with the in-crowd."

And who, I wondered, was the in-crowd? "You know," he said, "the Jewish guys."

That was my Pete Rose, and I couldn't get enough of it. And when the story broke that the commissioner's office had a megillah-full of evidence that Rose was betting on two-legged athletes, and hanging out with bad company (drugs were mentioned), I didn't want to believe it. He was offered a seven-year suspension and turned it down. But when the commissioner, Bart Giamatti, came back with a lifetime ban, with room for an appeal after one year, Rose took that bet. Giamatti died days later and his successor was Vincent, the guy who believes Rose was guilty of betting back when his name appeared on the lineup card.

For the next fouteen years, Rose kept telling people that baseball had it all wrong. Meanwhile, he squeezed a nice living out of a syndicated radio show, baseball card signings, a Florida restaurant ("My prison with a bar"), and who knows how many exactas. After his election in 2000 to baseball's all-century team, and being allowed to step on a major league field for the first time since he was placed on the permanently ineligible list in 1989, the crowd gave him a loud vote of confidence. There was the suggestion that Rose would be reinstated if he came clean, apologized, admitted that he bet on games, asked for help.

No, he wouldn't do any of that. Why should he? He was as innocent as a Little Leaguer. Until he squeezed a few more bucks out of a book. Yes, sir, he wrote, he was lying. Oy, was he lying.

He says he told the current commissioner, Bud Selig, in 2002 that he did bet. The conversation, as recounted in the book, went like this:

Selig: "How often?"

Rose: "Four or five times a week."

Selig: "Why?"

Rose: "I didn't think I'd get caught."

I believe that much. But I also believe his greatest crime is arrogance. He thought they would never kick Pete Rose out of the game. That in some cockeyed way he *was* the game—the all-time leader in hits (4,256), in games (3,562), not to mention in disdain.

On the book tour, when it was pointed out that his attempt at an apology had only warning-track power, his response was the kind that makes noses grow. "All I've been reading the last thirteen or fourteen years—I even heard George Bush say it—'Pete's got to come clean.' Well, I'm coming pretty clean." Now it's up to Selig to decide if "pretty clean" is clean enough. Rose insists Selig's in his corner. Or climbing the ring steps. Sitting in the same arena. Looking for parking. Something like that.

The commissioner has enough headaches. Hard to say when, or if, he'll sign off on the press release that will free Rose from casino-arrest and restore his place in baseball history. He can go along with Bob Feller, the Hall of Fame pitcher who said, "If you murder somebody and say you're sorry does that vindicate you? Rose is not sorry he gambled . . . he's sorry he got caught. He's a good hitter, an average manager, a liar, and a crook." Now there's a no-vote.

Or does Selig listen to Mike Schmidt, a former teammate,

who wants to see Rose get another chance. The book, Schmidt said, "wasn't the best showing of sorrow and regret. That's just something Pete isn't great at doing. But I know he truly is sorry and that he regrets everything."

They tell us it takes a big man, not necessarily a size forty-eight, to admit he's wrong. I didn't have a firsthand example of that until my friend Paddy Flood, a boxing manager, confessed to a robbery. We were walking along a midtown street when Paddy mentioned the last time he'd been down that particular street, decades ago, he was a teenager, a gang member. The gang broke into a car and hit the jackpot—bulging suitcases, jewelry boxes from Tiffany, expensive appliances. They were dividing the loot, Paddy said, "when I realized most of it was wedding gifts. I could just imagine how the couple felt when they got back to the car. It made me feel real bad."

When I said his teenage remorse spoke volumes about his basic deceny, Paddy began laughing. "I didn't feel bad that night," he said. "It just hit me when we came down this street."

Now you may say that confession doesn't count for very much. That there's a statute of limitations on mea culpas (see Robert S. McNamara). But there was no denying Paddy's sincerity all those years later. Rose and sincerity don't belong in the same sentence. Does that mean he belongs in hell? No, there are far greater crimes than arrogance. Maybe he goes to purgatory with a generous line of credit and a bookie whose phone lines are always busy. It is, come to think of it, one man's kind of hell.

PET PEEVES

These are the gnats and mosquitoes of our history. Mostly they just tick us off

Chickenhawk Warmongers. The American right wing is a hen house full of chickenhawks. They advocate war and build up military budgets, but somehow manage to miss fighting the conflicts they instigate. These war wimps talk tough and then hide in the National Guard, graduate school, or spend time skiing with supposed bad backs while the less-connected get blown up by roadside bombs. Here is the Chickenhawk Hall of Shame (feel free to add names as you think of them): George W. Bush (Head Chicken in Charge), Dick Cheney, Roy Cohn, Paul Wolfowitz, Newt Gingrich, George Will, Trent Lott, Rush Limbaugh, Donald Rumsfeld, Jeb Bush, Bill Bennett, Dan Quayle, Tom DeLay, Jerry Falwell, Brit Hume, Bill O'Reilly, Richard Perle, and the non-honorable senator from the great state of Georgia, Saxby Chambliss, who ran a slanderous campaign against Max Cleland, who lost three limbs while fighting in Vietnam. Chambliss's big issue was to question Cleland's patriotism!

Alfonse D'Amato. The former senator from New York gets our vote for the sleaziest lobbyist in the country. A man who brags about getting paid five hundred thousand dollars to make a single phone call to push a big-time real estate transaction, D'Amato gets paid fifteen thousand dollars a month by the home care industry to lobby against pay raises for workers making $7.50 an hour. Despite his near universal reputation as "Senator Shakedown" for his influence peddling prowess, the benighted voters of New York State somehow elected him three straight times. It took calling opponent Charles Schumer "a putzhead" (which alarmed the Jewish vote) to get him out of office, not that being a private citizen has slowed down D'Amato's strong-arm "can-do" approach to making money for his partners.

Don King. King has long been the boxing king of trickeration. The former numbers boss of Cleveland and convicted manslaughterer (he stomped and pistol-whipped one Sam Garrett to death over a six hundred dollar debt. Garrett's dying words were "Don, I'll pay you the money."), King is an equal opportunity exploiter of his often desperate gladiators. He has stolen money from Muhammad Ali and Mike Tyson as well as many a six-round pre-lim fighter. Not all go quietly, as witnessed by the more than forty lawsuits filed against him over the years. The number one bloodsucker in a business filled with sharks, King proves that boxing is one jungle where the lions are afraid of the rats.

The Reverend Al Sharpton. Despite his ever-winning one-liners on the campaign trail, the Rev. turns out to be a private COINTELPRO operative funded by right wing agents such as the loathsome Roger Stone to divide and confuse the Democratic Party. Stone funded much of Sharpton's ultimately humiliating 2004 campaign. The Rev. boasted he'd do as well or better than his predecessor and rival Jesse Jackson, but wound up mired in the low single digits, thereby ruining whatever slim credibility he had to begin with. As it turns out, refusing to apologize for his role in the infamous Tawana Brawley case might be the most principled stance Sharpton has taken in his long career, or at least the only one he's stuck to. To Al goes the "couldn't even have been a contender" award for his offensive insistance on representing himself as a meaningful force for change.

Jack Ruby. The exact role in the JFK assassination played by this strip club owner who shot Lee Harvey Oswald, ostensibly to show that "the Jews are tough," may never fully be known. But we do know that Ruby had extensive dealings with Santo Trafficante and Carlos Marcello, the supposed masterminds behind the alleged plot to kill the president. Whatever might have been in it for Ruby, he qualifies as a top member of the All-American Pawn In Their Game Flunky club. These are the underlings who act in the service of powerful, shadowy interests—in other words, the fools stuck holding the bag, or the smoking gun. James Earl Ray, the sub-humanoid killer of Martin Luther King, fits in here nicely, as do the killers of Malcolm X. These Wilmer-in-*The-Maltese-Falcon* figures include the idiot southern policemen cracking whips and labor head breakers, both pro- and anti-union, and many others. Just because the sucker suicide bombers of American history work for peanuts doesn't mean they should be absolved simply because they were "following orders."

Jane Fonda. A woman of shifting moods, the former Hanoi Jane, who directed her most revolutionary pronouncements at the poor-soul frontline grunts and draftees, made a quick costume change into a Ted Turner trophy wife doing the racist "tomahawk chop" in the front row at Atlanta Braves' games. Who knew it would be all downhill after *Barbarella?*

Jerry Rubin. Counter-culturist. The author of *Do It* urged flower children, among other zeitgeist worthy activities, to kill their parents and break every window available. Not taking his own advice, Rubin did none of these things, making a career change to personal wealth guru before being run over while jaywalking in Beverly Hills.

Leona Helmsley. The dark-hearted hotelier from New York who once said, "Only little people pay taxes."

Peter Bourne. Jimmy Carter's drug czar pioneered the use of poisonous paraquat spraying to kill marijuana fields, which was a rotten thing to do.

Mike "Coach K." Krzyzewski. Bobby Knight might throw chairs in public, but I don't even want to guess what this martinet does behind closed doors. The blue-faced hooligans of privilege filling Cameron Arena are bad enough without having to watch this guy's haircut every Final Four.

John Wayne. Wayne's best picture was *The Searchers*, in which he portrayed a crazed former soldier intent on killing his own niece because she slept with an Indian. It was the role he was born to play.

Abraham Foxman. The fund-raising wizard, national director of the Anti-Defamation League, is the shrillest of the anti-Semite hunters. His reflexive opposition to any and all criticism of Israel has done much to hamper realistic debate on the Middle East and any other issue dealing with the American Jewish community he claims to speak for. He might as well register as an agent of a foreign power.

Norman Podhoretz (plus wife Midge Decter, son John, and son-in-law Elliott Abrams, and the horse they rode in on). One of a number of people who really deserved a bigger entry in this book. Intellectual enabler of the neocon scourge, Podhoretz is the gnarly face that launched a million think tanks. The author of *Making It* saw the hand-writing on the wall before the final collapse of the liberal coalition, got out early and big-time. Probably the smuggest, most obnoxious essayist in the country, wife Midge, wet-kiss blower to Rumsfeld, is no better. Ditto Abrams, aka Elliott of Nicaragua, the nastiest of policy wonks. A bad bunch.

And, of course, no book like this would be complete without *George Steinbrenner* or the endlessly hated *Walter O'Malley*. For those who remember or care, it is an enduring joke about how the three worst people in the history of the world are Hitler, Stalin, and Walter O'Malley, the man who took the Dodgers out of Brooklyn. Recent research seems to prove that it wasn't all O'Malley's fault, that the famous Power Broker Robert Moses (the master builder/destroyer of New York, another prime American Monster) had a large hand in O'Malley's decision to move the ball club to Los Angeles. Maybe that's true, but why mess up a most perfect hatred? This is the man who traded Jackie Robinson (to the Giants!) for Dick Littlefield. A whole generation grew up in Brooklyn thinking the man's name was "son of a bitch" since they heard their relatives' endless references to "Son of a bitch, O'Malley."

CONTRIBUTORS

STEVE EARLE, unafraid singer-songwriter, most recently had the Powers That Be get their undies in a bunch over his song "John Walker's Blues." He is the author of *Doghouse Roses*, a collection of short stories.

DANNY SCHECHTER, known as the "news dissector," runs mediachannel.org among other forward-thinking information combines.

NAT HENTOFF, a national resource, is a full-time defender of the Constitution of the United States. He still enjoys a good Vic Dickinson trombone solo.

JOHN TURCHIANO is the publicity director of Local 6 of the Hotel and Restaurant Workers Union. He also keeps tabs on the right wing.

ISHMAEL REED, called the Charlie Parker of American fiction by Max Roach, has been enlightening and entertaining readers for years. His books include *Mumbo Jumbo* and *Freelance Pallbearers*.

LEW GROSSBERGER, never less than amusing in his far-reaching commentary, has long operated under the nom-de-plume Media Person.

KEVIN ALEXANDER GRAY ran Jesse Jackson's presidential campaigns in South Carolina in both 1984 and 1988. His work often appears on the Counterpunch website.

RAY ROBINSON, longtime magazine editor, is the author of many books, most recently, *Famous Last Words*.

ERROL LOUIS is a columnist for the *New York Daily News* and is currently completing law school.

NICK PILEGGI, alias St. Nick, is a longtime journalist and screenplay writer. His book *Wiseguy* became the film *Goodfellas*.

JACK NEWFIELD, a dean of American muckraking journalism, has been making life difficult for the crooked, the rich, and the powerful for several decades without showing any signs of slowing down. His recent book *The Full Rudy: The Man, The Myth, and The Mania* won the American Book Award.

ADA CALHOUN is currently an editor at Nerve.com. Her work has appeared in *New York* magazine.

THOMAS GOLTZ, world traveler and international bon vivant, is the author of *Azerbaijan Diary* and *Chechnya Diary*. He lives in Istanbul, Baku, and Montana.

JAMES RIDGEWAY writes the Mondo Washington column for the *Village Voice*. His always trenchant worldview is on display in *Blood in the Face*, which details the skinhead/white power movement, and *Red Light: Inside the Sex Industry*. His *A Pocket Guide to Environmental Bad Guys* was a partial inspiration for this current volume.

DAN BISCHOFF was the national affairs editor of the *Village Voice* and currently is the art critic of the *Newark Star-Ledger*.

TERRY BISSON has won both Hugo and Nebula awards for his widely acclaimed science-fiction novels, which include *The Pick-up Artist*, *Pirates of the Universe*, and *Bears Discover Fire*.

DARIUS JAMES, sometime poet laureate of expatriate Berlin, has written several books, including *Negrophobia*. He is currently at work on a comprehensive study of voodoo culture.

BRUCE STUTZ is the former editor-in-chief of *Natural History* magazine. His journalism has appeared in numerous magazines. He is currently at work on a comprehensive study of spring (the season).

JOE CONASON is a columnist for the *New York Observer* and Salon.com. His book *Big Lies* recently found itself on the bestseller lists. An earlier work, *The Hunting of the President*, was recently made into a film.

JIM CALLAGHAN is a regular contributor to the *New York Observer*.

GEOFFREY GRAY is a reporter for the *New York Times*.

STU LEVITAN is a writer, radio host, labor mediator/arbitrator, and chair of the Community Development Authority in Madison, Wisconsin.

JOHN PALATTELLA writes about poetry for *The Nation* and other publications.

MARK JACOBSON is a journalist and novelist. His recent books include *12,000 Miles in the Nick of Time*, the saga of a trip around the world with his family, and *The KGB Bar Nonfiction Reader*, a sampler of pieces from the long-running salon.

ART KLEINER, writer, critic, co-evolutionist, sage, has commented extensively on such modernist conundrums as responsible scenario planning and organizational learning.

His most recent book, *Who Really Matters*, is a guide to minefield of present day corporate culture.

JOHN HOMANS is the executive editor of *New York* magazine.

DANNY GOLDBERG is the chairman of Artemis Records and the author of the instructive *Dispatches from the Culture Wars: How the Left Lost Teen Spirit.*

LUCIUS SHEPARD is a classic fantasy and science-fiction writer as well as a cultural commentator. His newest book is *A Handbook of American Prayer.*

JAMES MARSHALL, aka The Hound, hosted a long-running, much beloved independent radio show in New York.

STUART MARQUES is the managing editor of the *New York Sun.*

LEGS MCNEIL, present at the creation of punk rock, is the author, along with Gillian McCain, of the music's bible tome, *Please Kill Me.* His oral history of the Los Angeles pornography industry will arrive shortly.

PATRICIA BOSWORTH, a contributing editor at *Vanity Fair*, has written biographies of Marlon Brando, Diane Arbus, and Montgomery Clift.

DENIS WOYCHUK wrote *Attorney for the Damned*, describing his experiences as a lawyer for the criminally insane. He now owns and operates the KGB Bar, noted New York literary watering hole.

TOM GOGOLA's work often appears in *The Nation*, *New York* magazine, and many other publications.

TODD GITLIN, is a professor at the Columbia University Graduate School of Journalism. He has written numerous books, including *The Sixties: Years of Hope, Days of Rage*.

CHRISTOPHER HITCHENS is a internationally renowned critic and author. His campaign to have Henry Kissinger tried as a war criminal was documented in the recent film *The Trials of Henry Kissinger*.

STEPHEN S. HALL, a contributing editor to the *New York Times Magazine*, has published several widely praised books on contemporary science, including *Commotion in the Blood* and *Merchants of Immortality*.

WILL BLYTHE, former fiction editor of *Esquire*, is currently at work on the definitive history of the class/basketball rivalry between the University of North Carolina at Chapel Hill (good) and Duke (bad).

JUDITH COBURN's newest book will detail her years as a war correspondent in Indochina, the Middle East, and Central America.

ARTHUR KEMPTON is the author of *Boogaloo*, which explores the interplay of the sacred and profane in modern rhythm and blues music.

VIC ZIEGEL, who covered the New York Mets down the stretch in 1969, writes a sports column for the *New York Daily News*.